PRAISE FOR *MONEY: MASTER THE GAME*

"Tony Robbins is a human locksmith—he knows how to open your mind to larger possibilities. Using his unique insights into human nature, he's found a way to simplify the strategies of the world's greatest investors and create a simple 7-step system that anyone can use on the path to the financial freedom they deserve."

—Paul Tudor Jones II, *founder, Tudor Investment Corporation, and legendary trader with 28 consecutive years of positive returns for his investors*

"Tony Robbins has influenced millions of people's lives, including my own. In this book he offers you insights and strategies from the world's greatest investors. Don't miss the opportunity to experience the life-changing value of this book."

—Kyle Bass, *founder of Hayman Capital Management and investor who turned $30 million into $2 billion in the middle of the subprime crisis*

"In this book, Tony Robbins brings his unique talent for making the complex simple as he distills the concepts of the best investors in the world into practical lessons that will benefit both naïve investors and skilled professionals."

—Ray Dalio, *founder and co–chief investment officer, Bridgewater Associates, #1 largest hedge fund in the world*

"*Money: Master the Game* will be a huge help to investors . . . Tony Robbins dropped by my office for a 40-minute appointment that lasted for four hours. It was the most provocative, probing interview of my long career, a reaction shared, I'm sure, by the other souls with strong investment values and sharp financial minds who populate this fine book. This book will enlighten you and reinforce your understanding of how to master the money game and, in the long run, earn your financial freedom."

—John C. Bogle, *founder, the Vanguard Group and the Vanguard index funds, #1 largest mutual funds in the world*

"This book is not the typical financial book in any way. It is packed with wisdom and vital philosophies to enrich your life. A lot of books out there have more sizzle than steak to offer. Tony's is different. This book will change your life."

—Dr. David Babbel, *professor of finance, Wharton School of the University of Pennsylvania*

"In this book, Tony masterfully weaves anecdote and expertise to simplify the process of investing for readers—priming their financial education and helping them effectively plan for their future."

—Mary Callahan Erdoes, *CEO, J.P. Morgan Asset Management, $2.5 trillion in assets under management*

"Tony Robbins needs no introduction. He is committed to helping make life better for every investor. Every investor will find this book extremely interesting and illuminating."

—Carl Icahn, *billionaire activist and investor*

"A gold mine of moneymaking information!"

—Steve Forbes, *publisher of* Forbes *magazine and CEO of Forbes, Inc.*

"You can't meet Tony Robbins, and listen to his words, without being inspired to act. This book will give you the strategies to create financial freedom for yourself and your family."

—T. Boone Pickens, *founder, chairman, and CEO at BP Capital and TBP; predicted oil prices accurately 18 out of 21 times on CNBC*

"Robbins's unrelenting commitment to finding the real answers to financial security and independence, and his passion for bringing the insights of the ultrawealthy to the average man, is truly inspiring. This book could truly change your life."

—David Pottruck, *former CEO of Charles Schwab and bestselling author of* Stacking the Deck

"If you're looking for answers and you're committed to creating financial freedom for yourself and your family, then Tony Robbins is your man. Get this book, change your life."

—Farnoosh Torabi, *award-winning author of* When She Makes More: 10 Rules for Breadwinning Women

"Sitting in the back of Financial Destiny nearly twenty years ago, I was a student of Tony Robbins's who had a dream to help teach and empower one million women to be smarter with money. Thanks to Tony, a year later I would be speaking on stage at his events, writing *Smart Women Finish Rich*, and ultimately creating a program that would reach millions of women worldwide. Today there are more than seven million copies of my *Finish Rich* books in print, translated into 19 languages. Tony changes lives, and he will change yours. I, like you, will be reading *MONEY* cover to cover, and sharing it with my friends."

—David Bach, New York Times *bestselling author; titles include* The Automatic Millionaire; Start Late, Finish Rich; Smart Women Finish Rich; *and* Smart Couples Finish Rich; *founder of FinishRich.com*

"We've been selected by *Forbes* as the most innovative company in the world for four consecutive years. Our revenues are now over $30 billion annually. Without access to Tony and his teachings, Salesforce.com wouldn't exist today."

—Marc Benioff, *founder, chairman, and CEO of Salesforce.com*

"Tony's power is superhuman . . . He is a catalyst for getting people to change. I came away with: It's not about motivation as much as it is allowing people to tap into what's already there."

—Oprah Winfrey, *Emmy Award–winning media magnate*

"Tony Robbins's coaching has made a remarkable difference in my life both on and off the court. He's helped me discover what I'm really made of, and I've taken my tennis game—and my life—to a whole new level!"

—Serena Williams, *18-time Grand Slam tennis champion and Olympic gold medalist*

"I was afraid that my success would take something away from my family. Tony was able to turn it around and show me that I've helped millions of people. Probably the most intense feelings I've ever had."

—Melissa Etheridge, *two-time Grammy Award–winning singer and songwriter*

"No matter who you are, no matter how successful, no matter how happy, Tony has something to offer you."

—Hugh Jackman, *Emmy and Tony Award–winning actor, producer*

"If you want to change your state, if you want to change your results, this is where you do it; Tony is the man."

—Usher, *Grammy Award–winning singer, songwriter, entrepreneur*

"Working with Tony Robbins, I felt unstoppable. From that moment on, there was zero doubt in my mind about what I wanted and how I was going to achieve it. I was so clear about what I wanted that I made it happen: I became world champion."

—Derek Hough, *dancer, choreographer, and five-time winner of ABC's* Dancing with the Stars

"Before Tony, I had allowed myself to be put in a position of fear. After meeting Tony, I made a decision not to be afraid anymore. It was an absolutely game-changing, life-altering experience. I'm so excited and thankful for Tony Robbins and the incredible gift that he gave me."

—Maria Menounos, *actress, journalist, and TV personality*

"What Tony really gave me, a kid sitting on Venice Beach selling T-shirts, was to take risks, take action, and really become something. I'm telling you as someone who has lived with these strategies for 25 years: I'll come back for more again, and again, and again."

—Mark Burnett, *five-time Emmy Award–winning television producer*

"What does this man have that everyone wants? He is a 6'7" phenomenon!"

—Diane Sawyer, *former* ABC World News *and* Good Morning America *anchor*

"Tony Robbins helps you take that first step to making real change in your life. I have a pretty good life, but all of us have aspects of our lives that we want to make greater. It's life-changing. It really is."

—Justin Tuck, *defensive end, Oakland Raiders,*
and two-time Super Bowl champion

"Tony Robbins knows the rhythm of success. He is an incredible source of inspiration, and his methods have improved the quality of my life. I only work with the best, and Tony is the best."

—Quincy Jones, *Grammy Award–winning musician, producer*

"Tony Robbins provides an amazing vehicle for looking at your life, mapping out a mission, and determining what's holding you back and what you need to move forward."

—Donna Karan, *legendary fashion designer, founder DKNY*

PRAISE FOR *UNSHAKEABLE*

"Remarkably, Robbins has produced a book that will appeal to both the beginner and the most sophisticated money jockey overseeing multibillions of dollars in assets. If there were a Pulitzer Prize for investment books, this one would win, hands down."

—Steve Forbes, *publisher of* Forbes *magazine and CEO of Forbes Inc.*

"Robbins is the best economic moderator that I've ever worked with. His mission to bring insights from the world's greatest financial minds to the average investor is truly inspiring."

—Alan Greenspan, *former Federal Reserve*
chairman under four sitting presidents

ALSO BY TONY ROBBINS

Life Force

Unshakeable

Money: Master the Game

Unlimited Power

Awaken the Giant Within

Notes From a Friend

THE HOLY GRAIL OF
INVESTING

**THE WORLD'S GREATEST INVESTORS REVEAL THEIR
ULTIMATE STRATEGIES FOR FINANCIAL FREEDOM**

TONY ROBBINS

WITH CHRISTOPHER ZOOK

SIMON & SCHUSTER

NEW YORK LONDON TORONTO SYDNEY NEW DELHI

1230 Avenue of the Americas
New York, NY 10020

First Simon & Schuster hardcover edition February 2024

SIMON & SCHUSTER and colophon
are registered trademarks of Simon & Schuster, LLC

Simon & Schuster: Celebrating 100 Years of Publishing in 2024

For information about special discounts for bulk purchases,
please contact Simon & Schuster Special Sales
at 1-866-506-1949 or business@simonandschuster.com.

The Simon & Schuster Speakers Bureau can bring authors to your live event.
For more information, or to book an event, contact the
Simon & Schuster Speakers Bureau at 1-866-248-3049 or
visit our website at www.simonspeakers.com.

Interior design by Ruth Lee-Mui

Manufactured in the United States of America

3   5   7   9   10   8   6   4   2

Library of Congress Cataloging-in-Publication Data has been applied for.

ISBN 978-1-6680-5268-6
ISBN 978-1-6680-5270-9 (ebook)

DISCLOSURE

CONTENTS

PART 1

THE SEARCH FOR THE HOLY GRAIL

Over the past ten years, I have had the privilege of authoring two #1 *New York Times* bestsellers on the topic of personal finance (*Money: Master the Game* and *Unshakeable*). They succeeded not because I am an expert in the field, but because I have one important thing . . . **access!**

Over four decades of work as a life and business strategist have earned me personal access to many of the world's most brilliant financial minds, many of whom happen to also be fans of my work. From Alan Greenspan to Ray Dalio to the late Jack Bogle to Paul Tudor Jones and countless others, I've had the pleasure of sitting down with titans of investing to extract the tools, tactics, and mindset that anyone, at any stage of life, can—and should—apply in the quest for financial freedom. Their generosity of time and principles helped me form a trio of "playbooks," and I encourage you to read the others if you have not already.

I began my deep dive into money mastery after the 2008 financial crisis when the world's economy was on the brink of collapse due to the reckless behavior and greed of a relative few. Nobody escaped the economic pain, myself included. My phone rang off the hook as I tried to coach friends and family through job loss, home loss, and obliterated retirement plans. From the barber to the billionaire, the storm tore through everyone's life with varying degrees of devastation.

Never one to be a victim of circumstance, I decided to take immediate action to become part of the solution. With a healthy dose of cynicism, I set out to answer the most important question facing a financially illiterate society. . . . **Is the game *still* winnable?** In the post–financial crisis world, could the typical investor win the game of investing? Could the average person become financially free even if they never sell a business, inherit a nest egg, or scratch a winning lottery ticket? **After interviewing over fifty of the world's most brilliant financial minds and boiling down hundreds of hours of interview recordings, the answer to the question was a resounding YES!** Although the titans I interviewed shared very different approaches, they all agreed on certain immutable laws and steps the investor needs to take (and avoid) to win the game.

Although there are many, the four of the most common principles among these greats were as follows:

1. **First, don't lose.** As Warren Buffett succinctly says, "Rule #1, don't lose money. Rule #2, see rule #1." If you lose 50 percent in a bad investment, you will need 100 percent return just to get back to even. One thing that all the most successful investors have in common is they know that they will indeed lose at times (yes, even Buffett). To mitigate this, they never get too far over their skis and risk too much on any one investment, which leads to the second principle . . .

2. **Second is the core principle of asset allocation**—i.e., spreading your assets among different types of investments with varying risk-reward ratios. When I sat down with the late David Swensen, the man who took over Yale's hundred-year-old endowment and grew it from $1 billion to $31 billion, he explained that your asset allocation accounts for 90 percent of your investment returns! **As you will learn, the ultra-high-net-worth and biggest institutional investors have a drastically different approach to asset allocation than the typical investor.**

3. **Third, wherever possible, look for opportunities with "asymmetric" risk reward.** Simply put, these investors look for investments where the potential reward far exceeds the downside risk. My good friend, and legendary trader, Paul Tudor Jones will only place trades where he believes the risk/reward ratio is 5 to 1.

He will risk $1 to make $5. This way he can be wrong more times than right and still succeed.

4. **Fourth and final is the principle of diversification.** You want to own a wide variety of investment *types* (stocks, bonds, real estate, private equity, private credit, etc.) across various asset classes, geographies, time frames, etc. . . .

My guess is, if you are reading this book, you are NOT the average **investor.** You (or your clients) have likely accumulated enough of a financial foundation to move beyond these core tenets and add some additional fuel to your investing fire. **As you will see in the pages ahead, alternative investments have generated outsized returns for the world's most astute investors. For example, between 1986 and 2022, private equity as a whole has outperformed the S&P 500 by over five percentage points annually (9.2% compared to 14.28%). That's a 50 percent plus greater return. Private credit, an alternative to bonds, has generated two to three times the income/yield.***

It is undeniable that the smart money uses high-quality alternative investments as the engine for greater diversification and accelerated growth. This is what the titans of finance do with their own personal capital. I know because they've told me. Over decades, I have fostered ongoing relationships with these "masters of the financial universe." For this book, we have interviewed a baker's dozen, thirteen of the most successful alternative investment managers that have generated extraordinary, compounded returns rarely seen by the general public. Folks like . . .

- **Robert F. Smith**—Founder of Vista Equity Partners, Smith is considered the most successful enterprise software investor of all time, managing over $100 billion and generating outstanding returns relative to the company's peers (over the past twenty-plus years). Vista's portfolio spans more than eighty companies, with ninety thousand employees. As of March 2023, the portfolio companies that Vista owns generate over $25 billion in annual revenue!

*https:/moneymade.io/learn/article/private-credit-vs-bonds

- **Bill Ford**—A pioneer in the world of private equity, Ford has grown General Atlantic's assets under management from $12 billion to more than $80 billion and expanded the firm's global presence. Over its history, General Atlantic has invested more than $55 billion in over five hundred companies within technology, financial services, healthcare, and life sciences.
- **Vinod Khosla**—Founder of Khosla Ventures, Vinod Khosla is a legend in venture capital. His early stage investments in disruptive technology companies propelled him from an immigrant with little means to a self-made multibillionaire. He is famous for turning a $4 million investment in Juniper Networks into a $7 billion windfall for his investors.
- **Michael B. Kim**—The "Godfather of Asian Private Equity," Kim has created the largest independent private equity firm in Asia, with a focus on China, Japan, and Korea. His astounding success for investors has also made him South Korea's wealthiest man.
- **David Sacks**—Founder of Craft Ventures, cohost of the *All In* podcast and original member of the PayPal "mafia" with Elon Musk and Peter Thiel. Sacks has invested in over twenty unicorns, including Affirm, Airbnb, Eventbrite, Facebook, Houzz, Lyft, Palantir, Postmates, Slack, SpaceX, Twitter, and Uber.

And many more!

These individuals play the money game at the highest possible level. Yet they play the game with an edge. **The edge of access!** Their status and professional networks **provide them with extraordinary access to unique investments that, frankly, 99.9 percent of people won't typically have access to.** Perhaps even more compelling, they tend to perform well in good times and in bad. **These investors have shown over and over that while they're not immune to the ups and downs of the economy, they know how to thrive, not just survive, during the economic winters.** Instead of being content to ride out the storm, they go shopping when prices are down. To them, a storm is an opportunity. It's one thing to make money when the markets rise; a rising tide lifts all boats. But to generate returns when markets are choppy? That's what separates the good from the great.

One of the "hall of fame" players in the smart money game is my friend **Ray Dalio.** Ray is the Tom Brady of "macro" hedge fund managers. The G.O.A.T. For those who aren't familiar, Ray is the founder of Bridgewater, the world's largest hedge fund ($196 billion*), with an astounding track record in both good times and bad. He was one of the first who predicted the Great Recession and took advantage. **In 2008, while the market melted down 37 percent, Bridgewater bucked the trend and gave investors a gain of 9.4 percent.** Their "Pure Alpha" fund has averaged over 11 percent annually since its inception in 1991 (compared to approximately 7 percent for the S&P 500).[†] Needless to say, when you consistently beat the market by wide margins for more than thirty years, you become one of the most sought-after hedge funds for the world's wealthiest. From the sovereign wealth funds of the richest countries on earth to the most influential billionaires, Ray is on speed dial to many of the world's most powerful.

In some of our earliest conversations, nearly a decade ago, he taught me what he considers the most important principle of successful investing. A principle of diversification to maximize reward and minimize risk. A principle that has guided my own personal investment strategy and, more important, provided the inspiration for the title and content of this third and final book in my financial trilogy: what Ray calls the **"Holy Grail" of investing.** A simple yet profound strategy that is rarely put into practice. I'm going to tell you how it works.

First, it's important to understand that most traditional portfolios hope to **reduce risk and maximize upside through the core principle of diversification: Don't keep all your eggs in one basket.** But unfortunately, this doesn't always work out as expected. This is because many of today's traditional investments are "correlated," which simply means they move up or down in unison.

Correlation measures how much investments move together in the same direction (positively correlated means they move in unison, while negatively

*https:/whalewisdom.com/filer/bridgewater-associates-inc
†https://www.reuters.com/business/finance/bridgewaters-flagship-fund-posts-gains-32-through-june-2022-07-05/#:~:text=In%20the%20first%20half%20of%202022%2C%20the%20S%26P%20500%20was,an%20average%20of%2011.4%25%20annually.

correlated means the opposite). Then you have varying degrees of correlation, meaning they move together but not in complete lockstep. **For example, stocks and bonds are generally uncorrelated. When stocks go down, it is helpful if bonds go up to give you some protection. However, correlations are always changing and can often throw some unexpected curveballs.**

In 2022, stocks and bonds both dropped simultaneously. While this is somewhat rare, it may not be an anomaly going forward. AQR, one of the world's most successful algorithmically driven hedge funds, believes that *"macroeconomic changes—such as higher inflation uncertainty—could lead to a reappearance of the positive stock–bond correlation of the 1970s, '80s, and '90s."* In August of 2023, a Bloomberg headline came across my screen that read *"Bonds are a useless hedge for stock losses as correlation jumps."*[*] The article noted that the positive correlation between treasury bonds and stocks is at its highest reading since 1996!

And it's not just stocks and bonds that have been shown to positively correlate lately. Publicly traded REITs (companies that own and manage real estate portfolios) tend to have a strong degree of correlation with stocks, despite being a different asset class. Between 2010 and 2020, REITs had an 80 percent positive correlation with the S&P 500.[†] Adding real estate to your portfolio might seem like a smart way to diversify, but in fact, your REITs and stocks are more likely to dance in unison. To be fair, REITs performed quite well over the period from 2010 to 2020. But here's the key point: when stocks came crashing down in 2022, REITs also took a tumble. So much for keeping a portion of your eggs safe and sound.

Likewise, cryptocurrency, often touted by its supporters as "digital gold" and a hedge against market volatility, has been moving in lockstep with stocks in recent years. In 2022, Bitcoin took a 65 percent plummet, from

[*]https:/www.bloomberg.com/news/articles/2023-08-02/bonds-are-useless-hedge -for-stock-losses-as-correlation-jumps
[†]https:/www.investopedia.com/articles/financial-advisors/030116/reits-still -viable-investment.asp#:~:text=REITs%20Offer%20Diversification%20 Pluses,through%20the%20end%20of%202020.

approximately $47,000 to nearly $16,000. The same year, stocks entered a bear market and inflation took root. A Georgetown University study found that "crypto assets followed the market's lead even more closely during periods of high market volatility, such as the Covid pandemic and Russia's invasion of Ukraine."* Who knows how it will perform in the future, but it certainly failed as a hedge of protection most recently.

The problem is that today most traditional diversification strategies tend to involve adding more and more positively *correlated* **investments!** Some investors, knowingly or not, seem to have given up on finding uncorrelated investments to help manage big swings. **One frightening headline recently came across my newsfeed: Older Americans, those in retirement or near to it, are forgoing bonds for protection and betting most or all of their future solely on stocks.** This is quite the gamble. The *Wall Street Journal* reported of clients at Vanguard, "one-fifth of investors 85 or older have nearly all their money in stocks, up from 16% in 2012. The same is true for almost a quarter (25%) of those ages 75 to 84."† **This abandonment of diversification is a high-stakes roll of the dice, but unfortunately, many American's feel they have no choice when their "diversified" portfolios don't act the part.**

So what is the "Holy Grail" of investing?

According to Dalio, the Holy Grail is a portfolio of eight to twelve *uncorrelated (or non-correlated)* investments which, together, will dramatically reduce risk without sacrificing returns. **Dalio demonstrates that a portfolio structured this way can reduce risk by as much as 80 percent while maintaining the same, or similar, upside potential.** He puts it this way:

> *"From my earlier failures, I knew that no matter how confident I was in making any one bet I could still be wrong—and that proper*

---

*https://www.institutionalinvestor.com/article/b8xcj9wtd1gjb5/Crypto-Is-Becoming-More-Correlated-to-Stocks-And-It-s-Your-Fault#:~:text=They%20found%20that%20the%20correlation,January%202016%20and%20January%202021
†https://www.wsj.com/articles/it-isnt-just-boomers-lots-of-older-americans-are-stock-obsessed-ca069e1a

diversification was the key to reducing risks without reducing returns.
If I could build [a portfolio filled with high-quality return streams that
were] properly diversified (they zigged and zagged in ways that balanced
each other out), I could offer clients an overall portfolio return much
more consistent and reliable than what they could get elsewhere."

This sounds simple enough, right? But there's one big challenge: Where do we gain access to so many high-quality noncorrelated investments? **Turns out, access is the tricky part—and that's precisely why I wrote this book.**

THE BILLIONAIRE'S PLAYBOOK

Since embracing the Holy Grail philosophy, I've developed a portfolio of publicly traded stocks combined with a large dose of unique alternative investments. For example, I am a fan of **private real estate** that affords steady income and tax benefits (e.g., depreciation). I am a fan of **private equity,** as nearly every great private company needs capital to grow, and private equity returns have consistently outperformed stocks quite handily. **Private credit,** when managed correctly, has proven to be a great alternative to bonds, especially at a time when rates are surging. I also sprinkle in some venture capital; it's higher risk but is always pushing the edge of innovation and disruption, which resonates with my inner entrepreneur.

As you may already know, once you reach a certain net worth, the SEC invites you into a special club. **They deem you an accredited investor when you achieve $200k in annual income or $1 million net worth (not including your home).** This affords you access to some, but not many, alternative investments. **The good news: At the time of this writing, there is legislation pending that will allow anyone to take a test to become "accredited" regardless of their net worth (more on this later in the chapter).**

The SEC bumps you up to **qualified purchaser** status when you have $5 million in total investments. This opens up the entire universe of alternative investments. But here's the rub . . . Just because you qualify, doesn't mean you can get in the door. **In fact, many of the best alternative investments are closed to new investors or, like a new, limited-edition exotic car, they sell out before they even hit the market.**

Earlier in my investing career, I experienced this frustration numerous times. The truth is, there seems to be simply too much demand—too much cash looking for a home in alternative investments. And who seems to be first in line? The biggest check-writing institutions in the world. Sovereign wealth funds, college endowments, and mega family offices throw their weight around and elbow out the individual investor.

My co-author, Christopher Zook, shared a funny anecdote from early in his career . . .

I had been waiting for the fax all morning. Yes, this was more than twenty-five years ago, in the days of the ancient facsimile machines. I had received a call the day before notifying me of the good news that my clients and I would be able to invest in a certain flagship private equity fund. We had been trying for years (to no avail) to get access to this specific manager as every fund was "over-subscribed."

Now the time had come to find out just how much of an allotment we would be given. We were finally going to get into the cool kid's club. My clients and I had pooled together approximately $5 million of our own money to invest. The fax machine began to make that unmistakable racket and spit a thin paper scroll onto the floor. My heart sank as I read that our total allotment (aka our allocation) was a whopping $250k. It was like getting a reservation at the best pizza place in New York only to be served a single slice to share with a crowded table of friends.

AN INSATIABLE APPETITE

The appetite for alternative investments in the areas of private equity, private real estate, and private credit seems insatiable. According to research firm Preqin, in 2006 approximately $1 trillion was being managed by private equity managers. **Today there is more than $6 trillion allocated to** private equity, with projections that the market will grow to more than **$14 trillion by 2025.** This "Great Migration" to alternatives seems unstoppable as the smart money is clearly re-allocating. Fewer public equities, more private equity. Less public credit (bonds), more private credit. Fewer public REITs, more private real estate.

My suspicions were confirmed by my dear friend and advisor Ajay Gupta. Ajay has represented my family for over fifteen years. By way of background, Ajay is the former (now retired) chief investment strategist for one of the largest independent investment advisors in the U.S., with approximately $200 billion in assets under management. He sold to one of the larger private equity firms, and he now runs Robbins Gupta Holdings, our joint family office.

One day, Ajay handed me a report from KKR, one the world's largest private equity firms. They had recently conducted a survey in which the world's wealthiest family offices, endowments, and pension plans all gave a peek under the hood. I was surprised by the survey participants' willingness to share their current asset allocation. It bears repeating that our asset allocation, how much we choose to invest and in which asset class, is the greatest driver to our investing success. This is a universal truth among every single investor I have interviewed over the past two decades.

As I scoured the KKR report, this was the most shocking statistic I saw . . .

Ultra-high-net-worth families (those with over $30 million) have nearly 46 percent of their assets in alternative investments, with only 29 percent in publicly traded stocks (see figure on page 13).* Alternative investments used to be a side dish in a portfolio; now they are more like the meat and potatoes. **And get this . . . of the money these groups had in alternatives, more than half (52 percent) was invested in private equity, with the balance nearly equally divided between real estate (25 percent) and hedge funds (23 percent).**

---

*https:/www.kkr.com/global-perspectives/publications/ultra-high-net-worth-investor-coming-age

ALTERNATIVES AS A % OF TOTAL ASSET ALLOCATION

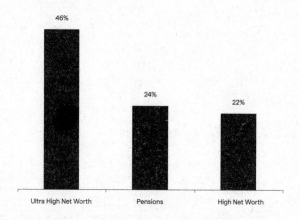

Data as of March 2017. Source: Willis Towers Watson Global Pension Assets Study 2017,
publicly available private wealth manager data. KKR 2017 HNW Survey

Why this profound shift toward alternatives? Well, these tea leaves don't take much reading . . .

On a global level, private equity outperformed public markets in thirty-five of the last thirty-five years (between 1986 and 2020)!*

As you can see in the figure below, as an entire asset class, private equity[†] produced average annual returns of 14.28 percent over the thirty-six-year period ending in 2022. The S&P 500 produced 9.24 percent. That's more than five percentage points greater in annualized returns, which translates into runaway compound growth. To put that into perspective, between 1986 and 2022, a hypothetical $1 million investment in the S&P 500 would have grown to **$26,310,105.** Not too shabby. But the same $1 million would have grown to a whopping **$139,604,229** with private equity! Keep in mind, these returns are the average for the private equity industry as a whole, but many firms have achieved far greater returns.

*Global PE vs MPME MSCI All Country World Index—Cambridge and Associates
[†]As measured by the Cambridge Private Equity Index. https:/www.cambridgeassoci ates.com/insight/us-pe-vc-benchmark-commentary-first-half-2021/

SIMULATED PERFORMANCE OF PRIVATE VS. PUBLIC EQUITY

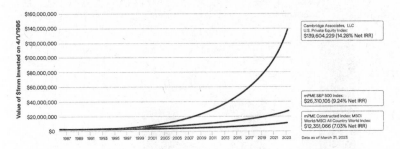

The index is a horizon calculation based on data compiled from 1,505 funds, including fully liquidated partnerships, formed between 1986 and 2022.

Private indexes are pooled horizon Internal rate of return (IRR) calculations, net of fees, expenses, and carried interest. CA Modified Public Market Equivalent (mPME) replicates private investment performance under public market conditions. The public index's shares are purchased and sold according to the private fund cash flow schedule, with distributions calculated in the same proportion as the private fund, and mPME NAV is a function of mPME cash flows and public index returns. "Value-Add" shows (in basis points) the difference between the actual private investment return and the mPME calculated return. Constructed Index: MSCI World/MSCI All Country World Index: Data from 1/1/1986 to 12/31/1987 represented by MSCI Index gross total return. Data from 1/1/1988 to present represented by MSCI ACWI gross total return. The timing and magnitude of fund cash flows are integral to the IRR performance calculation. Public indexes are average annual compounded return (AACR) calculations which are time weighted measures over the specified time horizon and are shown for reference and directional purposes only. Due to the fundamental differences between the two calculations, direct comparison of IRRs to AACRs is not recommended.

Sources: Cambridge Associates LLC, MSCI, Standard & Poor's.

PAST PERFORMANCE IS NOT A GUARANTEE OF CURRENT OR FUTURE RESULTS. Historical examples shown do not, nor are they intended to, constitute a promise of similar future results. The information and statistical data contained herein are taken from sources believed to be accurate and have not been independently verified by CAZ Investments. Historical examples are provided for information purposes only and are not intended to represent any particular investment.

As you can see, private equity performs well in good times, but it has also weathered many a storm. When we look at recent history, there have been three major market downturns (and subsequent recoveries). **The Internet Bubble Bursting of 2001, the Great Recession of 2008, and the COVID Pandemic of 2020. In all three cases, the "peak to trough" declines of the S&P 500 were far steeper when compared to private equity.*** A study by Wall Street behemoth Neuberger Berman summed it up nicely: *"Private Equity historically experienced a less significant drawdown, and a quicker recovery, than public equities in all three [downturns]."* **Case in point, in 2021, on the heels of the pandemic and a global supply chain crisis, private equity had one of its best years, producing pooled returns of 27 percent.† This is just slightly below the stellar performance of 33 percent in year 2020.‡** Private equity heavyweight Bain Capital wrote,

---

*As tracked by the US Private Equity Buyout Index of Cambridge and Associates
†https://www.mckinsey.com/industries/private-equity-and-principal-investors/our
-insights/mckinseys-private-markets-annual-review
‡McKinsey Private Markets Annual Review 2021

*"Private Equity blew the doors off in 2021 as trillions in pandemic-related stimulus produced a historic surge in dealmaking and exits."**

This explains the massive shift to private investments. They simply offer a greater opportunity set. You have to fish where the fish are. Increasingly, companies don't need to go public like they used to. They can get access to capital without dealing with the barrage of legalities and procedures that come with becoming publicly traded. In fact, according to the *Financial Times*,[†] **the number of publicly traded U.S. companies has fallen by nearly half, to around forty-four hundred, since the peak in 1996. That's just forty-four hundred companies for investors to consider,** and we all know many of them are mediocre at best when it comes to profitability, growth, and future prospects. **In fact, back in 2009, 81 percent of public companies were profitable (post IPO); by 2021, only 28 percent were profitable (post IPO).**[‡]

By contrast, there are tens of thousands of private companies growing, innovating, and disrupting. Approximately 80% of all companies with more than $100 million in annual revenue are privately held. **When you look at the total value of all publicly traded companies globally, you may be shocked to learn that the value of all companies held by private equity funds dwarfs public stocks by nearly 4 to 1!**[§]

Now, this is not to say that public stocks don't have a role in our portfolios. They absolutely do, and they are an important ingredient in many Holy Grail portfolios (mine included). Stocks allow anyone and everyone to become owners of our economy, not just consumers. You can own Apple, not just an iPhone. **And stocks allow us to access thousands of global companies, doing business in numerous geographies, with the ability to buy/sell their shares at the click of a button.** There is *not* a competition between public equity vs. private equity. **They are complementary!**

Numerous studies have shown that adding private equity to a typical stock-and-bond portfolio has the tendency to not only reduce volatility,

---

*https://www.bain.com/insights/private-equity-market-in-2021-global-private
-equity-report-2022/
[†]https://www.ft.com/content/73aa5bce-e433-11e9-9743-db5a370481bc
[‡]https://www.statista.com/statistics/914724/profitable-companies-after-ipo-usa/
[§]Prequin: World Federation of Exchanges

but also increase returns.* This is what it's all about: reducing risk (volatility) while increasing returns.

DEMOCRATIZATION

In addition to the many trillions already flowing into private markets, regulations are now being loosened.† Soon, hopefully, average investors will be able to invest in private markets through their 401k plans. This could add more rocket fuel to an already soaring industry. **And here is the best news of all. . . .**

As I mentioned earlier, it has always struck me as unjust that only those with enough net worth can participate in high-quality alternative investments. Heck, many wealthy individuals have become wealthy by selling a business—that doesn't necessarily mean they're sophisticated investors. On the other hand, there are plenty of folks with smaller checkbooks out there who have the desire and intelligence to play ball in private markets. It's my humble opinion that if someone is smart enough and understands the risks, they too should be able to join in. Luckily, Congress agrees. **At the time of this writing, the House of Representatives has passed a bipartisan bill that will allow anyone, even if they fall short of the wealth requirements, to become an accredited investor if they pass a test.** My hope is that by the time you are reading this, the legislation will have become law, and everyone will be able to access great opportunities.

As the bright future of alternatives began to take shape in my mind, my instinctual question was, **How can we participate in this broader trend of the trillions of dollars seeking out alternative investments? How can we ride this wave, this tsunami, beyond just being content with getting access to a handful of opportunities?**

Turns out, many of the best and brightest financial wizards have already figured out a way, and I assure you, most people have never heard of it.

---

*https:/www.nb.com/en/global/insights/investment-quarterly-asset-matters-private-equity-and-your-portfolio
†https:/news.bloomberglaw.com/daily-labor-report/private-equity-firms-are-winning-the-fight-for-your-401k

MY BIG BREAKTHROUGH

As many of you know, I have been coaching my dear friend Paul Tudor Jones for over two decades. Paul is considered by many to be one of the top ten hedge fund managers in history as well as an incredible philanthropist—his Robin Hood Foundation has donated more than $3 billion toward fighting poverty in New York City.

Nearly a decade ago, one of Paul's former partners (who has since launched his own successful fund) and I were having a conversation about alternative investments. I was commiserating over the common challenge of not being able to get into some of these great investment opportunities. **Getting an "allocation" in a highly sought-after private equity fund is the wealthy person's version of getting past the velvet rope at a hot new nightclub.** More often than not, people are left out in the cold, cash in hand.

Buddy to buddy, he decided to divulge what he does with a good chunk of his personal money. My ears immediately perked up. Here was a top-pedigree fund manager about to tell me what he does with his treasure. Like Tiger Woods telling you where he gets fitted for golf clubs. Better take note! He explained he personally uses a firm out of Houston, Texas, that was taking a slightly different approach. Texas? I thought a guy from Greenwich, Connecticut, would be using an elite firm from Wall Street, London, or Singapore. But like most brilliant financial folks that breathe rarified air, he would be found on the road less traveled.

He spent the next hour educating me on one particular approach that sounded like an exact answer to my question.

How can one participate in this seismic shift toward alternative investments?

As I scribbled notes as quickly as I could, he explained that instead of fighting to get into a fund as an LP investor (a limited partner), there was sometimes a way in which one could join up and become an owner of the entity known as the GP (general partner). The general partner is the actual operating company, also known as the asset manager, who manages the underlying investment funds. The GP is typically owned by the founders and the C-suite employees. *"One can actually buy a piece of the GP!?"* I asked, somewhat baffled. He nodded with the grin of a tenured veteran. This was a paradigm-shifting moment for me. After all, many of the financial titans I have interviewed became billionaires by owning their own asset management firms (and thus being the general partner).

It's no secret that the highest concentration of billionaires on the Forbes 400 are not from big tech or oil and gas. They are the moguls of private equity, private real estate, and private credit. These are the financial masterminds that often generate massive wealth for their clients (the LPs) and for themselves (the GP). These are the people that have mastered the game of money and manage tens or even hundreds of billions. These are the people that, given the opportunity, I want to sit shoulder-to-shoulder with as partners. Could it *really* be possible that I could own a sliver of their business of managing money, especially as trillions are flowing into alternatives? The answer, it turns out, is yes. This world, known as "GP stakes," has become increasingly popular among big institutional investors over the past decade but is only beginning to see mainstream coverage. A story in the *Wall Street Journal** summed it up with a headline: **"Buying Stakes in Private Equity Firms, Not Just Their Funds, Pays Big."**

Why does it pay big? . . .

The client of these firms, the investors/limited partners, pays the GP at least two different fees. First, they pay a management fee that is typically around 2 percent per year on the investment amount. Second, if the investment fund performs well, the firm typically gets 20 percent of the profits. So for the top-tier firms that make investors happy, the firm itself is a wealth-building machine for its founders and owners.

As my brain worked to process what I had just learned, I launched into a game of twenty questions. He boiled it down for me, explaining that becoming a minority/passive owner in an asset management firm (the GP) has three distinct benefits . . .

1. Cash Flow—Predictable income is a wonderful thing. If you run a business, you know how rare, and wonderful, it would be to know in advance that you'll have stable, predictable revenue for years.

---

*https:/www.wsj.com/articles/buying-stakes-in-private-equity-firms-not-just-their-funds-pays-big-1542542401#

Welcome to private asset management. A typical asset management company (GP) manages numerous funds on behalf of investors (LPs). The investors often agree to "lock up" their investments for longer periods of time in exchange for the potential of outsized returns. This creates a long-term horizon for the manager, giving them plenty of time to make the best possible decisions. While putting the investors' money to work, the manager is entitled to a management fee (typically 2 percent per year of all dollars invested). **When investors agree to specific "lock-up" provisions (typically between five and ten years), the asset manager knows they will generate predictable and contractually secured management fee revenue throughout that period. That translates to reliable cash flows for the owners of the firm—in this case, that would include us!** Even better, this steady stream of income will also rise as the firm increases the amount of the money it manages!

2. A Piece of the Profits—As mentioned, in exchange for making their investors money, **the GP receives a handsome percentage of the profits, typically 20 percent, on all the capital they manage.** This is known as carried interest or performance fees. Making money on other people's money, while still giving them great benefits, is a win-win situation that can create outsized returns for the GP (us again!).

3. Diversification—In the wise words of Nobel Prize laureate Harry Markowitz, **"diversification is the only free lunch."** Owning part of the asset management company gets you tremendous diversification. **Why? Because a typical firm manages numerous funds.** Each of those funds has a unique start date or "vintage," which means they are spread across various market/economic cycles. Beyond that, each of those funds contains its own portfolio of companies/investments spread across various industries, sectors, geographies, and stages of growth. This is diversification at the highest level.

There is a fourth and final overarching benefit. Sometimes, a private asset manager will go public or be sold to a larger firm. In this case, the owners, with whom you and I sit shoulder-to-shoulder, may receive a multiple on the equity they own upon the sale. There are a lot of additional benefits that you will learn as you read on, but needless to say, at this point in my conversation I was leaning forward in my chair. It all sounded very appealing (and a little too good to be true). I couldn't help but wonder . . .

Why in the world would a private asset manager sell a stake in their business?

His answer? You need to meet Christopher Zook.

HOUSTON, WE HAVE AN OPPORTUNITY

I was taken aback when I first met Christopher because the first thing he told me was that he was inspired to start CAZ Investments more than thirty years ago after listening to my original *Personal Power* cassette series. (Yes, those ancient cassettes!) It was 1991, and he was working for a major Wall Street bank at the time. He drew a line in the sand and told his wife that within ten years he would launch his own firm. In 2001, true to his word, he launched CAZ Investments—only to be greeted by the post-9/11 bear market. But as you will learn, Christopher is not easily discouraged, and he is an incredibly effective hunter of opportunity, regardless of the market conditions. In addition, he is extremely well respected in the world of alternative investments. **In 2019, the Texas governor appointed him to the state's Pension Review Board, where he serves as the chair of the Investment Committee.**

CAZ Investments is not your typical investment firm. A refreshing candor and a get-your-hands-dirty work ethic are reflective of its deep Houston roots. Under Christopher's more than two decades of leadership, they have forged their own unique path. They had to, because Christopher knew that in order to compete with the big institutions, he'd need to rethink the old, stale model.

Over more than two decades, Christopher and his team have built a network of high-net-worth families that bind together as an "insti-vidual" and use their collective purchasing power to negotiate access to unique investment opportunities. Once again: Access is the name of the game when it comes to alternative investments. As Christopher explained it to me, *"Our role is to wake up each and every day and curate exclusive opportunities for our network of investors to consider (they can always choose to invest or pass). In return, our investors have agreed to lock arms as a unified front. We pool our money for each new opportunity and write a single check that will move the needle as much as any major institution."*

Today, the firm has more than three thousand high-net-worth clients across the globe as well as numerous investment advisory firms who participate in its curated opportunities. The firm has grown to be one of the top 200 allocators to private equity investments worldwide, ahead of major institutional investors like the endowments of Columbia, Duke, and MIT.*

Over dinner, Christopher briefed me on the numerous investment opportunities that have been funded by his network over two decades. I was thoroughly impressed at the scope of timely and thematic opportunities the firm brought to its network. From shorting subprime mortgages during the housing crisis to energy opportunities during an oil crash to buying fractional interests in NBA, NHL, and MLB teams. This list goes on. But it's in the world of "GP stakes" where **CAZ has grown to become one of the biggest players, with ownership in more than sixty prominent private equity, private credit, and private real estate firms that span the globe.**

After extensive due diligence, I became a client, and my family office partner, Ajay Gupta, joined the CAZ board. Over the years, the more we spent time with Christopher and his team, the more we fully appreciated his firm's method of reviewing more than fifteen hundred opportunities each year only to invest in a handful of the best and most timely investments. The team at CAZ was instrumental in helping me assemble my own personal Holy Grail portfolio. I decided I wanted to amplify Christopher's voice and wisdom within my network, and Christopher afforded us the opportunity to join a few dozen others in becoming minority shareholders in CAZ itself. I am not actively involved in the business, but I am passionate about being armed with knowledge about these investment trends, how and where the smart money is moving, and how to capitalize on timely opportunities.

*Source: PitchBook Data as of April 2022

LET'S SPREAD THE WORD

In the middle of 2022, the world was undergoing a major sea change as the era of zero interest rates came to an abrupt end. Persistent inflation, a supply chain crisis, the Ukraine-Russia war, and numerous other factors were sending ripples through the markets. I reached out to my Rolodex of financial titans (many of whom we interviewed for this book), and none were fearful. In fact, they were excited. They sensed opportunity. **For example, while bonds were crashing, rising rates were actually *helping* private credit firms (some of which I own a GP stake in) make substantially higher returns because the rates they charged adjusted upward. Prior to rate hikes, many businesses were accustomed to paying 5–6 percent to private credit lenders; once rates took off, those same businesses were required to pay north of 11 percent as the loans adjusted to the current market rate. Same borrower, same loan—but with a surge in profitability for the lender.**

I recall sitting on my back patio, staring at the ocean, feeling grateful for the principles that Dalio and numerous others had taught me along my journey. Grateful for the strategies I was deploying in my own Holy Grail portfolio. Grateful for the platform I have to share all the insights I have learned through my access. In that moment I knew that Christopher and I needed to write this book. There was simply too much important and empowering material for us to share. Too many interesting strategies to be revealed and explored. Too many voices of seasoned and successful veterans that needed to be heard. I picked up the phone and told Christopher that we needed to write this book for two reasons . . .

1. Between the two of us, we have unique access to many of the most brilliant and successful minds in the alternative investment space. **Folks like Barry Sternlicht, founder of Starwood Capital. Sternlicht has built a global real estate investing empire that spans thirty countries, with more than $115 billion in real estate assets under management. Folks like Wil VanLoh, founder of Quantum Energy, one of the largest private energy investors, with an astounding track record (despite investing**

in an asset class that has major volatility). **Speaking with him was incredibly interesting, especially considering the world's focus on renewables and the opportunities they present.** These incredibly engaging conversations embody the timeless truth that **knowledge is power when it is not only learned but applied.**

2. **Even in the circles of high-net-worth families and the advisors that represent them, there is a general lack of awareness regarding the breadth of the possibilities alternative investments represent.** This was once true for me, and I know it's true for many successful people in my inner circle. Far too often, individuals working with well-intentioned advisors only see a limited set of opportunities, which are often preselected by the advisor's parent company. **We want everyone, investors and advisors alike, to be equipped with the tools, awareness, and opportunities that many of the world's greatest investors are using for their own Holy Grail approach.**

SEVEN UNIQUE STRATEGIES

So let's dive in! This book is divided into two parts. **In Part 1, each chapter is dedicated to a specific alternative investment strategy (or category).** We selected *seven unique strategies* that have created extraordinary returns over long periods of time. **Each of the seven strategies is an entirely uncorrelated investment opportunity, which is why we selected them from the universe of potential options.** We will launch this rocket by first covering GP stakes in more depth. Then we'll reveal how investors can now take part in one of the only legal monopolies in North America: professional sports ownership. Relatively recent rule changes have opened the door for investors to own a portfolio of numerous teams across Major League Baseball, Major League Soccer, the National Basketball Association, and the National Hockey League. These teams have incredibly durable revenue models that have the advantage of powerful tailwinds. **They've evolved from making money off beer and butts in seats to being multifaceted global empires that command billions in streaming rights, sponsorships from those involved in legalized gambling, hotel and restaurant**

revenue, and much more. This is just a taste of what's to come. Every one of the other strategies we present is equally exciting!

In Part 2, we sit down with an all-star lineup of expert asset managers. Collectively, they manage more than half a trillion dollars! They generously took the time to share their origin stories and the instincts, techniques, principles, and strategies that guided them to unimaginable success. We ask each of them to share what *they* think of as the Holy Grail of Investing. Their answers are diverse, surprising, and profoundly wise. So let's turn the page and begin with GP stakes to discover why tens of billions in smart money are chasing this strategy. . . .

A Note from the Authors: We, Christopher and Tony, wrote this book in tandem, conducted the interviews together, and collaborated to bring you the absolute best information. Thus, instead of passing the baton between chapters or paragraphs in the remainder of the book, we decided to write with one clear and unified voice.

CHAPTER 2

GP STAKES

A PIECE OF THE ACTION

"The best route to riches? Finance and investments. More than a quarter of the wealthiest people in America made their money in this industry, which includes hedge funds, private equity and money management."
—Forbes*

"Do you want to bet on a horse or own a piece of the entire racetrack?"

Since CAZ Investments began investing in GP stakes nearly ten years ago, we have acquired a minority stake in more than sixty different household names in private equity, private credit, and private real estate. All told, we have billions of investor capital allocated to GP stakes, making our firm one of the world's biggest investors in the space. I tell you this not to brag, but because I have an intimate understanding of the many good reasons why a firm would be willing to sell a minority passive interest to investors—particularly if those investors are strategic. We will dive into those reasons in the pages ahead, but first, let's explore what makes these asset management businesses so attractive.

*https:/www.forbes.com/sites/rachelsandler/2021/10/26/nearly-half-of-americas-richest-billionaires-have-fortunes-in-these-two-industries/?sh=79ec65d7445b

THE REVENUE ENGINE

When buying a stake in any type of business, we have to understand its revenue engine. How will the business make money? Let's take a minute to understand the business behind the business.

Most private asset management firms are set up in the same way. The fund(s) they manage is (are) pooled capital from numerous investors. When setting up an investment fund, the firm will often use a legal entity called a limited partnership, and thus, the investors are considered limited partners in the fund. Then there is the asset manager, which is responsible for managing the money. This is the general partner (GP). The GP is the asset management firm/entity that is responsible for creating, marketing, and managing multiple fund vehicles.

To recap, the GP is normally paid at least two distinct sources of revenue for their management services:

1. **Management Fee**—An annual management fee that can range between 1 percent and 3 percent of the total capital being managed (2 percent is the standard at the time of this writing). This is paid regardless of how the fund performs.
2. **Performance Fee**—Sometimes called a carried interest or incentive fee, a performance fee is paid out as a percentage of the fund's investment gains. The standard incentive fee is 20 percent of the profits.

Let us take a simple example of just how attractive these asset management businesses are from a revenue standpoint. Imagine ABC Private Equity, a hypothetical firm that manages a $1 billion fund. The firm will receive 2 percent a year (or $20 million) in management fees, typically for a minimum of five years. That is a total of $100 million in revenue that is as close to guaranteed as one can contractually get. This management fee revenue creates consistent cash flow payments for the general partners (which includes you if you own a stake in the GP). A GP stake will typically produce annual cash distributions in the range of 5 percent to 10 percent annually, beginning on day one of the investment. So, for instance, if you were to make a $1 million investment in a GP stake, it would generate between $50,000 and $100,000 annually in management fee income payments. (For the investment nerds like us, this means it effectively eliminates the J-Curve.*)

Next, let's assume the fund does a reasonably good job and doubles the value of its portfolio over those same five years—$1 billion becomes $2 billion. The investors (LPs) are happy, and the firm is entitled 20 percent of the $1 billion profit. That's $200 million. Not too shabby.

So let's summarize the total revenue potential for the GP. . . .

$100 million in management fees

+

$200 million in performance fees

=

$300 million in gross revenues (per billion in asset managed)

These are incredible economics that are rarely seen in any business on the planet—and that's why we love being partners in these asset management firms. Keep in mind, the example above is relatively conservative. Many top-tier managers have generated much higher returns, resulting in extraordinary revenue for the general partner.

On top of extremely attractive revenue models, these businesses are also highly efficient and extremely profitable when it comes to economies of scale. **A firm of twenty people managing $1 billion can double the size of the funds it manages without coming close to doubling its head count.** I am personally aware of a firm with a mere seventy-five employees that has $47 billion under management. Remember the example above with $300 million of potential revenue per billion? You can quickly do the math and see why these firms that manage multiple billions can be wealth-generation machines for the general partner (and those of us who own GP Stakes).

*In typical private equity investing, the J-Curve means investors in a fund initially show "losses" while their capital is being put to work to buy assets in the fund. This is followed by a reversal once the gains start to materialize, creating a J-like curve on a graph.

To capitalize on economies of scale, most successful firms will launch a new fund every one to three years, adding an additional revenue stream to the firm with each new fund. Firms that have been around for decades, and have multiple business lines, may have twenty or more funds under management. **This is where the math becomes exponential, and we start to understand how the Forbes 400 is dominated by the founders of these types of firms.**

SMOOTHING OUT THE RIDE

In the southwest of France, near the Garonne River, exists one of the most renowned winemakers in the world . . . *Château Lafite Rothschild*. They produce some of the most expensive Bordeaux wines ever made. As a Bordeaux lover myself, I can tell you that certain years, or vintages, are much better than others. The same is true with private investment funds.

Firms will typically raise a new fund every few years, a new "vintage." Each new fund will purchase a diverse set of investments. For example, each private equity fund may acquire somewhere between five and fifteen companies. Without knowing how each of those companies/assets will perform or the economic times/market cycle in which the fund was launched, the performance of each vintage can vary drastically.

But unlike wine, as an investor, you do not know which vintage will be great until *after* you have already spent the money. You have to invest first—and then wait—before seeing the results of the "harvest." **This is precisely why most institutional investors will be invested across numerous vintages managed by numerous managers. This strategy offers greater diversification and ensures exposure to as many vintages as possible.** Needless to say, this is a tall order for an individual investor. Even very wealthy individual investors do not have pockets deep enough to participate in numerous vintages across multiple managers, so they naturally end up with more concentrated risk by investing in a small number of funds.

By contrast, by owning a GP and moving up the ladder to the position of the general partner, one inherits what we call "Vintage Diversification." Why buy one vintage year from Lafite Rothschild when you

can buy a piece of the whole vineyard? Since a typical firm has numerous funds and vintages, the GP stake in said firm will earn its proportional share of profits generated from their entire lineup of funds (past, present, and future). If one specific vintage or fund does not perform as well as expected, it is less damaging to the GP stake, as the firm will typically have numerous funds with different vintages.

To take it one step further, different asset management firms focus on different industries and geographies. From consumer tech to real estate to healthcare to aerospace to enterprise software to hospitality and beyond. While many of these firms are located in the U.S., some are located, or have offices, across the globe. They hunt far and wide for opportunities. While some economies are suffering, others are thriving, so being unconstrained by geography is a huge advantage.

Now imagine a portfolio of dozens of GP stakes with some of the world's most effective and proven asset managers across various market segments. This is the approach our firm takes, and it provides numerous benefits, including . . .

- Diversification by the types of firms you own (private equity, private credit, private real estate, etc.)
- Diversification in the unique expertise (e.g., aerospace, healthcare, software, retail, fintech . . .) of the funds in which you own a GP stake.
- Diversification by the geographic focus (U.S., Europe, Asia, etc.) of the firms in which you own a GP stake.
- Diversification across the vintages/funds (past, present, and future vehicles) managed by the firms in which you own a GP stake.
- Diversification among the portfolio of companies (or assets) within each individual fund/vintage managed by the firms in which you own a GP stake.

Thus, a portfolio of numerous, high-quality GP stakes can offer investors consistent cash flow along with "asymmetric" risk/reward. That's fancy for limited downside with greater upside. This level of uncorrelated diversification is financial heaven for those looking to align with Dalio's Holy Grail philosophy. In fact, many of the nation's top investment advisors are beginning to utilize GP stakes in their clients' portfolios. Creative Planning (managing more than $200 billion in assets), repeatedly ranked #1 investment advisor in the country by *Barron's* and CNBC, is a big believer in alternative investments and GP stakes. "GP stakes are a very unique way for our clients to get access to top-tier private equity from an entirely different angle and experience the benefits of ownership" said Peter Mallouk, president of Creative Planning.

ENTERPRISE VALUE

One final benefit of buying a GP stake derives from the growth in the enterprise value of the firm itself. As the firm grows its "assets under management," and corresponding revenue, the value of the GP stake can be expected to increase. Consulting giant McKinsey reported that *"total assets under management across private markets reached an all-time high of $9.8 trillion as of June 30, 2021, up from $7.4 trillion 12 months prior."* Most industry experts agree this trend is likely to continue.

When private equity, private credit, or private real estate firms raise new capital to manage, this corresponds to increased cash flows from management fees (typically 2 percent annually) as well as increased potential for profit distributions for performance fees. Some of the firms we have purchased stakes in over the years have grown reasonably well, while many more have grown exponentially. One of the private equity firms in which we own a stake had $13 billion under management when we bought it; today they are managing more than $100 billion! The exponential revenue from the management fees and performance fees has made this an extraordinary business to own.

So how does one realize the growing value of the GP stake? Well, this naturally leads to the question *"What happens if I need to get out? How can I get liquidity in the future?"* Outside of the income stream paid to investors, it is true that GP stakes are generally considered illiquid. That said, there are a couple of ways to generate liquidity should you want to sell your position . . .

1. Certain vehicles will periodically provide a "tender offer" for your ownership position. This simply means they will buy you out at the current "net asset value," or NAV, of your position.

2. You will likely be able to sell your positions in a "secondary" transaction depending on the quality of the asset. This means you could sell your position to a third party for a mutually agreed upon price. This is a common occurrence in the alternative investment space (and a topic we cover in more depth later in Chapter 9).

3. Many firms are eventually acquired by other industry players, which creates a harvest event for all the owners of the business. This is often at a significant multiple on the business's profits.

4. Some firms choose to go public, which provides owners of GP stakes with publicly traded stock.

LEAD WITH ALIGNMENT

This all sounds good so far, right? But if you're like me, you might be wondering about the elephant in the room . . .

> *Why in the world would a successful private equity firm, private credit firm, or any private asset manager sell a piece of their business?*

We have to rewind a clock a bit to find the answer. The year was 2013. Bain Capital, one the largest private equity firms in the world, had just announced that it was raising more than $4 billion for their first new fund since the 2008 financial crisis. But what could have been just another typical announcement sent shock waves into the private asset management industry. **Bain boldly declared that it would put $800 million of its own capital into the fund.** This was capital that belonged to Bain's general partners, a group made up of Bain executives and partners that ride the elevator every day. **They were signaling to the world that they were willing to put their money where their mouths were. If they win, then you win; if they lose, then you lose too.** Remember, the backdrop to this bold announcement was a financial industry that had nearly imploded thanks to the reckless behavior of many Wall Street firms who brought our economy to the edge of collapse. **In an age of unaccountability, Bain had stepped up and declared that serious personal capital commitments were the way of the future for investors that were understandably trigger-shy.** They were willing to lead with alignment.

To many, Bain Capital launched a new era. Today, following their example, it's customary for firms (the GP) to invest a significant amount of their own personal capital in every fund they manage. This can be tens or even hundreds of millions in each fund/vintage.

In practice, this approach becomes very cash-intensive for these firms. Let's say XYZ Private Equity makes a 5 percent commitment of their own GP capital into each and every fund they launch. That means that for every $1 billion raised from investors, XYZ has to pony up and invest $50 million of their own cash. If they launch a new fund every two to three years, and each fund is larger than the last, these firms can easily run into a cash crunch—especially since it can take five to ten years for each fund to fully liquidate and return the rewards back to investors (including the firm's GP). Ironically, they become victims of their own success. **The better the firm does—i.e., the more funds they raise—the more capital they have to come up with. Enter GP stakes.**

When a firm sells a minority-interest GP stake, there is a clear "use of proceeds" established. That means the firm is committed to doing something specific with the proceeds from selling the GP stake. Most typically, the proceeds are used to help fund the customary "GP commitments" to the funds they manage.

Thus, investing in GP stakes is never a cash-out-and-sit-on-the-beach-sipping-piña-coladas situation. These investments are structured with alignment to add fuel to a rocket already in orbit. The GP stake investor wins by owning a piece of a high-quality operating business, and the firm wins by bringing in much needed capital that will help accelerate the growth in enterprise value.

Despite good reasons as to why an asset management firm might sell a piece, **the world of GP stakes is relatively small.** After all, the universe of high-quality private asset managers is very limited, and the percentage of their firms they are willing to sell averages about 18 percent.* A *Forbes* article[†] from 2022 explains it well:

> *Opportunities are rare—even within the institutional space. Access for retail investors will likely always be extremely rare—at best— but can be invaluable as a financial vehicle: affording performance that is not only uncorrelated, but generates unmatched absolute risk-adjusted performance. Nothing else comes even close.*

The author is spot-on. GP stakes are indeed rare and always finite in capacity. **Moreover, access to GP stakes in a business is generally limited to investors who have long-standing relationships with said firm, as the management teams are understandably cautious as to who they want as their minority partners.** One thing is for certain, as the world of private asset management continues to grow, there will undoubtedly be more high-quality firms that will be selling a minority interest.

For individuals who want to access a portfolio of GP stakes, there are only a handful of vehicles available. If you are looking for more information on GP stakes, feel free to reach out to our team by visiting us at **www.WhyGPStakes.com.**

ADDING MORE VALUE THAN ANYONE ELSE

I have lived my life, both personally and professionally, with one core guiding principle: Do more for others than anyone would ever expect. **Add more value than anyone could possibly imagine, and you will have raving fans, not just satisfied clients.** If you have been to any of my live events, where we spend twelve-plus hours a day in full immersion, you know this to be true. When interviewing the most successful investors in the world, there is an important distinction between the traders and the private equity folks. Traders are looking for arbitrage. They are looking to

*http:/arc.hhs.se/download.aspx?MediumId=4842
†https:/www.forbes.com/sites/forbesfinancecouncil/2022/11/18/gp-stakes-what-you-should-know-about-designer-financial-structures/?sh=3957bbbd57a2

create "alpha," or added returns, by buying and selling assets at the right exact time.

Private equity folks take a different approach, one that is more aligned with my life philosophy. They aim to buy good businesses and make them better. Once they buy a business, they look for all of the ways in which they can add value to the company. Whether that means taking advantage of economies of scale, bringing in new leadership, improving supply chain procurement, implementing stronger best practices etc. . . . In the early days of private equity, it is true that there were ruthless takeovers of distressed companies, but the industry has evolved in the many decades since. **The very best in the world today are looking to grow good businesses.** This was exemplified in the interview with Robert Smith of Vista Equity Partners, which you'll find in Chapter 10. His firm has spent more than two decades creating a playbook for all of the companies they acquire. The playbook is a proven set of systems and tools that will undoubtedly add value to any company lucky enough to become part of the Vista ecosystem. This is why I have a kinship with the incredible souls we have interviewed for this book. They truly care about the businesses and the employees they partner with. They are brilliant at engineering added value, and they are rewarded handsomely for doing so—as are their investors.

Now it's time to jump into the exciting world of professional sports ownership. **These conglomerates have outperformed the S&P 500 over the last decade and are incredibly resilient during difficult economic times.** But until recent rule changes, ownership was limited to the biggest billionaires. **Then, the game changed!** Turn the page, and let's discover another uncorrelated investment and the power of professional sports ownership . . .

CHAPTER 3

PRO SPORTS OWNERSHIP

SWINGING FOR THE FENCES

*"Sports have the power to change the world. It has the power to
inspire, the power to unite people in a way that little else does."*
—Nelson Mandela

**In March of 2012, the Los Angeles Dodgers made headlines by selling
for an eye-popping record price of $2 billion.** The most recent compa-
rable sale was that of the storied Chicago Cubs, which went for "just" $850
million. The new Dodgers ownership group included my dear friend and
partner Peter Guber (co-owner of the Golden State Warriors and LAFC,
the Los Angeles Football Club), Mark Walter (CEO of financial powerhouse
Guggenheim Partners), and NBA hall-of-famer Magic Johnson.

**Most economists expected the Dodgers sale price to be closer to
$1 billion.** On the surface, $2 billion seemed well outside the ballpark of
reality, and the experts took immediate issue with it. Andrew Zimbalis, an
acclaimed sports economist and college professor, scoffed at the sale, saying:
"Keep in mind, in addition to the price, the new ownership group will have
to invest something in the neighborhood of $300 million to refurbishing
Dodger Stadium and that price does not include $150 million for the sur-
rounding real estate. At the end of the day, you have to question this deal."

Mark Rosentraub, a professor of Sports Management at the University of
Michigan, didn't hold back in his scathing criticism, saying: "It's the craziest
deal ever; it makes no sense. [The price] is over $800 million more than what
pencils out for a profitable investment for a baseball team. If making money
doesn't count, this is a great move."

Having had a front row seat to Peter's brilliance in business for the past thirty years, I knew there had to be more to the story. First, a little background: Peter is the former CEO of Sony Pictures and founder of Mandalay Entertainment. **His legendary movies include** *Midnight Express,* *Rain Man, Batman, The Color Purple, Gorillas in the Mist, Terminator 2, Groundhog Day, City Slickers, A Few Good Men,* **and many more!** In addition to being cinematic classics (receiving a cumulative fifty Academy Award nominations), **his films have grossed more than $3 billion worldwide.**

I reached out to Peter and asked what he was cooking up. Why would he be willing to pay such an astronomical price? He said, "Tony, I don't want to spoil the surprise. Just wait till you hear the upcoming announcement in the news and then give me a call." I don't know what I'd expected; of course, a legendary movie producer would leave me with a cliffhanger!

The sports economists and various talking heads were served a giant slice of humble pie as they read the press release. . . .

*"Dodgers and Time Warner agree to more than $7 billion TV deal."**

This was the largest TV deal in sports history—even more eye-popping when you remember it was solely for the *local television* rights and the formation of a new regional Dodgers Network. **A $2 billion acquisition for $7 billion in expected revenue less than one year after the purchase.** The world of sports was floored. In the decade that followed, the Dodgers became a baseball powerhouse, delivering their home city a World Series title in 2020, their first in more than thirty years.

VANITY OR VALUE

For much of the last century, a sports franchise was the ultimate vanity purchase. Any billionaire can buy a plane or a yacht, but there are only thirty (or thirty-two) sports teams in each of the major leagues (NBA, MLB, NFL,

*https://www.cbssports.com/mlb/news/report-dodgers-time-warner-agree-to -more-than-7-billion-tv-deal/

NHL, and MLS). As we will uncover here, there have been relatively recent rule changes (as of late 2019), that have opened the door for very specific types of investment funds to buy a minority stake in not only one but numerous teams. Whether you are a sports fan or not, these global businesses have some unique characteristics that make them extremely attractive as part of one's Holy Grail strategy.

That said, a sports team is more than a trophy asset. There's something much deeper and more meaningful about it. Owning a team means owning a place in our culture. Sports transcends color or creed. It transcends our borders. It transcends socioeconomic status. It binds us together with friends and family. It gives us a tribe to root for as they go to "battle" on the field. Sports give us reprieve from the daily grind. A chance to win no matter how hard our day has been. **With winners and losers, triumphs and tragedies, sports are an undeniable part of the heartbeat of humanity.** They also happen to be incredibly lucrative.

Through much of the twentieth century, sports were almost exclusively an in-person live event business. Revenue from ticket sales and concessions were the main drivers of value. But media revenue was always important, even from the earliest days. **In 1897, the first "sale" of broadcast rights took place.** The baseball teams got Western Union to offer free telegrams for their traveling players in exchange for allowing their games to be telegrammed into saloons. Western Union ultimately started paying teams for telegram rights. Patrons in saloons nationwide waited with bated breath to see the updated scores posted every mid inning. Many team owners were worried that telegrams would decrease ticket sales, but in reality, the media got the assist in exploding baseball's popularity. The forever marriage between sports and media was solidified.

After telegrams, radio and newspaper coverage became integral to sports and their fanatics. People from all walks of life huddled around radios to listen to the crackled sounds of their favorite team in the heat of battle. **Then, on August 26, 1939, came the first televised baseball game.** Announcer Red Barber called a game between the Cincinnati Reds and the Brooklyn Dodgers. **This was at a time when there were only about four hundred television sets in the entire New York area! In 1946, just seven years later, the New York Yankees became the first team in history to** sell their local television broadcast rights, for $75,000, or about $1.14 million in today's dollars. By this time, the number of TV sets in U.S. homes had grown to eight thousand. This rapidly increased to 45 million homes by 1960!

In 1979, a channel entirely dedicated to sports was launched. Many predicted its failure, but ESPN gained immediate traction. Twenty-four seven coverage shifted sports into another gear. **Fast-forward to 2002, and the media rights for baseball exceeded "gate revenue" for the first time in history.***

The last two decades have seen an explosion of technology, all of which has added fuel to the sports business fire. High-speed internet, social media, smartphones, and streaming services have shrunk the globe and brought unprecedented accessibility to nearly any game, anywhere. Sports has evolved from a ragtag business of hot dogs and ticket stubs to a global content production and distribution machine.

MONEYBALL

Sports as an "asset class" is a relatively new concept. Only since the early 2000s have leagues and their teams grown into sophisticated global enterprises. Before we look under the hood of these multifaceted empires, let's explore their performance from an investor's point of view.

Between 2012 and 2022, the S&P 500 returned approximately 11 percent annually. The Russell 2000 (an index comprised of small cap stocks) returned 8 percent annually. Over the same period, **the big four leagues (NBA, MLB, NFL, and NHL) combined generated a staggering 18 percent compounded return (See chart on page 39).** What's more, there is very little leverage used (per league policy), so these returns are not "juiced up" in any way.

Even more interesting is the fact that the performance of sports franchises seems to have very little correlation with the public markets. (For the investment wonks, the correlation was 0.14 between 2000 and 2022.) **Low leverage and low correlation are a very attractive one-two punch for any Holy Grail portfolio.**

*https:/eh.net/encyclopedia/the-economic-history-of-major-league-baseball/

ANNUALIZED RETURN FROM 2012-2022

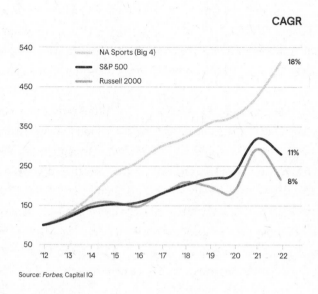

CAGR

Legend:
- NA Sports (Big 4)
- S&P 500
- Russell 2000

18%
11%
8%

Source: *Forbes*, Capital IQ

Let's dive a little deeper . . .

Between 2002 and 2021, the average price for an NBA team rose 1057 percent! By comparison, the S&P 500 returned a total of 458 percent over that period. Moreover, 2023 was a blockbuster year for record-breaking NBA transactions . . .

- **The Phoenix Suns sold for a record $4 billion to my friend and mortgage mogul Mat Ishbia.**
- **Milwaukee Bucks owner Marc Lasry sold a minority stake that put a $3.5 billion value on the team.**
- **Michael Jordan sold his majority stake in the Charlotte Hornets for $3 billion (while still holding on to a small minority position!). This was more than ten times his original investment of $275 million, made in 2010.**

Other leagues have also offered great returns (based on previous and current sale prices). **Major League Baseball teams generated an average total return of 669 percent between 2002 and 2021, and the NHL generated**

467 percent over the same period. North American Major League Soccer, the new kid on the block, is now considered the fifth major league and hit a major milestone in 2023 with its first $1 billion valuation, for the LAFC (Los Angeles Football Club).* Full disclosure: We (Peter Guber and Tony) were founding investors in the launch of LAFC, and we are so proud of the team winning the 2022 MLS Cup in Hollywood fashion with a penalty kick shootout!

As we enter an era of higher inflation, wealth preservation and purchasing power are the name of the game. In this regard, sports franchises seem to be highly defensive investments. (Yes, we plan on using as many sports analogies as possible in this chapter.) Looking to history, we can see that sports have thrived during other inflationary periods, like the 1970s and early 1980s. During the stretch from 1968 to 1982, the S&P 500 generated a 7 percent annualized return, while the enterprise value of the Big 4 teams grew at a 16 percent annualized growth rate. **Case in point: in August of 2022, the Denver Broncos were sold for a North American sports franchise record of $4.65 billion during the fastest interest rate hiking cycle in U.S. history.**

Bottom line, over the past hundred years, these leagues have survived pandemics, lockouts, world wars, player strikes, depressions, recessions, and everything in between. They are incredibly durable assets. The leagues and their teams are evolving before our eyes, and the opportunity to partake is finally open to investors like us.

> *"I don't know which SAAS (software as a service) company will be around in 5 years, but I know that 50 years from now, there will be a World Series in October."*
> —Ian Charles, Arctos Sports Partners

MULTIPLE STREAMS OF INCOME

When looking at a sports team as an investment, there are two main revenue categories: league revenue and team revenue. Let's break these

---

*https:/bleacherreport.com/articles/10063920-lafc-tops-forbes-list-of-mls-team-values-1st-billionbillionbillion-dollar-franchise

down and explore why teams have such economic resiliency, making them great assets to own in a Holy Grail portfolio. (And don't worry, I will explain how we can get access in the pages ahead.)

1. Teams Receive a Portion of League Revenue—The leagues have always been responsible for negotiating the national (and international) broadcast rights and sponsorships (i.e., the deep voice that tells you "The Ford F-150 is the official truck of the NFL"). **League revenues are divided equally between all the teams, so they work together to extract the highest possible price for the broadcast rights and sponsorship.** And recent changes in consumer behavior have given the leagues more leverage. **Networks and their advertisers are becoming increasingly desperate as "cord cutting" is eroding their ability to reach their target customers via cable television. In other words, the number of people watching cable is dropping. Live sports are the only broadcasts that buck this trend. Sports are easily the highest-rated programs on all networks. As a result, advertisers covet sports programming because live TV is nearly the only place where large audiences will be willing to watch ads. In 2019, ninety-two of the top one hundred highest-rated programs on TV were sporting events.*** The leagues know this. And they've leveraged this dynamic into massive media rights contracts that drive revenue to the leagues. **A second driving force is the increasing popularity of North American sports throughout the rest of the world,** from Europe to China. The NFL will have a record five regular season games on European soil during the 2023 season. The NBA schedule now includes games in Mexico City, Japan, and Paris. North American sports are also going viral worldwide on social media; **the NBA recently surpassed more than 75 million followers on Instagram, and 70 percent of those followers are located outside of the United States.**

*https:/www.sportsbusinessjournal.com/Journal/Issues/2021/01/11/Media/Top-100 .aspx

The third driving force behind surging league revenues is the streaming wars. Apple, Amazon, Netflix, and YouTube are battling it out to become the dominant streaming player, and all of them covet the rights to live sports. **Not only do sports attract viewers, they also require very low production cost relative to coming up with the latest binge-worthy series. You don't need actors, you don't need an expensive set, you just set up the cameras and go.** The cumulative annual broadcast rights for the Big 5 leagues totaled $7.6 Billion in 2014.**It is estimated that this figure will be $16.6 billion in 2024.** As the streaming wars wage on, sports will easily be the biggest beneficiary.

2. Teams Generate Their Own Revenue—In addition to their sizeable annual revenue share from the league, each team has numerous other ancillary revenue sources that they keep for themselves. As you will see, beers and butts in seats are only two pieces of this profitable pie . . .

   Local Media—Local television has a ratings problem. They are victims of market disruption that is attacking from all angles (streaming, YouTube, social media, etc.). Frankly, sports are a lifeline for these antiquated local networks. **Compared to typical programming, sports generate two to four times the ratings. And since every team retains the revenue from selling their local media rights, this can be quite lucrative. (Just think back to that $7 billion deal for the local LA Dodgers Network.)** Many teams have followed LA's lead by creating their own local networks or partnering in joint ownership deals with local television networks.

   Real Estate—**Many sports teams own their venue and pick up all the additional revenue from concerts, events, e-sports, and more.** Brilliantly, many teams have also bought up much of the surrounding real estate. **The neighborhood around a stadium or ballpark where there can be hundreds of events annually is a fun and energetic environment for young professionals with disposable income.** From parking garages to hotels to apartments to retail, the teams are quickly becoming vertically integrated to capture as much of the peripheral revenue as possible.

Licensing/Sponsorships—When I (Christopher) walk around the Astros ballpark in Houston, I marvel at the number of local sponsorships. Signs of local businesses are plastered everywhere, including the name of the stadium itself, "Minute Maid Park." Local restaurants, breweries, and coffee shops are included in many venues and receive massive credibility by being the official "fill in the blank" for their local team. This team connection lends to measurable brand loyalty.

Tickets/Concessions—Last time I went to a game, I saw people paying $12 for a hot dog. The line was twenty people deep and nobody complained about the price. **These teams have perfected the science of sales to a captive audience who seem not to mind—or are at least willing to accept—the astronomical prices.** In 2008, New York Yankees and Dallas Cowboys owner Jerry Jones announced a joint venture called Legends Hospitality. They realized their teams were so good at maximizing food, beverage, and merchandise sales that they should offer their management services and strategies to other venues/teams around the globe. They leverage economies of scale, sophisticated logistics tools, and consumer behavior data analytics to lead teams and their venues into the twenty-first century. **The point is that these teams operate at the highest level of retail sales expertise and know exactly how to get all the juice out of the proverbial orange.** Today, the company has clients across the NFL, MLB, and the NBA, and they've also expanded to UFC (Ultimate Fighting), Wimbledon, and numerous Premier League Soccer venues.

Luxury Boxes and Suites—For decades, luxury boxes have provided high-margin foundational income streams for sports team. My friends Peter Guber and Joe Lacob, and our partners at the Golden State Warriors, broke the mold with their recently opened state-of-the-art sports and entertainment arena, the Chase Center. This $1.4 billion work of art sits right on Mission Bay and incorporates eleven acres of shops, restaurants, and bars, as well as a five-acre waterfront park. The contemporary venue is as nice as any five-star hotel and creates an elevated, dare I say luxurious, experience. With over two hundred live events and games per year, they have created a cash cow. Their luxury suites go for as much as $2.5 million per year and require a minimum contract commitment of ten years. Silicon Valley tech companies and Venture Capital firms fought tooth and nail to get their hands on a finite number of suites, making it the hottest ticket in town. From valet parking to suites catered with champagne and sushi buffets, teams are leaning into elevated VIP experiences that command much higher ticket prices.

Gambling—In 2018, the Supreme Court ended a ban on the expansion of the sports gambling industry. Whereas **sports gambling was once confined to the sports books of Vegas, as of August 2023 it is now legal in thirty-five states.** By all accounts, this is a modern-day gold rush. **In 2021, sports gambling doubled, with over $57 billion wagered.*** From TV commercials to endorsements to jersey patch sponsors, the increased advertising income from sports betting companies has added significant revenue for leagues and teams alike. While I am personally apprehensive about the societal implications of legalized gambling, the ship has sailed, and gambling will only become an increasingly inextricable part of professional sports.

A SEAT IN THE OWNER'S BOX

Becoming an owner in a professional sports team is no small feat. First and foremost, the league will vet you from every angle. Are you a moral risk? A headline risk? A financial risk? For many years, the league required owners to be individuals. They had once allowed institutions and media companies (e.g., Disney owning the Anaheim Mighty Ducks), but such firms proved unreliable as owners due to issues in their primary businesses and frequent

*https:/www.americangaming.org/new/2021-commercial-gaming-revenue-shatters -industry-record-reaches-53b/

turnover among their management. So, for many years, ownership was limited to mega-wealthy captains of industry like Steve Balmer (Microsoft), Dan Gilbert (Rocket Mortgage), Joe Lacob (Kleiner Perkins), Charles Johnson (Franklin Templeton), and so forth.

Then, in 2019, Major League Baseball changed their policy. They cleverly realized that their teams, these platforms, had evolved into highly sophisticated enterprises with valuations beyond what even the wealthiest of the wealthy might be willing to pay. **Furthermore, while most teams had a single controlling owner, there were numerous smaller individual owners/investors who were along for the ride but didn't have any operational control. These individuals, many of whom were older, needed a path to liquidity, either for diversification reasons or estate planning.**

So MLB passed a new rule to allow certain types of investment funds to purchase a minority stake in a team so long as a long list of criteria were met and, most importantly, so long as the firms avoided conflicts of interest. Initially, many expected this rule change to open the floodgates for private equity firms who, for the reasons outlined in this chapter, would love an opportunity to invest. **However, numerous hurdles made many firms ineligible. For example, they were prohibited from owning any other businesses that had a conflict (e.g., sports gambling or sports agency).** Heck, many of the biggest moguls in private equity already had a personal stake in a team, thus disqualifying their firms immediately. When the dust settled, only a handful of private equity firms remained eligible. Those firms have since raised and deployed billions in capital to buy minority interests across all major sports leagues (with the NFL being the last remaining to open its doors to fund investors).

Today, qualified individual investors now have a path to ownership in professional sports. Instead of investing in a single team, some of these pooled vehicles hold a diversified basket of numerous teams across all the eligible major leagues **(MLB, the NBA, the NHL, MLS, and the Premier League).** *Bloomberg* **reported that the Fenway Sports Group (which owns the Boston Red Sox, the Pittsburgh Penguins, Liverpool), the Sacramento Kings, the Golden State Warriors, and the Tampa Bay Lightning (NHL) are just a few of the organizations that have brought**

on a private equity investor.* And according to PitchBook, more than a third of Europe's Big 5 soccer leagues are now backed by private equity.†

Holding numerous teams, across multiple leagues and geographies, creates significant uncorrelated diversification. And as a bonus, owning a share of a team can offer tax benefits as depreciation or amortization may flow through to investors in the fund. Now we have a better understanding of why many of the world's wealthiest own sports teams. They aren't just a trophy investment. In fact, after many decades in alternative investments, I would consider pro sports ownership an absolute all-star with an incredible stat line: a globally diverse, noncorrelated investment that has proven to be durable over a century.

To learn more about accessing these opportunities, you can visit **www.WhyProSports.com.**

LEADERS IN LENDING

As we shift gears to the world of private credit, you will likely feel a second bolt of lightning. Most investors only use traditional bonds when it comes to the fixed income portion of their portfolio. But you aren't most investors! Like Neo in *The Matrix*, you are now seeing the alternative reality. **This is where the smart money has been using private credit for decades as a safer and less volatile way to generate double-digit income returns.**

So let's dive in and discover why private credit is poised for massive growth as interest rates rise and banks tighten their lending appetites . . .

---

*https://www.bloomberg.com/news/articles/2022-03-24/private-equity-funds-encroach-on-sports-owners-box
†https://pitchbook.com/news/articles/european-soccer-us-private-market-capital

CHAPTER 4

PRIVATE CREDIT

LEADERS IN LENDING

*"As fewer companies have gone public in recent years, the number
of private companies has grown commensurately, providing a
larger pool of private firms looking for access to capital."*
—CNBC, *Demystifying Private Credit*, June 21, 2023*

In 2022, trillions in value were eviscerated as the value of bonds collapsed. Like tens of millions of Americans, you may have felt the sting in your portfolio. **And yet, while the traditional investor was losing sleep holding publicly traded bonds, the smart money was once again living in an alternative reality. They were generating healthy returns with the "fixed income" part of their portfolio while suffering minimal or no losses.** Welcome to the world of private credit.

For those unfamiliar, private credit is a way for established businesses to borrow money without using a bank. **For the investors like us, whose capital is being lent, this can generate two to three times the income return of traditional bonds and can serve as another noncorrelated income strategy in our Holy Grail portfolio. Why is creating a stable income stream so important?**

The ultra-wealthy are fully aware that assets will fluctuate in value. **But you cannot "spend" assets. You spend cash.** When markets drop, lots of people quickly become asset heavy and cash poor. They do not want to sell

---

*https://www.cnbc.com/2023/06/21/op-ed-demystifying-private-credit-amid-a-fro
zen-ipo-market.html

their assets when the market is down, but they can become forced to if they don't have sufficient income/liquidity. **This is why I live by the mantra** *"income is the outcome."* **Building a critical mass of assets that pay you a handsome income stream gives you the crucial stability you need to survive an economic winter.**

<u>**In the pages ahead, we explore how private credit has grown from just $42 billion in assets under management in the year 2000 to over $1.5 trillion today!***</u> **As banks continue to clam up and tighten their lending purse strings, the industry is expected to grow to over $2.3 trillion by 2027.** Ahead, we will explain how investors can take advantage of private credit, but first, let's go back in time and discover why private credit became a favorite smart money strategy.

SHIFTING WINDS

> *"The 60/40 Portfolio Is Delivering Its Worst Returns in a Century"*
> —*Wall Street Journal*, October 14, 2022

For many decades, a time-tested strategy for most ordinary investors has been the 60/40 portfolio (60 percent stocks, 40 percent bonds). Aside from providing income, or yield, bonds have historically served to cushion a portfolio in years when stocks are down. **But in 2022, the cushion was yanked out from under investors and they landed flat on their behinds.** Stocks and bonds *both* plummeted as interest rates rose and the economy began to slow down. Stocks and bonds moving in lockstep, also known as correlation, is exactly what you DON'T want in bear markets. **And 2022 was the first year in history when stocks and bonds both went down by the same magnitude (-22 percent annualized by October 31 of 2022).†** **The seven largest stocks in the S&P 500 went down an average of 46**

---

*https://www.bloomberg.com/news/articles/2019-09-22/how-private-credit-soared
-to-fuel-private-equity-boom-quicktake
†Data as of October 31, 2022. Using S&P500 and Barclays U.S. Aggregate for bonds. Assuming yearly rebalancing *2022 return corresponds to annualized YTD return.

" You have a balanced investment portfolio.
Everything you own is losing money equally. "

percent. Put it all together, and the 60/40 strategy experienced one of its worst performances in nearly a hundred years.* Since then, stocks and bonds have become even more correlated, not less. *Bloomberg* reported that "bonds are a useless hedge for stock losses as correlation jumps."†

Prior to COVID, investors hunting for yield were forced to take bigger risks as they waded into deeper and more dangerous waters. **With such low interest rates, and such low income returns on traditional bonds, many investors were tempted into buying riskier, higher yielding junk bonds, cleverly re-branded as "high-yield" bonds.** But don't let the name fool you: These so-called high yield bonds were paying a measly 3.97 percent in

---

*https://www.wsj.com/livecoverage/stock-market-news-today-2022-10-14/card/the
-60-40-portfolio-is-delivering-worst-returns-in-a-century-yrOrYOfkthrBQhSbf5By
†https://www.bloomberg.com/news/articles/2023-08-02/bonds-are-useless-hedge
-for-stock-losses-as-correlation-jumps

the summer of 2021. **Contrast this with private credit, which was paying 9 percent income during the same year.***

For sophisticated investors there was an uneasiness when it came to low-yielding junk bonds and how they had proliferated into the portfolios of ordinary investors. Like a dog sensing an earthquake minutes before the tremors, those who were paying attention knew something was not right. At that point in time, interest rates had nowhere to go but up, which meant the price of lower-quality junk bonds would then collapse. The risk-reward ratio was so out of whack that we knew the winds would eventually shift. And shift they did.

On November 9 of 2021, *Bloomberg* wrote . . .

"U.S Junk Bonds Set $432 Billion Record"†

Not even a year later, on October 22 of
2022, the same outlet wrote . . .

"Global Junk Bond Sales Drop Most Ever With No Signs of Recovery."‡

While bond values were collapsing with rising rates, many of the biggest institutions were enjoying the benefits of private credit. Instead of losing, their income payments from private credit were steadily rising along with interest rates.

THE ALTERNATIVE REALITY STRIKES AGAIN

*"A bank is a place where they lend you an umbrella in fair
weather and ask for it back when it begins to rain."*
—Robert Frost

---

*https://www.forbes.com/sites/forbesfinancecouncil/2023/03/30/private-credit-investing-current-opportunities-and-risks/?sh=368627993821
†https://www.bloomberg.com/news/articles/2021-11-09/u-s-junk-bonds-set-432-billion-record-in-rush-to-beat-rates#xj4y7vzkg
‡https://www.bloomberg.com/news/articles/2022-10-24/global-junk-bond-sales-drop-most-ever-with-no-signs-of-recovery

"How would you like to dabble in some very
high quality junk bonds?"

For decades, the deepest pockets of smart money have invested massive
sums in "non-bank" lenders that generate much higher returns than
traditional bonds. This is the world of private credit. Private equity is
to public equities what private credit is to bonds.

While big businesses like Amazon, Google, and Tesla have no problem
securing loans from big banks or selling publicly traded bonds to raise capital, there is a huge swath of middle-market companies that have to look
elsewhere. But we're not talking about your local hardware store or florist
borrowing money to make payroll. According to the Corporate Finance In-
stitute, **U.S. middle-market companies have between $100 million and
$3 billion in revenue, with anywhere between one hundred and twenty-
five hundred employees. Believe it or not, there are over two hundred
thousand companies in the United States that fit this category!**
We all know that when it comes to lending, banks have extremely tight
fists. If you have ever bought a home, you are all too familiar with the financial prostate exam required. But loans are a necessity for successful businesses, which rely heavily on them to fund operations. They have to pay all
sorts of bills up front—rent, payroll, inventory—and wait a bit for the revenue to come in. But bank loans aren't always available, or sufficient. **After**

the 2008 global financial crisis, banks were further handcuffed by regulators, diminishing their ability to issue loans, and many companies were left with one option to keep the cash flowing: private credit.

The recent boom in private equity has poured even more fuel on the private credit fire. When a private equity firm buys a company, they will often use some form of leverage (like an individual putting a mortgage on a new house). Where does that leverage come from? By now you won't be surprised to learn that a very large percentage of these mergers and acquisitions are financed by private credit firms.

THE 3 PILLARS OF PRIVATE CREDIT

It's worth repeating that just twenty-three years ago, the world of private credit topped $42 billion in total loans. After enduring the Internet Bubble and Great Financial Crisis, the evaporation of bank loan availability has resulted in a private credit boom. **At the end of 2022, the global private credit market exceeded $1.5 trillion. Research firm Preqin estimates the industry will grow to over $2.3 trillion by 2027 as traditional banks further retrench.**

This trend only looks likely to accelerate. In early 2023, Silicon Valley Bank collapsed nearly overnight. Numerous other regional banks followed suit. The rapid rise in interest rates had caused a collapse in their bond portfolios. Private credit firms don't face the same risks (as explained ahead). This is why many firms see a "golden moment" in this space in light of bank failures.* Moreover, regional banks account for close to 80 percent of commercial real estate loans, and with vacant office buildings piling up, we could see a major calamity when those loans come due in coming years and defaults begin to domino. **All of this points to the continued use of private credit firms who are unbound by many of the constraints of traditional banks.**

One thing is clear: Private credit is solidifying its position as a dominant force for middle-market companies' lending needs. These firms

---

*https:/pitchbook.com/news/articles/blackstone-first-quarter-earnings-private -credit-pe are incredibly cautious but willing to lend if the risk-reward ratio makes sense. They are fast, flexible, and creative with when, where, and how they lend. The result is often a much better risk-reward situation for investors like you and me who are putting up our capital. Let's explore the three pillars of private credit, and why private credit has grown to be a sought-after asset class from an investor's point of view:

1. Higher Rates of Return—Private credit offers substantially better rates of return (aka higher yields) than other debt instruments and has **proven its ability to do so in both low and high interest rate environments.** From 2015 to 2021, when interest rates were held at historic lows, private credit still managed double-digit returns! **As you can see in the figure below, in 2021–22, private credit loans (aka direct lending) provided more than double the yields of junk bonds, and often with better protections.**

2. Private Credit Typically Has Less Interest Rate Risk—Loans made to private companies usually have floating rates that adjust with market rates. So when interest rates rise, so do the payments made by the borrower. Private credit usually makes it hard for borrowers to lock in low fixed rates for extended periods, which serves

DIRECT LENDING: HISTORICALLY HIGHER RETURNS

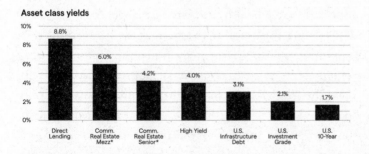

Asset class yields

Source: BofA Securities, Bloomberg Finance L.P., Clarkson, Cliffwater, Drewry Maritime Consultants, Federal Reserve, FTSE, MSCI, NCREIF, FactSet, Wells Fargo, J.P. Morgan Asset Management. *Commercial real estate (CRE) yields are as of September 30, 2021. CRE - mezzanine yield is derived from a J.P. Morgan survey and U.S. Treasuries of a similar duration. CRE - senior yield is sourced from the Gilberto-Levy Performance Aggregate Index (unlevered); U.S. high yield: Bloomberg US Aggregate Credit - Corporate - High Yield; U.S. infrastructure debt: iBoxx USD Infrastructure Index capturing USD infrastructure debt bond issuance over USD500 million; U.S. 10-year: Bloomberg U.S. 10-year Treasury yield; U.S. investment grade: Bloomberg U.S. Corporate Investment Grade. Data is based on availability as of May 31, 2022.

as great protection for the lender/investors, even as they reap rewards in the form of higher returns. **This design can be very meaningful during periods of high inflation, and it is precisely why hundreds of billions are pouring into private credit despite intense inflationary headwinds.**

3. Private Credit Can Provide Stability Through Difficult Markets and Has Experienced Low Default Rates—Private credit portfolios have proven that they can weather storms quite well. **In the eighteen-year period from June of 2004 through June of 2022, which included both the Global Financial Crisis and the COVID pandemic, loss rates for private credit loans averaged around -1 percent of loans per year, a number most banks would envy.** Furthermore, a study of the period between 1998 and 2018 showed that **the worst five-year period for private credit still produced positive returns for investors. Why?** There are really two main reasons:

First, because private credit lenders often hold their own loans (as opposed to selling them off to third parties), **they truly have their own money at risk.** This incentivizes them to adhere to strict credit research and underwriting standards—and they do. These lenders can be very picky about who they lend to, and they often choose only the highest-quality borrowers. **They can also be choosey about which *types* of companies they lend to, granting loans only to businesses in the more recession-proof industries (e.g., consumer staples, healthcare, infrastructure, etc.).**

The second appealing feature of these loans is the protections that the lender can build in. When private credit firms issue loans to companies, the transactions are typically structured as "senior secured loans." **This simply means that the lender is first in line to get paid back in the event the company has trouble.** Private credit firms are also extremely creative, and they often include specific covenants, protections, and collateral requirements that give them a high degree of confidence in making sure they do not lose money.

Remember Buffett's #1 rule of investing? DON'T LOSE MONEY! **You can see in the figure below that even in its absolute worst five-year**

HISTORICALLY CONSISTENT PERFORMANCE

Lowest 5-Year Annualized Performance (1995–2022)

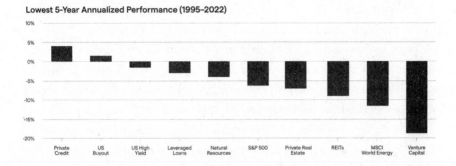

Source: Burgiss. Private Credit=Burgiss US Private Debt Funds Index. US Buyout=Burgiss US Buyout Funds Index. US High Yield=ICE BofA US High Yield Index. Leveraged Loans=Credit Suisse Leveraged Loan Index. Natural Resources=Burgiss US Natural Resouces Funds Index. S&P 500=S&P 500 Total Return Index. Private Real Estate=Burgiss US Real Estate Funds Index. REITs=S&P United States REITs. MSCI World Energy Total Return. Venture Capital=Burgiss US Venture Capital Funds Index. All data is taken from sources believed to bereliable but cannot be guaranteed.
PAST PERFORMANCE IS NOT NECESSARILY INDICATIVE OF FUTURE RESULTS.

period, private credit still made money! Pretty impressive when you stack it up against other asset classes.

FROM CONCEPT TO EXECUTION

"Nobody ever mastered any skill except through intensive, persistent and intelligent practice."
—Norman Vincent Peale

By now it should be clear why the biggest institutional investors find solace in their private credit investments. **They understand that income is the outcome! To recap, these are the three primary reasons why the smart money has diversified into private credit for consistent income.**

1. Low correlation to public markets (think Holy Grail)
2. Attractive risk-adjusted returns with floating rate protections as interest rates rise
3. Strong lender protections against default (e.g., senior position to be paid back first)

So now that we understand private credit conceptually, what is the best strategy for an investor wanting to allocate a portion of their portfolio to private credit? While there is no one-size-fits-all, we can certainly share our perspective, as we have invested in private credit for decades.

First and foremost, selecting an excellent private credit manager is crucial. Why? Because each manager must have deep expertise in sourcing, underwriting, and executing on hundreds of loans to create a diversified basket for their underlying investors. The success of these loans is highly contingent on the skill set of their underwriters, which the best firms have developed over decades. In Part 2 of this book, we interview David Golub of Golub Capital. David is one of the best performing private credit managers in the world, with more than $60 billion in assets under management and a consistently stellar track record.

There are numerous categories and subcategories of private credit that we do not need to dive into here; however, the chart below shows the impressive, industry-wide, average returns (CAGR = compound annual growth rate) of different private credit strategies across different geographies.

Our firm's philosophy is never to bet on just one horse in one race. We prefer to build partnerships with managers across multiple private credit strategies that create immense diversification across numerous types of loans, with varying risk profiles, across various sectors and

PRIVATE DEBT HISTORIC AND FORECAST PERFORMANCE

Performance	CAGR (2015–2021)	CAGR (2018–2021)
Private debt	9.37%	11.44%
Private debt—direct lending	6.83%	7.98%
Private debt—distressed debt	9.18%	12.64%
Private Debt—other	11.74%	14.28%
North America—private debt	8.92%	12.09%
Europe—private debt	9.88%	9.62%
APAC—private debt	10.09%	11.42%
Rest of World—private debt	13.44%	16.26%
Diversified multi-regional private debt	14.29%	21.30%

Source: PREQUIN

geographies. In short, we do not want to feel turbulence in case one specific strategy has a higher than normal default rate. Having multiple partners and multiple lending strategies helps smooth out the ride and create more predictable returns.

Is there a downside to private credit? The tradeoff in private credit is liquidity. While you still receive your monthly or quarterly income payments, it usually takes three to five years to fully harvest your investment—a relatively long time compared to bonds, which can be sold at the click of a button. This is because private credit lenders normally hold the loans they make to maturity. But that is precisely what also provides the predictability that investors have grown to really appreciate from this asset class.

To learn more about the specifics of private credit, you can visit our informational page: **www.WhyPrivateCredit.com.**

As we turn the page, we dive into one of the most important aspects of our ability to survive and thrive on this plane . . . energy! We are in the midst of an energy revolution, turning toward a combination of renewables (wind, solar, etc.) and new innovative technologies that can reduce or eliminate carbon from traditional fossil fuel burning. **With the biggest institutions and world governments throwing their weight behind this category, there is tremendous opportunity for investors.**

CHAPTER 5

ENERGY

THE POWER OF OUR LIVES (PART ONE)

"Energy is the key to human progress."
—John F. Kennedy

A Quick Note: The topic of energy is robust to say the least! As a result, we have dedicated two chapters to adequately cover it. In Chapter 5, we will set the stage and get an understanding of our current global energy situation. In Chapter 6, we will cover some of the investment opportunities that are unfolding as the world embarks on a multitrillion-dollar energy revolution.

SHARED PROSPERITY

The story of human progress is a story of energy. Prior to our ability to efficiently harness energy, we lived brutally short lives of survival. We spent our time hunting, gathering, and lighting fires to keep us warm and cook our food. This was our way of life for millennia. Aside from the elites, the vast majority were poor, illiterate, uneducated, diseased, and malnourished. Both then and now, these are the plagues of a population without energy.

Once we figured out how to harness energy, life on this planet began a steady march toward progress. Not perfection, but progress. Life became much easier when we invented new methods of heating, lighting, and transportation. The transition from wood to coal single-handedly launched the Industrial Revolution. The steam engine transformed travel and trade in one fell swoop. In the 1890s, Nikola Tesla developed AC power generation and dazzled the world when he used it to power a hundred thousand lights at the Chicago World's Fair. **Fewer than forty years later, American households were filled with electric appliances, tools our ancestors would have only dreamt of.**

In 1990, nearly 1.9 billion people (35 percent of the world population) lived in extreme poverty, defined as living on less than $2 per day. Today, just a few decades later, this figure has fallen to 782 million people (or 10 percent of the world population). World Bank Group president Jim Yong Kim said, *"Over the last 25 years, more than a billion people have lifted themselves out of extreme poverty, and the global poverty rate is now lower than it has ever been in recorded history. This is one of the greatest human achievements of our time."* This great feat would have never been possible without access to energy. **Energy is the rope by which the poor can pull themselves up; it is also the rope that we, in the developed world, must let down. It is the foundation for employment, education, food security, clean water, basic healthcare, internet access, entrepreneurship, global trade, and shared prosperity. Energy is the precursor for industry; and just as our bodies need oxygen, industry needs energy.**

Today, we have two important realities to contend with:

First, we are experiencing an energy revolution wherein renewable sources of clean(er) energy are taking over market share from less clean energy sources. This trend is going to continue, but, according to numerous experts we interviewed, traditional fossil fuels will likely never be fully replaced. This may come as a shock if you were thinking society would flip a switch and rid itself of fossil fuels. This is certainly how it sounds when renewables are discussed in the media. However, as we will cover later in the chapter, the more likely outcome is that technological innovation will make existing fossil fuels much cleaner and greener. In fact, technologies that can do just that already exist, but it will take time for them to scale.

Second, the growing world population, and the billions of people in emerging economies like China and India, will need *all* forms of energy to meet ever increasing demand. Case in point, China currently generates 63 percent of its electricity from coal. That's down from 77 percent in 2000,* but coal in China isn't going anywhere any time soon. The Climate Action

*https:/www.eia.gov/todayinenergy/detail.php?id=53959

Tracker reported that coal production [in China] reached record levels in 2022 for the second year running. And while the entire world retired 187 gigawatts of coal plants between 2017 and 2022, the Chinese have added 113 gigawatts of new coal-powered plants in the last two years alone.* The Paris Climate Accords notwithstanding, China has recently permitted 180 new coal mines to be built and at the time of this writing is permitting two new power plants per week.† In February of 2023, the Center for Research on Energy and Clean Air reported that *"the coal power capacity starting construction in China was six times as large as that in all of the rest of the world combined."*

The fact is, India and China, with nearly 3 billion people combined, are going through their own Industrial Revolution with no intention of slowing down. They are keenly aware that energy drives industry and that industry will usher hundreds of millions from poverty into the middle class. President Xi Jinping says climate goals *"can't be detached from reality"* nor come at the expense of Chinese energy and food security.

NET ELECTRICITY GENERATION IN CHINA BY FUEL TYPE (2000–2020)

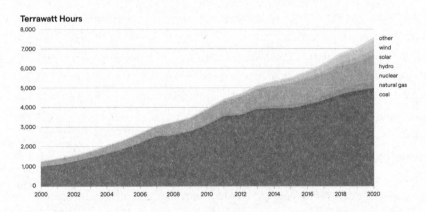

Data Source: U.S. Energy Information Administration, International Energy Statistics

*https://www.wsj.com/articles/john-kerry-china-climate-economy-xi-jinping-bei jing-e50b9ef4?mod=hp_trending_now_opn_pos1
†https://energyandcleanair.org/publication/china-permits-two-new-coal-power -plants-per-week-in-2022/

SEPARATING FACTS FROM FEELINGS

Upon hearing the words "energy transition," one might naturally think that we are switching from fossil fuels to renewables. Nothing could be further from the truth. Modern man has always been "transitioning" to different forms of energy, which is why the word "transition" is an unfortunate misnomer. Energy expert Wil VanLoh, whom you will hear from in Part 2 of the book, believes that energy "addition" would be a more apt term. Why? VanLoh explained that when we look at history, we can see that it takes a very long time for new energy sources to be adopted, and that they have never fully replaced the previously dominant forms of energy. He laid out the data showing that we are currently undergoing the fifth energy addition/transition in modern history. Let's take a look . . .

1. In the mid-1800s we began transitioning from wood to coal. It took fifty years for coal to reach 35 percent of global energy market share. While coal has lost market share (as a percentage) relative to other energy sources, **in 2022 we used more coal than EVER in history.** Coal remains the largest source of energy for electricity and is vital to the production of concrete, steel, paper, and more.

    In the early 1900s, following the production of Henry Ford's first Model T, we began transitioning from coal to oil. It took fifty years for oil to reach 25 percent of global energy market share. **In 2023, we are on track to use more oil than any year in history, with 2024 projected to be even higher.***

2. In 1938, the U.S. passed the "Natural Gas Act" to regulate the transition from oil to natural gas. It took natural gas fifty years to reach 25 percent of global energy market share, and as with oil, **2023 will mark another year of record demand, with 2024 demand expected to grow as well.**[†]

---

*https://www.reuters.com/business/energy/opec-upbeat-over-2024-oil-demand-outlook-despite-headwinds-2023-07-13/
[†]https://www.iea.org/reports/gas-2020/2021-2025-rebound-and-beyond

The 1960s saw the beginning of the proliferation of nuclear power. Nuclear peaked out in 1977 with roughly 5 percent of global energy market share, but it looks poised to make a serious comeback. (More on that later!)

Around 2010, society began the move toward wind, solar, and other renewables. Today, after thirteen years and nearly $1 trillion invested, **these renewable sources provide just 3 percent of the world's energy needs.**

Given the choice, we all want cleaner forms of energy, and we can surely get there with innovation. But we also need to understand just how much time it takes for new sources to gain substantial market share. And this, my friend, presents tremendous investment opportunity.

EXPONENTIAL DEMAND

When we look at the future, experts foresee two unavoidable variables that will impact energy demand . . .

1. Population Growth—The global population has grown from 2.5 billion in 1950 to more than 8 billion today. The International Monetary Fund (IMF) predicts that the global population will continue to surge, reaching 9.7 billion by 2050.*
2. Middle-Class Growth—As the world marches forward, **a combination of technology, advances in healthcare, and access to energy will propel billions from relative poverty into the middle class.** People who earn more, spend more. And they undoubtedly use more energy.

Point being, we aren't dealing with a static amount of energy usage; we are dealing with ever-increasing demand. The world's population currently uses about **100 million barrels of oil per day,** and that number is only expected to grow. **By 2050, most experts believe that the total global energy demand will increase by roughly 50 percent.** This is a reasonable estimate considering demand grew by 50 percent between 1990 and 2020.

*https:/www.imf.org/en/Publications/fandd/issues/2020/03/infographic-global -population-trends-picture

State-owned oil company Saudi Aramco is one of the greatest beneficiaries of this ever-increasing demand. **They ranked #2 on the Fortune Global 500 largest companies in the world, with revenues of $604 billion in 2022.*** These revenue numbers dwarf Amazon (#4 on the list) and Apple (#8) and could put the company in the top spot (over Walmart) as soon as next year if they continue to grow at the current pace.

As Mark Twain said, *"history doesn't repeat itself, but it rhymes."* When we look to the future, most experts absolutely predict that renewables will grow as a percentage of our global energy supply. Renewables will gain market share—as new energy sources always have during periods of energy addition—but will likely never replace existing fossil fuel energy sources. Quite the opposite in fact. **According to the U.S. Energy and Information Administration (EIA), the use of natural gas, coal, oil, nuclear, and renewables will ALL expand to meet demand by 2050.** (See chart below.)

Every year, I (Tony) host an intimate financial event for my foundation's largest donors. We gather to hear from a who's who of financial experts, former presidents, policy-makers, and more. Much like this book, we sit at a proverbial table of titans to gain wisdom about the future and how they can capitalize.

GLOBAL PRIMARY ENERGY CONSUMPTION BY ENERGY SOURCE (2010–2050)

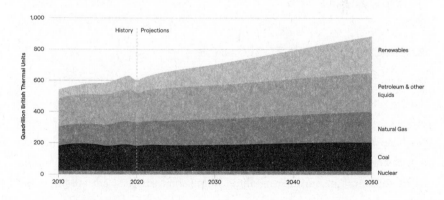

Source: U.S. Energy Information Administration, International Energy Outlook 2021 Reference case
Note: Petroleum and other liquids includes biofuels.

*https:/fortune.com/2023/08/01/saudi-aramco-profitable-oil-company-trillions/

Jamie Dimon is the CEO of J.P. Morgan, the world's largest bank and a company that has committed to net-zero emissions by 2050. He graciously accepted my invitation to the event, and much of our discussion was devoted to the future of energy. To suggest he is a proponent of the green energy movement is an understatement. He shared with me how **J. P. Morgan established a clean energy allocation that is on track to finance $1.1 trillion in clean energy projects by 2030! He is also pressuring Congress to expedite the permitting of green energy technologies. And yet, Dimon explained to the audience, he may have been early in his desire to switch energy sources:** *"The lesson that was learned from Ukraine is that we need cheap, reliable, safe, secure energy, of which 80 percent comes from oil and gas. And that number's going to be very high for ten or twenty years."* Driving oil and natural gas prices higher is a punitive measure that is actually making matters worse by forcing nations to switch their coal plants back on. In a letter to J.P. Morgan's shareholders Dimon wrote *"using (natural) gas to diminish coal consumption is an actionable way to reduce CO_2 emissions expeditiously."*

For those who may cringe at the thought of more fossil fuels in the interim, not to worry. **There are countless billions pouring into carbon capture (and storage) technologies that, although not yet totally scalable, will make the use of fossil fuels far greener.** We will highlight a couple of exciting breakthroughs in Chapter 6.

Let's drill down a bit . . .

SUN AND WIND IN THE FORECAST

Wind and solar are the core technologies for renewable energy generation, but they face significant headwinds . . . pun intended. First and foremost, there are winners and losers from a geographic perspective. The wind must blow *intensely* if you want to use wind power. The sun must shine *intensely* if you want solar. Partly cloudy skies with a light breeze ain't going to cut it. To be clear, I am not talking about home solar panels, I am talking about industrial-strength solar fields that can power a grid.

In the U.S., there are huge swaths of land rich in howling wind (the middle of the country) and scorching sunshine (the Southwest). But that's not the case for most of the world. In fact, the vast majority of the world is considered unsuitable for industrial-strength wind, solar, or both. Most of the world's cities with populations over 1 million are not ideally suited for industrial-strength, renewable power generation. Thus, any solar or wind farms that power them must be placed far away, and transmission lines have to be built to transport the electricity. This is less than ideal and incredibly expensive when compared to other available sources. I don't mean to take the wind out of anyone's sails, but at the end of the day, there is a consensus among experts that solar and wind have very real limitations at scale. Among other reasons, this is why China and India are doubling down on nuclear.

NUCLEAR POWER

Only three nuclear reactors have come online in the United States over the past three decades, partly because the horrors of Three Mile Island, Chernobyl, and Fukushima left an indelible impression on a generation. While nuclear disasters are intolerable, it is also important to balance the memory and lessons of these disasters against new, safer nuclear technologies and the environmental impact of all other types of energy. From burning coal to mining critical minerals for electric cars, nearly all forms of energy have their dirty downsides. As the wise Thomas Sowell once said, *"There are no solutions, only tradeoffs."* This certainly applies here, as nuclear is still the cleanest, densest form of energy known to man. From a technology perspective, many of the reactors in use today are using decades-old technology, and the accidents that occurred were all relics of history. To be fair, we must look at today's technology and safety standards to judge nuclear. This is where small modular reactors (SMRs) come into play.

After decades of innovation, experts believe that SMRs hold great promise. About the size of a small commercial airplane these reactors are tiny compared to the massive traditional reactors you probably imagine when you hear the words "nuclear power." **They are far safer and have numerous fail-safes in place to avoid a catastrophe.** Unlike traditional reactors, which can take a decade to build, SMRs can be quickly built and assembled in a factory and delivered by truck to their final destination. This allows them to be placed in isolated areas and sites with limited access to water. **If** units like these become ubiquitous, we are talking about cheap, green energy for huge portions of the global population.

In 2022, the first U.S.-based small modular reactor was approved by regulators for construction in Idaho. There are now multiple companies developing incredibly efficient SMRs that will produce as much electricity as older, much larger, reactors—**and they'll do it with just 1 percent of the land that other renewables (wind, solar, hydro) would require to produce the same amount of electricity!**

There are numerous companies in the race to create next-generation nuclear technologies (including SMRs), which is important because as a global community, we are way behind the curve. If we are serious about getting to "net-zero," most experts believe that nuclear will need to be a major part of the solution. And yet nuclear tends to be divisive due to the tension between its potential dangers and the fact that it is the greenest form of energy we can produce. Case in point: For years, environmental groups pushed to shut down the Indian Point nuclear reactor, which supplied nearly 25 percent of New York City's power. They argued that it could be replaced by renewables like wind and solar. In 2021, the plant was shuttered, and the unintended consequences began to stack up. The state reported that since the closing, 89 percent of its electricity now comes from natural gas and oil, up from 77 percent the previous year when both of Indian Point's reactors were running.* Certainly not the outcome that environmentalists had in mind.

This anti-nuclear position also backfired in Germany. By 2022, they had retired all their nuclear plants. Exacerbated by the war with Ukraine and the elimination of Russian natural gas, the Germans have had to resort to re-igniting their coal plants, replacing green nuclear energy with dirty energy. Then, in another desperate move, they disassembled a large wind farm to expand their coal mining operations!†

Many nuclear proponents suggest that Germany should have looked to their French neighbors who get 70 percent of their energy from nuclear.

---

*https://www.lohud.com/story/news/2022/07/22/new-york-fossil-fuels-increase-after-indian-point-nuclear-plant-shutdown/65379172007/
†https://www.theguardian.com/world/2022/oct/26/german-windfarm-coalmine-keyenberg-turbines-climate

WHO IS BUILDING NUCLEAR REACTORS?
Top 10 countries by nuclear capacity under construction

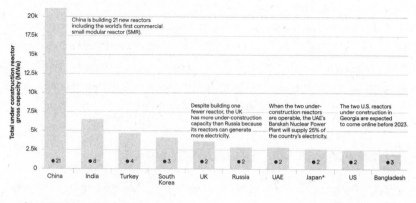

● Reactor Under Construction ▪ Reactor Under Construction

Source: World Nuclear Association

Instead of closing down plants, France has six new reactors coming online before 2050. The French have also pioneered an incredible strategy for recycling nuclear waste and maximizing its useful life span.

In April 2023, Finland switched on a new nuclear plant. **The plant was so effective at creating an abundance of affordable, green energy that prices dropped below zero for a short period!** Now the country can use as much energy as it pleases and know that it's nearly 100 percent green. China and India also understand that nuclear is a vital part of their own green future. Aside from growing energy demands, both countries acknowledge that they are facing major air quality and pollution issues. As the world presses forward with ESG commitments, China and India have made abundantly clear their need to balance their environmental concerns with their growing economy. They have indicated they will do this by going nuclear, and China is easily winning the race. Bolstered by deep government pockets and the absence of obstructionists, China is currently building twenty-one nuclear plants. In addition, they are investing half a trillion dollars to build 150 reactors in the next fifteen years!* This pace of expansion is unlike anything the world has seen.

*https://www.bloomberg.com/news/features/2021-11-02/china-climate-goals-hinge-on-440-billion-nuclear-power-plan-to-rival-u-s

India is also moving at warp speed, currently building an impressive eight nuclear plants. Even oil-rich Saudi Arabia has plans to build sixteen reactors over the next two decades. Contrast this with the U.S., which has just two under construction. U.S. regulators need to move swiftly if we plan on leading the nuclear technology revolution. Most experts believe that environmentalists and politicians need to be looking at this technology through a modern lens. We don't judge the safety of cars based on models built in the 1950s. The same should hold true for nuclear power!

GREEN MACHINES AND THE RACE FOR MINERALS

Electric vehicles (EVs) are having their moment in the spotlight. With Tesla leading the way, every car manufacturer has jumped into the EV revolution. But while electric cars are greener on the road, it's undeniable that producing them is incredibly taxing on the environment. The same is true of wind turbines and solar panels. The reality is that "green machines" must be manufactured using traditional sources of energy. Oil, natural gas, and coal are needed to produce the necessary concrete, steel, and plastics. **For example, the energy equivalent of one hundred barrels of oil is required to fabricate a single EV battery that can store the equivalent of one barrel of oil.** Then we have the vast amount of critical minerals that are needed for batteries, solar panels, transformers, generators, and other inner workings of these green machines. The process of finding, mining, refining, and transporting these minerals is not at all green. Consider these facts . . .

- Nearly five hundred thousand pounds of earth are dug up and processed to create just one one-thousand-pound EV battery. This mining is often done with heavy, diesel-burning equipment.
- A standard EV battery contains about 25 pounds of lithium, 30 pounds of cobalt, 60 pounds of nickel, 110 pounds of graphite, and 90 pounds of copper.
- An EV battery contains one thousand times more cobalt than a smartphone.
- By 2030, more than 10 million tons of batteries will become garbage each year.

"Naturally, there's a trade-off for its exceptional fuel economy."

To be clear, electric vehicles, wind farms, and solar panels are indeed an important part of renewables. But the entire supply chain needs to be de-carbonizing if we are going to be intellectually honest. China has the most EVs in the world, but most of them are charged using electricity from coal. Can we really consider coal-powered cars "green"?

The bigger point I am making is that we need to separate fact from fiction, marketing from reality. We all want clean energy and to take care of our planet. And yet we must digest some difficult realities. One of those realities is the control of critical minerals by often adversarial countries.

TOTAL(ITARIAN) CONTROL

In the early 2000s, China saw the writing on the wall. They could see that the world was committing to greener technologies and knew that every one of those green machines would require critical minerals. Without substantial deposits in their own country, the Chinese government spent hundreds of billions to lock up control of numerous mining operations around the world. Notably, they flexed their power (and wallets) with the sometimes corrupt governments of Africa, a continent rich in natural resources. The Congo was China's primary conquest.

Cobalt is used in nearly every smartphone, tablet, laptop, and EV, to give batteries stability and keep them from overheating. The Democratic Republic of Congo has more cobalt deposits than the rest of the world combined. In fact, nearly 70 percent of the world's known supply is buried in the Congo's shallow red earth, where its easily accessible. (Somewhat ironic, considering that, according to the World Bank, only 19 percent of the population in the Congo has access to electricity.*)

It is estimated that fifteen of the nineteen major mines in the Congo are controlled, either directly or indirectly, by China. Some of them are the size of a European city! Most disturbing are the human rights abuses taking place. The Congo has a sad history of exploitation and slavery dating back to the late 1800s. Around 1890, there was a "bicycle craze" as millions of people around the world began to ride. Believe it or not, the earliest bikes had steel and/or wooden wheels—so it was a big deal when, in 1888, inventor John Dunlop patented a new form of pneumatic rubber tire. And his invention really took off when automobiles entered the scene. Demand for rubber exploded, and the Congo just so happened to have rubber trees as far as the eye could see. Under the colonial oppression of Belgian King Leopold II, untold numbers of Congolese villagers were forced into slavery as deforestation ravaged their lands. The Congo became the world's largest rubber exporter, and yet the people remained impoverished. Published in 1899, Joseph Conrad's famous novel *Heart of Darkness* documented the horrific tragedy of a population stripped of their freedom and a land devoured for commercial purposes.

Today, the Congo is being ravaged once again—not for rubber, but for cobalt. Around the world, tech companies buying the cobalt are often told by wholesalers that the supply chain is clean. This turns out to be untrue for most of the mining operations. Thanks to the courageous work of investigative journalists like Siddharth Kara (author of *Cobalt Red: How the Blood of the Congo is Powering Our Lives*), we now know what the bottom of our supply chain really looks like. Many of the mines are run on the backs of

*https:/www.trade.gov/country-commercial-guides/democratic-republic-congo
-energy#:~:text=Despite%20millions%20of%20dollars%20of,one%20percent%20
in%20rural%20areas

modern-day slaves. Under the eye of armed militia, men, women, and children dig endlessly for cobalt. They scavenge with sticks, pickaxes, shovels, and rebar, all the while being exposed to toxic carcinogens. For twelve hours a day, hundreds of thousands of Congolese toil in the heat to make a dollar or two. Just enough to barely survive.

So proponents of the electrification of everything must also grapple with the true meaning of ESG: Environmental, Social, and Governance. Does each letter carry the same value? If the environment is being destroyed in the Congo (and elsewhere) while hundreds of thousands of natives are enslaved, could one possibly argue that the end justifies the means? Ultimately, big tech will need to wake up and address these issues in unison. **Their purchasing power can demand reform so workers can be paid and treated fairly.** We also must keep working on newer technologies that may not need some of these critical minerals. For example, solid-state batteries and other cobalt-free batteries are being implemented. Tesla is now using cobalt-free batteries in 50 percent of their cars and has indicated they want to completely remove cobalt from their products. Hats off to Elon, but other issues remain.

THE RUSSIA-CHINA BLOC

Russia, a country flush with natural resources, including substantial reserves of critical minerals, has joined forced with China in a mutually beneficial relationship. For example, while China has brought hundreds of billions to Africa, Russia has installed the muscle with paid mercenaries. These are the enforcers hired by governments to keep the populations in check.

Obviously, this China-Russia bloc is giving pause to world leaders who can see that the two have an iron fist of control around our mineral supply. Meanwhile, other not-so-friendly regimes also have a level of control of critical minerals. Consider China, Russia, Iran, Kazakhstan, North Korea, and Venezuela. These six totalitarian regimes have dominant control over the minerals (see chart below) we require for cell phones, tablets, EV batteries, solar panels, windmills, and more. This brings up a host of questions. *How do we secure a safe and reliable supply chain? How do we ensure human rights are prioritized? How will we satisfy increasing demand for critical minerals if environmental policies keep us from mining in our own country?* These

Source: USGS, World Nuclear and Statista

are questions that do not yet have great answers but will undoubtedly need to be navigated.

AN ELECTRIFIED WORLD

In 2022, California mandated that by 2035 all new vehicles sold in the state must be zero emissions (electric, hydrogen, etc.).* Ironically, not long after the announcement, California had a heat wave and pleaded with people to avoid charging their electric vehicles for fear of overloading the aging electrical grid. This begs the honest question . . . Can California's grid handle a fifteen-to-thirtyfold increase in electric cars? **It's estimated that the state will need to triple their power generation in the next decade to do so.** To put that into perspective, California is generating nearly the same amount

*https://ww2.arb.ca.gov/news/california-moves-accelerate-100-new-zero-emission -vehicle-sales-2035

of power as they did thirteen years ago.* Even a small increase is challenging enough, and this is likely why the energy commission has not released any plans on how it might go about this monumental task.

Elon Musk, founder of Tesla (the largest EV manufacturer in the world), has been quite vocal about his concern that there is "insufficient energy" for the U.S.'s goals and that we could reach a shortage in as little as two years. He predicts that our electricity demand is going to triple by 2045 and most recently shared his concerns at a conference with the nation's largest utilities. When you consider that demand has historically only increased 2 to 3 percent per year, it's easy to see why the power companies are woefully underprepared for the coming surge.

While California and twelve other states are legislating this EV mandate, the rest of the world seems intent on pushing for a similar outcome. The United Nations target of zero net emissions, known as the 2050 net-zero goal, states *"The Net Zero Emissions Scenario sees an electric car fleet of over 300 million in 2030 and electric cars accounting for 60% of new car sales."* Every manufacturer is rapidly creating new electrified versions of existing models, from the Ford F-150 Lightning truck to the upcoming electric Corvette.

NEW EV CAR PRODUCTION TARGETS

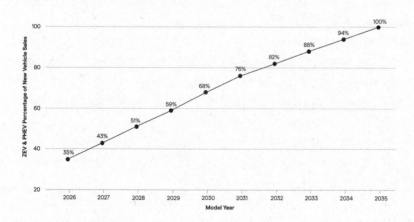

*https:/www.energy.ca.gov/data-reports/energy-almanac/california-electricity -data/2021-total-system-electric-generation

Currently, there are roughly 2.5 million electric and hybrid vehicles out of a total of 290 million cars on the road (less than 1 percent) in the United States. The total number of electric cars in the entire world is 16.8 million out of roughly 1.44 billion total cars (also about 1 percent). **So with a goal of 300 million zero-emissions cars by 2030, we are talking about an unprecedented level of demand for the critical minerals needed.** Is that even doable? The challenges for such lofty goals are very real indeed.

Let's start with a glance at history. **No extractive industry (oil, gas, gold, iron ore, etc.) has EVER been able to increase global supply production by 100 percent in a single decade.** Mining is expensive, laborious, time-consuming, and a regulatory nightmare, particularly in developed nations where human rights and environmental impact studies are prioritized. A newly discovered deposit can often take many years to come online and actually start producing the raw materials needed.

Setting aside the trillions in required investment, environmental experts believe that mining the critical minerals required to produce 300 million zero-emissions vehicles may put an extraordinary burden on planet earth. When you add in the mega wind farms, industrial storage batteries, and thousands of acres of solar panels, the amount of minerals required to reach a goal of *"net-zero by 2030"* is staggering. The figure below shows the exponential demand for the various minerals required.

Take lithium for example. It's estimated that we will need eighteen times more lithium than the current amount being mined today. But lithium is not the only mineral we will need for constructing our green tech. We will need two times more copper, seventeen times more graphite, and eleven times more nickel than we currently produce today.*

Again, we have never in history been able to double the supply of any extractive mineral within a ten-year span. "Dig faster" does not seem like a viable plan.

When I discuss this *"never before in history"* scenario with energy experts, there is almost unanimous consensus that this an impossible feat. A noble goal? Yes. Great talking point for politicians? Sure. **But we must take into**

*IEA Critical Mineral Outlook

CURRENT VS FUTURE DEMAND FROM CLEAN ENERGY USES (OF TONS)

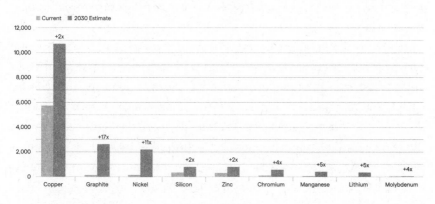

Source: IEA Critical Minerals Outlook

account the realities of what the earth will yield for us and what other costs, both human and environmental, will be incurred.

Now, depending on your presuppositions, many of the facts I have laid out thus far might be hard to digest. I think we would all love to flip a green switch and decarbonize our planet. Numerous experts and I actually believe this is possible with new innovations over the long haul. But in the interim, there will be numerous investment opportunities in an asset class where rising demand seems inevitable.

WHO DRANK ALL THE MILK?

Back when my son was living at home, I would often open the refrigerator door to find a near-empty milk carton in the fridge. It seemed like no matter how much milk we bought, the container always dwindled faster than we could replace it. Living with a teenage boy in your house is analogous to our current energy situation. Bear with me here.

Energy, like the milk within a specific carton, is finite and must be replaced. Now think of an oil or natural gas reservoir. Once we pop the top, it contains a certain amount we can extract before it is dry. **Energy companies and their investors must spend hundreds of billions, in advance, to explore and bring new projects online just to keep up with the world's current thirst.**

But what happens when we dramatically stop spending to generate new production? What happens when we fail to replace our supply for the current and growing demand? We may all find out sooner than later.

In June of 2014, oil prices surged to $107 a barrel. Then, in a dramatic turn of events, prices plunged to $44 just six months later. These rapid losses were devastating, and the biggest energy companies tightened the reins on spending as they licked their wounds. Around the same time, the ESG movement began to really gain steam. With noble goals, they unfortunately put out some incredibly unrealistic timelines. Instead of looking for innovative technology to make oil/gas/coal cleaner, the movement focused on ending fossil fuels, an aim that was even echoed by then presidential candidate Biden, who promised, *"I guarantee you. We're going to end fossil fuel."*

Energy companies were between a rock and a hard place. Institutional investors that had historically funded exploration of new replacement energy sources were pressured to avoid fossil fuel investments like the plague. CEOs of big energy were also under tremendous pressure. They were being told by board members and large shareholders, both explicitly and implicitly, NOT to spend so much on new replacement energy projects. Instead, they were encouraged to return their excess cash to investors either through dividends or share buybacks. **Thus, investments in discovering and extracting new supply dropped by nearly 50 percent in subsequent years.** To put it into perspective, before 2014, the major oil companies invested about $700 billion per year in replacement energy. Since 2014, they have spent only about $300 to $350 billion globally.

Critics argue that less spending on new "upstream" projects is a good thing. A green thing. But in reality, experts believe that it could be setting us up for a chain reaction of higher energy prices, higher food prices, and less national security. This was Jamie Dimon's earlier point regarding the unintended consequences of short-term moves that could actually inhibit everyone's long-term net-zero goals.

SEVEN SAUDI ARABIAS

As mentioned before, the world's energy use shakes out to about **100 million barrels (or barrel equivalents) per day.** To put that into perspective, a football stadium would hold about 2 million barrels. That total use equates to fifty football stadiums' worth of oil EVERY DAY. **That adds up to 36.5 billion barrels every year just to keep our world's economic engine running. Population growth and economic expansion mean demand is expected to grow by 1–2 percent, or 365–700 million barrels, per year.**

But how much do we deplete the existing supply each year? How much does the proverbial milk carton go down? This is the trillion-dollar question . . .

The global "supply decline rate" is 7–8 percent per year. This means that existing fossil fuel reservoirs and deposits are losing 7–8 percent of their total finite capacity per year. **That's 7–8 million barrels of daily supply that we need to replace EACH AND EVERY year just to keep pace with current demand, not to mention attempting to meet the future growth of demand. Wil VanLoh is the founder of Quantum Energy Partners, one of the largest private energy investors in the world. He framed the current situation best: "This is the equivalent of needing to find seven new Saudi Arabias' worth of energy production in the next twenty years."** Simply put, by slowing our replacement energy spending over the past decade, we find ourselves behind the eight ball. VanLoh also believes that the lack of replacement spending over the past several years is just now beginning to show up in prices.

Bottom line: Depleting finite projects with not enough spending to replace them is a recipe for constrained supply, higher energy prices, higher food prices, and higher consumer prices.

TIME TO PLACE OUR BETS

Now that we have parsed fact from fiction, we can see that there will be tremendous opportunity in the years ahead. In fact, many of the experts I speak to believe that we may be entering a Golden Age for energy investing. For fossil fuels, there will be shrinking supply and increased demand, likely leading to increased prices. For wind, solar, and nuclear, there will be accelerated adoption and trillions invested in innovative companies. And finally, for green technology, there are numerous decarbonization innovations coming online that will likely allow us to continue to use fossil fuels in a much greener way!

Let's explore these opportunities in Part Two! . . .

CHAPTER 6

ENERGY

THE POWER OF OUR LIVES (PART TWO)

*"Energy can neither be created or destroyed, it can
only be changed from one form to another."*
—Albert Einstein

ENERGY FOR ALL

It should not be contentious to say that less pollution is better for this beautiful planet we share. We should all be striving for greener solutions through heavy investment into renewables as well as through innovation within traditional fossil fuels (i.e., carbon capture).

Yet, as laid out in Part One, experts agree that we are living with the tension of two undeniable realities . . .

1. Demand for all forms of energy will continue to grow, fossil fuels included.
2. The burning of coal, natural gas, and oil creates a significant and impactful amount of CO_2 in the earth's atmosphere, and we should reduce it using the ***best means possible***.

The "best means possible" is where experts have major disagreements. In March of 2023, the U.N. secretary general called for "ceasing all licensing or funding of new oil and gas" as well as "stopping any expansion of existing oil and gas reserves."

While we all may want 100 percent green energy yesterday, the world is like a giant neighborhood. We need all nations to cooperate and work together. But not everyone is singing from the same sheet of music; that is, everyone has a vastly different time frame for achieving carbon neutrality. It is a delicate balance of not harming the environment while also not harming people and their ability to make a living, cook food, secure transportation, and so forth.

China, India, and many other developing nations know that flipping the off switch on fossil fuels is entirely unfeasible. Experts warn that drastic measures would send the world into a catastrophic global depression where hundreds of millions might die of starvation. Jamie Dimon of J.P. Morgan reiterated in a congressional hearing that "stopping oil and gas funding would be a road to hell for America." Remember, it takes approximately 36 billion barrels of oil per year to keep our global economic machine running, which means we can't pull the plug abruptly.

So is this really humanity's binary choice? Be destroyed by the U.N.'s prophecy of a *"climate change time bomb"* or cease using all fossil fuels immediately and be relegated to a life of green poverty? Most experts believe that a balanced point of view is what is needed. We need to strive to find innovative solutions that can keep the world on its current path of population growth and the eradication of extreme poverty worldwide. **We must deliver the cleanest energy possible to as many people as possible to drive global economic growth and food security. And we must do so in a cost-effective way.** Innovation has always been and will always be the answer to these types of problems. **As the saying goes, the Stone Age didn't end because they ran out of stones.**

THE WORLD'S FIRST NEAR ZERO-EMISSIONS NATURAL GAS PLANT

Rodney Allam is a chemical engineer who, at eighty-two years young, prefers to do his calculations on graph paper with a pencil and standard calculator. As the chief inventor at 8 Rivers, Allam attempts to look at energy problems quite differently. His unique approach has earned him numerous patents as well as the distinguished Global Energy Award (2012).

While most are trying to figure out how to capture and sequester carbon dioxide, Allam wondered if we could use it to our advantage. In 2013, he patented a revolutionary method for capturing nearly 97 percent of the carbon dioxide that is created by the burning of natural gas. Here is how it works . . .

In today's standard method, natural gas is burned to generate heat. The heat generates steam, which spins a turbine. A spinning turbine equals electricity. This process accounts for about 40 percent of the electricity generated in the U.S. The problem is that the by-product of burning the gas is carbon dioxide that is emitted into the atmosphere. The same is true with coal, although coal is significantly dirtier.

Allam wondered if instead of using steam to power the turbine, he could capture and compress the CO_2 and use *that* to spin the turbine. What if he could create a closed loop system in which most of the CO_2 would never be emitted to the atmosphere? If it worked, it would create nearly zero-emission natural gas! Over time, he refined his calculations and ultimately patented his incredible innovation. Then it was time to move from paper to plant. Working with a company called NetPower, Allam set out to complete a proof of concept and build the first near-zero-emissions natural gas power plant. They fired up the test facility in 2018, and after a few years of testing and refinement, they successfully connected it to the Texas power grid! Now they are working on building their first full-scale plant in West Texas. *(Disclosure: To be clear, we are NOT investors in NetPower at the time of this writing.)*

While NetPower is currently at the front of the pack, this type of innovation story is happening all over the world. There are literally hundreds of innovative companies with potential or proven solutions that accomplish carbon capture (and storage). From giant CO_2-sucking fans to take it right out of the air, to companies that pump excess carbon into underground rock formations for storage, they are at various stages of development (and feasibility), but the broader point is clear . . . according to experts, it will likely be innovation that will get us to net-zero, not the complete elimination of fossil fuels. In the meantime, there will be numerous investment opportunities as the world wrestles with reality vs. rhetoric. Let's drill down . . .

"OIL THAT IS, BLACK GOLD. TEXAS TEA!"

If you ask one hundred people who is the largest energy producer in the world, many will guess Saudi Arabia. But many would be wrong. **The United States is the world's largest oil and gas producer. We produce about 22 percent of the world's supply, with Russia (15 percent) and Saudi Arabia (9 percent) in second and third place.* Not only are we the largest, but we are also the cleanest (relatively speaking). Case in point, U.S. natural gas is about 30 percent cleaner than Russian natural gas.**[†] The same is true for oil. Have you ever seen a flame that is constantly burning at the top of an oil rig? This was a common sight for us Texans once upon a time. This burning flame is the result of a practice called flaring, which burns off the excess methane gas created when drilling for oil. **Methane is a far more potent greenhouse gas than CO_2,** which makes flaring quite filthy. This is why the U.S. has been leading the charge to end the practice and has reduced flaring intensity by 46 percent while still growing production.[‡] Unfortunately, countries with less environmental regulation have increased flaring over the past decade. **For example, Venezuela has eighteen times the flaring emissions when compared to the U.S. Point being, not all energy is created equal.** The U.S. has the most stringent regulation and environmental impact laws.

Aside from working to generate the cleanest versions of our fossil fuels, **our energy independence and standing as the world largest producer gives us a tremendous advantage in terms of economic security, food security, and national security.** For the past few decades, our world has become increasingly interdependent. Often for the sake of profits, the West has exported jobs in exchange for cheaper products. **We have also exported**

---

*https://www.washingtonpost.com/climate-environment/2022/10/08/us-is
-worlds-largest-oil-producer-why-youre-going-pay-more-gas-anyway/#:~:text
="We%27re%20the%20world%27s%20largest,100%20million%20barrels%20
per%20day.
[†]https://clearpath.org/our-take/where-american-gas-goes-other-clean-energy-can
-follow/
[‡]https://thedocs.worldbank.org/en/doc/1692f2ba2bd6408db82db9eb38
94a789-0400072022/original/2022-Global-Gas-Flaring-Tracker-Report.pdf

emissions by allowing developing countries with cheap labor to pollute their own air and water while making the products we purchase. We tend to forget that if climate change is a global issue, polluting other countries doesn't solve the problem. We all live in a global "cul-de-sac," and pollution has no borders.

Then, along came COVID. If nothing else, the COVID pandemic pulled back the curtain on the fragility of our global economic machine. We learned quickly that our supply chains are almost entirely outside of our country, and thus, outside of our control. From pharmaceuticals to furniture, we could not get what we needed—anyone who has tried to buy a car over the past few years will know exactly what I'm talking about. Empty store shelves gave us all an eerie feeling. We took for granted that re-stocking would never be an issue . . . until it was.

After this wakeup call, countries have already begun to *onshore* critical elements of their supply chain and bring industry home. From food to microchips to equipment manufacturing, this de-globalization will require domestic energy. Countries with energy independence are positioned to thrive. And those with excess energy beyond their domestic needs will be dominant forces with the ability to be a "net exporter" to allies.

While the American energy industry has been persona non grata as of late (for all the reasons laid out in Part One), American energy stands to become critically important to our nation's prosperity in the decades ahead. We will have an incredible advantage as we lead the way in both in the implementation of renewables and innovative solutions for greener fossil fuels.

Let's explore a handful of themes where experts believe opportunity will emerge. Please note that many of these themes can be accessed in both public markets and private markets (for those that qualify). **Energy is notoriously volatile, so proceed with caution. Case in point, CAZ Investments never invests directly in energy without a strategic partner that has boots on the ground, decades of experience, and a proven track record.**

OPPORTUNITIES FOR INVESTMENT IN ENERGY AHEAD

1. Private Equity—**Approximately ten years ago, just 15 percent of the oil rigs operating in the U.S. were considered private equity–funded, with the balance owned by the big publicly traded companies. Today, more than 50 percent of the rigs running are private equity–backed.** They generate relatively predictable cash flows, and more conservative firms will also often pay for a hedge against falling prices, which effectively locks in profits. That said, private equity energy firms are still experiencing reluctance from institutional investors, which means that well-positioned investors can get greater access to quality opportunities than ever before. **Later in the book, we will glean some wisdom from two of the more successful energy investors in the world: Bob Zorich, cofounder of EnCap Investments and Wil VanLoh, of Quantum Energy Partners. Both firms have outstanding multi-decade-long track records.**

2. Undervalued Publicly Traded Oil and Gas Companies—In 2016, the S&P 1500 oil and gas exploration companies were trading at thirteen times their EBITDA, which is a fancy acronym for profits (EBITDA: Earnings Before Interest, Taxes, Depreciation, and Amortization). **At the time, this multiple was higher than the financial, industrial, and healthcare segments.** Despite the oil and gas sector's rebounding financial performance, they have fallen out of favor for the reasons previously discussed and now trade at a paltry 4.7 times EBITDA. Based on the realities laid out in this book, many energy experts believe this to be one of the more undervalued asset classes in the world today.

3. Refineries—In June of 2022, an article popped up in my inbox. **Mike Wirth, the CEO of Chevron was being interviewed by** *Bloomberg* **and dropped a bomb.* Noting that no new refineries have been built in the U.S. since the 1970s, he grimly**

---

*https:/seekingalpha.com/news/3845705-no-new-refineries-likely-ever-built-again-in-the-us-chevron-ceo-warns forecast, *"My personal view is that there will never be a new refinery built in the United States."*

Against the backdrop of rising demand and growing populations, this could present a disaster for consumer prices but also a good opportunity for investors. Refineries play a critical role by turning crude oil into products like gasoline, diesel, and jet fuel. **More than 4 million diesel-powered freight trucks keep our stores stocked and Amazon packages coming each day. There are more than 22 million flights each year that require immense amounts of jet fuel. When airlines pay more for fuel, you pay more to fly. When truckers pay more to fill their tanks, you pay more at the register.**

In April of 2022, when some California refineries shut down for seasonal maintenance, gas prices jumped to near-record levels. What happens if or when such shutdowns become permanent? According to Laura Sanicola at *Reuters*, *"Since the onset of the global pandemic, the US has lost nearly 1 million barrels per day of oil refining capacity, with more set to be shuttered in the next few years."* In 2022, the *Washington Post* reported that *"five refineries have shut down in the past two years, reducing the nation's refining capacity by 5%."* **Five percent may seem small, but it was enough to send a supply shock wave through the system. As gas prices skyrocketed, a desperate U.S. government called on refineries to increase supply, but they were already running at near peak capacity.**

So now the obvious question. **Why in the world would we be shutting down refineries in the face of increasing demand?**

Historically, refineries are boom-and-bust businesses. They make a boatload of profits when prices surge and take significant losses when prices collapse. Now, with decades-old equipment, refineries are staring down the barrel at two bullets. **First, it requires billions to modernize these aging refineries, and it can take a decade to complete the renovation. Second, refiners are having a hard time raising capital for these renovations in the current environment, so some have simply chosen to scrap their facility and sell the valuable real estate to developers. As** we continue to lose refining capacity, we could see significant price increases as demand continues to grow.

4. Liquefaction—**Cheap, reliable, and relatively clean natural gas can be a powerful tool for decarbonization. Between 2009 and 2015, the U.S. reduced its emissions more than the next eight countries combined—all because of natural gas. Transporting natural gas is where it gets tricky. Standard natural gas can be moved in pipelines, but those take ages to construct and are geographically constrained to wherever the pipes go. Enter liquefied natural gas, or "LNG" for short. Natural gas can be liquefied when cooled to -260 degrees Fahrenheit. Once liquefied, it can be transported in cargo ships and trucks equipped with sophisticated cryogenic storage. Then, once it reaches its final destination, it is reheated and turned back into gas form. It's a pretty incredible innovation when you stop and think about it. But here's the issue: There is no new liquefaction capacity coming online in the near future.** We simply don't have enough facilities that can accomplish this complex task to keep pace with demand. In early 2023, the Federal Energy Regulatory Commission reported that *"tight LNG supply contributed to rising international prices, which reached record levels."* **Are you starting to see a theme here?** When reality collides with the wishful thinking of bad policy, prices tend to surge.

   Consider that at the time of this writing, Europe is paying six to ten times higher gas prices than it was a year ago because 40 percent of its natural gas used to come from Russia. That valve is quite literally closed now due to sanctions and the damage to the Nord Stream Pipeline. **According to Reuters, the U.S. is poised to become the world's largest LNG producer in 2023, just ahead of Australia.* We will have a distinct advantage, but the question of liquefaction capacity still remains.**

5. Private Credit for the Energy Industry—As we covered previously,

---

*https:/www.reuters.com/business/energy/us-poised-regain-crown-worlds-top-lng -exporter-2023-01-04/

private credit has stepped in to lend money to companies when banks cannot or will not. Some of these companies are oil and gas companies. **Many banks have signed "net-zero pledges," which is a self-imposed proclamation limiting their lending to fossil fuels companies. While some banks are still lending discriminately, it is not nearly enough to keep pace with the billions of required capital. Once again, this creates opportunity for savvy investors in a very capital-intensive industry.**

CREATING A NET-ZERO WORLD WITH CLEAN CARBON TECHNOLOGIES

Imagine the best of all worlds . . . **If we could convert the already abundant resources of oil, coal, and natural gas to 100 percent net-zero green energy, we could have a cleaner planet while simultaneously providing billions of global citizens with the energy they need—not only citizens in developed nations, but also those in emerging nations that need cheap and abundant energy to power their economy and pull themselves out of poverty.**

One company in which I (Tony) am personally involved is Omnigen Global. **Their mind-blowing technology, which revolves around hydrogen, is poised to change the game. Although it's not currently a public company or available to invest in, it can give you a sense of the kind of groundbreaking innovation that many companies around the world are striving for in order to guide humanity to clean and cheap energy.**

When it comes to green energy, hydrogen is considered by many experts to be the "Holy Grail." **When hydrogen burns, the only byproduct is water vapor! However, creating, storing, and transporting hydrogen is expensive, with a current market cost in the range of $10,000 per ton. Compare that to the current cost of coal, which is about $100 per ton. That said, hydrogen has been commercially generated since 1783 and is now crucial for manufacturing everything from steel to semiconductors to fertilizer.**

There are three main methods for producing hydrogen and, as you'll see, not all hydrogen is created equal.

- Steam Reformation: Natural gas is reacted with steam to produce hydrogen. This is the cheapest method, but it produces significant greenhouse gases.
- Water Hydrolysis: Water is split into hydrogen and oxygen using electricity. However, the source of electricity can be both dirty and expensive—sometimes up to 2.5 times more expensive than the value of the hydrogen created.
- Pyrolysis: Fossil fuel (or biomass) is heated to high temperatures (1500–1800 degrees Fahrenheit) to produce hydrogen. Previous forms of this technology are much too expensive to be commercially viable, and they still generate a significant amount of carbon waste product and greenhouse emissions.

Since there are varying levels of environmental friendliness, there are universal color assignments applied based on how the hydrogen is made. For example, "Blue" and "Grey" hydrogen are made with natural gas but still release significant emissions when produced. "Green" hydrogen, considered the most environmentally friendly, is made with renewable energy sources, but isn't truly green at all. For example, if solar power is used to create the electricity, we know that the manufacturing of those panels has a substantial carbon footprint. **The solar panel manufacturing process requires the mining and transportation of critical minerals (dominated by China), the use and disposal of hazardous caustic chemicals, and dirty industrial furnaces. The panels will eventually fail over time and could ultimately end up in a landfill.** The *Harvard Business Review* estimates that retired solar panels could total 78 million tons of waste by 2050 because recycling them is not yet cost-effective.*

As I mentioned above, transporting hydrogen is a monumental and costly feat. **While coal can be shoveled onto a train or ship, hydrogen must be cooled to -253 Celsius—just twenty degrees warmer than absolute zero, at which all matter is essentially motionless! Then it must be highly pressurized to more than 10,000 psi. Even after all that, more than 10 percent is typically lost from leakage during transport.** The

*https:/hbr.org/2021/06/the-dark-side-of-solar-power

sophistication and cost of this process, from end to end, presents very real challenges to the broad use of hydrogen for the globe's energy needs. That was until a couple of brilliant material scientists started asking better questions. Ask better questions, get better answers.

What if we could use our existing power plants to generate clean and abundant hydrogen? Since those power plants are already connected to the grid, the massive costs from cooling, pressurization, and sophisticated transportation wouldn't be required.

In addition, what if we could utilize existing fossil fuels (coal, oil, and natural gas) to generate hydrogen in an entirely green way—i.e., with no CO_2 released whatsoever—thereby delivering the abundant clean energy that the world desperately needs and demands?

What if we could deliver truly green hydrogen, what the inventors call "Quantum Hydrogen," at the same price as today's traditional energy sources?

Like all great pioneers that came before, these scientists viewed the "impossible" from a different angle. They started from the belief that there must be a solution, while the "experts" stood by, arms folded, rooted in their skepticism. Truth be told, I was also skeptical until I visited one of the largest coal distribution plants in Pennsylvania that, for many years, has been doing the seemingly impossible. There I met Simon Hodson, founder of Omnigen Global, who had invited me to witness the technology in action with my own eyes. As a material scientist, Simon holds a staggering 140 issued patents.* For example, he developed some of the strongest concrete in the world and licensed his technology for use in the construction of New York's Freedom Tower. Simon was also instrumental in pioneering advancements in horizontal drilling. Horizontal drilling is the primary reason why the U.S. became a dominant force in global energy (from what was known as the Shale Revolution).

Simon also introduced me to his partner, Dr. Nansen Saleri, another brilliant scientist from the field of energy. For nearly a decade, Dr. Saleri was head of reservoir management for Saudi Aramco, the most profitable company in history. During his time there, Dr. Saleri was the chief architect

*https:/patents.justia.com/inventor/simon-k-hodson

for optimizing output from Ghawar, the world's largest oil field, and also pioneered AI-driven smart technology in this field. Together, Simon and Dr. Saleri have worked to bring this technology to light.

I had spoken to Simon and Dr. Saleri numerous times by Zoom, but seeing is believing. I walked into the nondescript metal building where Omnigen had been testing and refining their novel technologies for four years (in partnership with Consol Energy, a company that generates the coal and natural gas for nearly one-third of the electricity used in the U.S.).*

I put on ear protection before stepping inside the building, as the sound was deafening. The door swung open and there stood what Simon calls "Quantum Reformers." These three-story-tall systems can break down coal, oil, or natural gas at 5,500 degrees Fahrenheit (and with zero oxygen prevalent). That's about half of the temperature of the surface of the sun! Their major breakthrough was figuring out a way to keep the system itself from disintegrating at such temperatures—as any engineer could tell you, that's no easy feat. This is part of their proprietary twist on a process called Pulse Pyrolysis. Other Pulse Pyrolysis systems exist, but none can perform at these temperatures, do it without generating carbon waste products, or do it in a cost-effective manner.

When inserted into the Quantum Reformer, fossil fuel is instantly vaporized by the extreme temperature. This separates the fossil fuel into its individual elemental parts (carbon and hydrogen). The "Quantum Hydrogen" is then captured in near pure form and directed right into the power plant for green electricity generation. No transportation needed! **The most amazing part is that Omnigen believes they can accomplish this with no incremental cost to the electricity after the plant has been converted! Said another way, they believe they can produce hydrogen approximately 90 percent less expensive than that produced by other methods.**

But what happens to the carbon? **The carbon is captured (or sequestered) and turned into high-quality graphite!** Thousands of pounds of graphite flakes come out the other end of the equipment as it cools. Said another way, the "waste" by-product of the process is a valuable critical mineral.

Graphite is used in everything from solid state to batteries to nuclear

*https:/www.consolenergy.com/about/

reactors. **As electric vehicle popularity has grown, the cost of graphite has surged more than 50 percent since 2020.** As we learned in the last chapter, China controls 86 percent of the world's graphite. **Unlocking the ability for everyone else to create huge amounts of low-cost graphite will be critical for supply chain issues and the worlds' goals for electrification.** Case in point, Tesla and other EV manufacturers are desperately trying to secure graphite from sources other than China, both for supply chain diversification and to make sure that buyers get the U.S. tax credits (which they become ineligible for if manufacturers secure minerals from "foreign entities of concern," China included).*

The high-grade graphite created by this process is composed of a high percentage of graphene. **Graphene is an incredible material that is just one atom thick, two hundred times stronger than steel, light as paper, and conducts electricity better than copper!** Scientists at MIT were recently experimenting with layers of graphene and figured out that if layered at a "magic angle," graphene turns into a superconductor—a rare class of materials able to conduct electricity with no energy loss and zero heat![†]

Previously, graphene has been prohibitively expensive, with prices running as high as $200,000 per ton! If it were cheaper, it would be used ubiquitously for its superior characteristics. However, the fact that high-grade graphite is effectively a by-product of the Omnigen process could dramatically drive down the cost. Once this happens, Omnigen believes that abundant graphene supply will become significantly more viable, perhaps even unleashing its own wave of exciting new innovations.

At the time of this writing, Omnigen Global has purchased a large coal-powered plant in West Virginia that it will be retrofitting. They are under contract with numerous others. For some perspective, there are approximately 225 coal-fired power plants in the U.S. and more than 1,100 in China (where two new power plants are being permitted every week). Many of the coal plants in the U.S. are struggling to stay alive, with potential shutdowns looming (despite the hard to swallow fact that we need this electricity to power our homes and businesses). Thousands of jobs at the newly

*https:/www.ft.com/content/46e5c98e-f9cd-4e88-8cd5-23427522c093
†https:/news.mit.edu/2022/superconducting-graphene-family-0708

acquired plant will now be saved. A true godsend for those workers and their families.

The U.S. regulatory environment, along with lack of capital invest-ment, is accelerating the closure of U.S. coal plants that currently generate 25 percent of the nation's electricity. Thousands of jobs and the families they support are at risk. **But why close these crucial en-ergy sources (that are already connected to the grid) if we can con-vert them into net-zero green power–generating machines?** And how about the thousands of coal plants worldwide, particularly those in develop-ing nations that have no intent to close their doors? While I am thrilled to be a part of this particular company, this technology will likely be one of the many game-changing innovations that we will need to power our planet to net-zero. Naturally, we are very hopeful that Omnigen will be able to ac-complish everything they believe they can, as it would be game-changing. Time will tell if the science and technology will scale for widespread use, but rest assured we will be rooting for them!

TECHNOLOGY DRIVES ABUNDANCE

In 1973, I was a thirteen-year-old eighth grader. In just a few short years, I would be able to get my driver's license and have my first taste of freedom. Then came the Arab Oil Embargo. Fuel shortages meant a rationing pro-gram where you could only get gas on days that corresponded to the last number on your license plate. Lines at gas stations often stretched for miles, and the scarcity created a palpable tension. My friends and I wondered if we would ever get to drive a car as experts prophesied a world which would soon go dark. I can still remember that gut-wrenching anxiety.

My eighth-grade shop teacher was a man in his mid sixties who could best be described as a bit of a curmudgeon. One day, he read a doom-and-gloom speech from renowned scientist Thomas Huxley about the end of our world as we know it. Huxley discussed how the *"oil supply is diminishing, and it is not improbable that there is a day in the not too distant future when it will be entirely exhausted."* My stomach sank. I would never drive a car. I figured I may as well start saving for a horse.

Then the teacher asked a classmate to come up the front of the room and read aloud the date on the speech. He shuffled to the front, squinted at the small print, and with a puzzled look read, "1868?" **The speech was about the diminishing supply of** *whale oil* before the turn of the century.

In dramatic fashion, the teacher reminded the class that **necessity is the mother of invention. When humanity hits a roadblock, we figure out a way forward. We always have and always will. There will always be solutions when people care enough. When humanity focuses its collective brain power toward innovation, nothing is impossible. As we know, humans went on to invent petroleum and vegetable oils to replace the whale oil. Then came coal, natural gas, nuclear, wind, solar, and more.**

I have never forgotten that powerful moment when the wisdom of my levelheaded teacher prevailed. We can never forget that scarcity is eliminated with technology. It is technology that drives abundance. This has been proven throughout history, over and over again. And yet purveyors of doomsday theories, who fail to recall history, seem to be the loudest voices. Unfortunately, fear sells.

As an example, in the 1968 book *The Population Bomb*, author Paul Ehrlich warned of coming mass worldwide starvation due to arrive in the 1970s. He couldn't have been more wrong. Then, in 1981, the *New York Times* wrote an article entitled "The Coming Famine." The author wrote, *"The world is on the brink of a food crisis"* and *"the population explosion is outpacing food production, and the result will be widespread starvation."*

Fast-forward to today, and according to the United Nations, the number of undernourished people in the world has fallen from 1.9 billion in 1990 to 821 million in 2019. That's a 50 percent decrease! This was entirely driven by innovation and new technologies. Sure, we must do a better job at distribution and supply chain waste, but with time, technology will help mitigate those issues as well.

TIME TO LEAD

During challenging times, leaders maintain a committed capacity to envision something better. If you are reading this book, it's my bet you are a leader. A leader of a company, your community, your church, your family, or even just yourself. **In my experience, there are three mandates of a true leader.**

First, **leaders see things as they are, not worse than they are.** Many people default to seeing things as worse than they really are. Some of these folks call themselves skeptics, but in reality, they are scared. It takes no courage to sit back and view the world through a lens of cynicism, waiting for the worst to happen.

Second, **leaders see things as better than they are,** the potential of how things *could* be. Leaders don't lie to themselves about the current situation, but they must have a vision. **As the wisdom of Proverbs says,** *"Where there is no vision, the people will perish."*

And finally, **leaders make it the way they see it.** They make their vision a reality with courage and hard work. Fortunately, there are people all over the world, folks like Simon and Dr. Saleri, who are laser-focused on solutions to support our energy needs while also taking care of the planet we have so graciously been entrusted with. Solutions are here, and more are coming! Remember that when you read the next "whale oil" headline.

In the meantime, the realities of our energy demands will create tremendous opportunities for investors. Energy may certainly find itself as part of your own personal Holy Grail portfolio.

As already mentioned, in Part 2 of this book, we will hear from Wil Van-Loh of Quantum Energy and Bob Zorich of EnCap Investments, two of the largest private energy investors in the world. They will share their vision and ideas for how one can take advantage of our current climate (no pun intended).

For more information on energy and the items we covered here, feel free to visit **www.WhyEnergyNow.com.**

BETTING ON THE OUTLIERS

Now let's take a look at venture capital, a subset of private equity that is willing and able to take gigantic risks on early stage companies in order to bring about massive change and disrupt the status quo. In fact, many venture firms are investing in breakthrough green technologies that we discussed in this chapter. Venture firms have some serious intestinal fortitude, knowing that the vast majority of the companies they invest in will likely fail. But the ones that survive could very well be the next Google or Tesla. Let's turn the page and dive into this exciting segment, which is the tip of the spear for global innovation.

CHAPTER 7

VENTURE CAPITAL AND DISRUPTIVE TECHNOLOGY

"Technology is a force that converts scarcity into
abundance, over and over again."
—Peter Diamandis

In 1996, Vinod Khosla saw a highly improbable opportunity. The internet was just beginning to take root, and Juniper Networks was a startup with a bold prediction. The founders believed that if high-speed internet was the future, everyone would need to buy the necessary equipment (IP routers). This was at a time when everyone used dial-up, Google did not yet exist, and there were fewer than one hundred thousand websites worldwide. (Today there are over 2 billion websites and growing.)

The founders of Juniper Networks had approached Khosla for a significant venture investment. He began his due diligence, and every major telecommunications company he spoke to said they didn't really see the need for ubiquitous high-speed internet access. **Undeterred and, like all great VCs, something of a contrarian, Khosla knew it is not always smart to listen to the customer.** As Henry Ford famously said, "If I would have asked them what they wanted, they would have said faster horses." **Khosla trusted his instincts, believing that high-speed internet was the way of the future and that telecommunications companies would ultimately need to buy a whole heck of a lot of Juniper's equipment.**

Khosla and his partners at the venture capital firm Kleiner Perkins plunked $4 million into the startup. **That single investment returned $7 billion in**

profits for their investors. To this day, it remains one the most successful investments in venture capital history. **Returns like this are few are far between, but the hunt for high-risk/high-reward opportunities is the business of venture capital in a nutshell.**

As a quick refresher, venture capital is a subset of private equity. But whereas traditional private equity tends to focus on established companies with significant revenue and profits—i.e., good companies that can be made better—venture capital usually focuses on early stage private companies that might have little to no revenue, but big potential to disrupt the status quo down the line. **However, investing in startup companies, which are prone to failure, is a high-risk endeavor. It is often said that about one in ten venture investments survives.** But the one that does survive, if truly a home run, offsets all the other losers and then some. **Stomaching this level of risk isn't everyone's idea of a good time. Most high-net-worth individuals have an average of 1–5 percent of their portfolio in venture capital.** Some certainly have more, but others choose to avoid it altogether as it sometimes requires nerves of steel.

As a rule of thumb, Khosla looks to generate a minimum of ten to fifty times his original investment. He is looking for moonshot companies that face enormous odds but will, if successful, reshape the future (and produce a substantial return on his investment). His extraordinary track record, both as an entrepreneur and a venture capitalist, has earned him a place among the Forbes 400 wealthiest individuals, a far cry from his humble roots in rural India.

RENTING MAGAZINES

The son of an army officer, Khosla grew up at a time when technology was only available to the elites. He still didn't have a TV or telephone in his home when he left for university. Instead, he would rent magazines and get inspired by innovative entrepreneurs on the other side of the globe. He was deeply moved by the story of Andy Grove, a Hungarian immigrant who moved to Silicon Valley to join the founding team of Intel. The company went on to become one of the biggest chip makers in the world.

At age thirty, just two years out of Stanford Business School, Khosla founded Sun Microsystems with investments from Kleiner Perkins and Sequoia, both landmark Silicon Valley venture firms. The company took off like a rocket, and within five years, Sun Microsystems had over $1 billion in annual sales! Khosla ultimately decided that managing a company was not as exciting as helping find, fund, and foster the next disruptive technology. He became a partner at Kleiner Perkins, where he made some extraordinary investments in small startups like Amazon, Google, and Twitter.

In 2004 Khosla decided that he only wanted to invest his own personal fortune and created Khosla Ventures to do so. His mission was to help companies with bold ideas in healthcare, infrastructure, robotics, transportation, augmented reality, and artificial intelligence. In 2009, he decided to let certain outside investors come alongside him, although he remains the largest investor. Talk about alignment!

To say Khosla Ventures has done well is quite the understatement. They are consistently recognized as one of the top performers in Venture Capital and have helped build over forty unicorns. (A unicorn is a startup that goes from zero to a billion or more in valuation.) They were early investors in companies many of us use every day: Affirm, Instacart, DoorDash, Stripe, Opendoor, Impossible (foods), and OpenAI (the company behind ChatGPT). Another notable Khosla Ventures investment was Square. Jack Dorsey (founder of Twitter) approached Khosla with a new idea to disrupt the antiquated credit card processing industry. He had just four employees at the time. Today, the company has a valuation north of $40 billion.

Later in the book we have the privilege of sitting down with Vinod Khosla for an interview. Full disclosure: We are big fans of Khosla, and CAZ Investments has a strategic investment relationship with the firm.

IT'S NOT ALL UNICORNS AND RAINBOWS

Although Vinod Khosla is a success story worth highlighting, the overall performance of venture capital has been choppy and less predictable. According to Preqin, there are 5,048 venture capital funds in the market globally. This adds up to a very saturated market, and for every Khosla Ventures, there are dozens of firms that perform quite poorly. Although the world tends to glamorize the many successes of venture investing, we can't gloss over the many epic failures. Because of its somewhat speculative nature, venture as an industry is often guilty of jumping on the latest trends and buying into hype. FOMO (fear of missing out) is quite prevalent when there is a race to be on the cutting edge. WeWork is perhaps one of the best examples of a company that capitalized on the herd mentality within venture capital. The company would lease office space, make it trendy inside, and rent desks to younger folks that loved a coworking environment. But instead of valuing it as the real estate business it was, the charismatic founder marketed WeWork as the *"world's first physical social network."* Venture firms clamored to get a piece of the company at each fundraising round. It was a frenzy, and WeWork became one of the largest renters of commercial space in the country, with over 11 million square feet to pay for.

Flying too close to the sun, the company's valuations soared to a preposterous $47 billion prior to their filing to go public. When Wall Street finally got a look under the hood, their financials told a story of a company with an entirely unsustainable business model that was bleeding cash. Ultimately, WeWork's financial prospects imploded. In November of 2023, the company filed for bankruptcy, sending shock waves through the industry. The company has a total valuation of just under $100 million, leaving behind it a wake of capital destruction.

When it comes to venture capital, the disparity between the all-stars and "the rest" is extremely large. **Between 2004 and 2016, the top 10 percent of venture capital firms generated returns of 34 percent annually.** This was the golden age, the era that gave us the invention of the iPhone, YouTube, Uber, and hundreds of other disruptive tech companies. **The bottom 10 percent of venture firms lost money during this period, with average returns of -6.50 percent. The middle of the pack did not do much better than traditional stocks. The NASDAQ 100, which consists of the largest one hundred tech stocks, generated returns of just over 10 percent annualized; the median return for venture firms was just over 12 percent (see figure below). Let's not sugarcoat it: Mediocre returns like those are not worth the tradeoff of having your money locked up in a fund for a decade.**

It's no accident that the same VC firms seem to appear at the top of the performance lists each and every year, both in terms of the number

Returns for Venture Firms (2004–2016)	Annualized Returns
Top Decile	34.60%
Top Quartile	22.40%
Median IRR	12.15%
Bottom Quartile	3.36%
Bottom Decile	-6.50%

Source: Cambridge and Associates

of successful companies they have invested in, as well the returns generated from the companies they have exited. I attribute this to a unique dynamic I call the "flywheel of success."

THE FLYWHEEL OF SUCCESS

If you are investing in a strategy where you expect to lose nine out of ten times, you need a few things to be successful . . .

1. Deep Pockets—Diversifying across lots of different companies requires very deep pockets. Individual investors who bet on their brother-in-law's tech startup have horrific odds compared to the professionals who allocate their portfolio across numerous companies.
2. Longevity—The most successful venture firms have numerous vehicles and launch new funds every two to four years (as a new vintage). This gives them diversification across market cycles. Spreading their investments out over time also improves the odds of one of their funds containing the next Facebook, SpaceX, or Salesforce.
3. Deal Flow—Startup entrepreneurs inevitably aim to secure investments from the best venture capital firms, who can provide

invaluable wisdom and guidance in addition to funding. When a top-tier firm makes an investment, it sends a message of confidence to the marketplace, which helps entrepreneurs raise capital, hire talent, and win customers. Therefore, the top venture firms are *invited* to invest in hot startups; the less successful firms must go deal hunting, resulting in adverse selection and poor performance relative to their peers.

The smart money knows this "flywheel" dynamic well, which is why the wealthiest investors (and institutions) almost exclusively invest with the top-tier firms. In 2022, approximately 73 percent of all new capital raised went to experienced venture capital firms that have successfully created and managed a minimum of four fund vehicles (aka vintages) in their history.

Naturally, the burning question is: **How in the world does an individual investor get access to top-tier venture capital firms?**

Top-tier venture firms will often have a "stated" minimum of $10–25 million for prospective investors. Even this is a bit misleading, though, as top firms are typically oversubscribed, meaning no new investors are allowed in—even those with giant checkbooks. Therefore, the only route for most investors is to partner with firms like ours, which have existing relationships in place. Individuals, and their advisors, can leverage our buying power and long-standing relationships. And by locking arms with our clients as one single investor, we're able to negotiate the best fees and other benefits, such as priority position to invest directly in some of the VC's winners (also called co-investment opportunities). In fairness, we are not the only firm that takes this approach, so as an investor, I would look at two important criteria before jumping in with a firm . . .

1. Are the total "all in" fees reasonable when you add the cost of the venture capital manager and the partnership that is providing access. Top-tier venture capital managers get paid well, but the organization providing you with access should be getting some preferential treatment because of their purchasing power.

2. Is there an alignment of interests? Do the access provider and its shareholders have their own personal capital at risk? Or are you

using an access "platform" that could care less how the investment performs?

The next logical question: **Is now the right time for you to invest in venture capital?**

DRY POWDER

As I write this, venture capital is experiencing a harsh winter. The tech sector has been hit hard in both public and private markets. Certain venture funds will experience rough waters ahead as their portfolio companies struggle to survive. And yet, spring always follows winter. A bull market follows a bear market. This season of austerity has created a return to healthy investing practices. In an environment where valuations are more reasonable, companies will be more prudent with their purse strings.

Many of today's biggest and best venture firms have an incredibly optimistic outlook. **First of all, the global venture community has hundreds of billions in cash (aka dry powder) ready to invest when the right opportunities come along.** Second, companies these days are waiting longer to go public, which means there is more time for value creation. This means better returns for investors as well. **Get this . . . since 2008, the average time for a company to go from launch to IPO has doubled to almost ten years.**

ACCELERATION OF INNOVATION

As we look to the horizon, **we see that we are heading into the greatest acceleration of innovation in the history of humanity,** and venture capitalists are the tip of spear. They take massive risks, and sometimes they lose big. But when they win, they win big, all while funding the next generation of life-changing innovation. Imagine a world without smartphones, personal computers, or the internet. **Companies like Apple, Amazon, Zoom, Tesla, Spotify, Airbnb, Facebook, Twitter, and SpaceX were all funded by venture capital.** There are hundreds more that have transformed our daily lives, all thanks to the bold risk-takers in venture capital.

Today, we are on the cusp of more groundbreaking, life-altering innovation. From artificial intelligence (AI), to robotics, to 3D printing, to astonishing advances in precision healthcare, the future is bright for mankind. Let's take a moment to highlight just a few of the incredible innovations that will birth thousands of new companies and create massive increases in quality of life around the world.

- Artificial Intelligence (AI)—The fastest-growing internet application in history is NOT Facebook, Instagram, or Twitter. It is in fact, ChatGPT, an AI platform in which we are investors. Within a few months of its launch, ChatGPT garnered 100 million users. *Forbes* describes ChatGPT as a *"clever ask-me-anything tool [that] has been the go-to-resource for advice on just about any topic it's been trained on and can complete complex tasks like debugging code, doing research and writing articles in an endearing human-like tone."* You are likely already using it or one of its competitors (e.g., Google's Bard).

  As those of us in the knowledge and service economies can already see, AI will make people more productive than ever. However, there is a legitimate fear that certain jobs could be eliminated as a result. While the debate is contentious on both sides, those at greatest risk are those who do not lean in and use AI to augment their work and become more efficient. The traditionalists who dig their heels in and cling to the ways of old are most at risk of becoming obsolete.

  Experts believe that doctors, lawyers, medical researchers, screenwriters, and computer programmers are just a few of the professionals that will be able to move faster than ever. AI will also be able to assist teachers. **Khan Academy, the popular free online education platform, recently launched Khanmingo, described as a "world class AI tutor for anyone, anywhere." Their technology powers an infinitely scalable solution of AI tutoring while also acting as a teacher's assistant for traditional education environments. Since high-quality education is the great equalizer, this could be wonderful for society as a whole.**

We are in the early stages of AI, but its force as a disruptive, yet incredibly helpful, technology is already clear. It will likely become as integral to our lives as the smartphone.

AI has already taken the world of venture capital by storm. **The New York Times writes that the "gold rush into startups working on 'generative' artificial intelligence has escalated into a no-holds-barred deal-making mania."** As we now know, the vast majority of these startups will be dismal failures, but the next Google, Apple, or Facebook is likely being created by two people in a garage at this very moment. This is where venture capitalists can usher in the next wave of innovation with their willingness to take risky bets on startups with the possibility of a gigantic asymmetric upside.

- Healthcare Advances and Precision Therapies—Neuralink, a breakthrough company cofounded by Elon Musk, has surgically installed a coin-sized brain-computer interface that "uses thousands of small electrodes embedded in the brain to read signals emitted by neurons and transmit them to a computer." This technological innovation has far-reaching implications. **The company's first goal is to successfully restore someone's vision, even if they were born blind! Next, they will work toward restoring motor function in paralyzed patients. Musk believes the implant could also help address other neurological disorders, like Parkinson's, Alzheimer's, and tinnitus.** This is truly the stuff of science fiction made real, and it has the potential to dramatically improve the quality of life for millions around the world.

Dr. David Sinclair, a leading Harvard geneticist, has answered a hotly debated question: *What drives aging?* **In 2023, he and his team demonstrated their ability to speed up or even reverse aging in cells and restore signs of youth in mice.** *Time* magazine explained that *"reversibility (of the cells) makes a strong case for the fact that the main drivers of aging aren't mutations to the DNA, but miscues in the epigenetic instructions that somehow go awry."** Sinclair

*https:/time.com/6246864/reverse-aging-scientists-discover-milestone/

and his team have figured out a way to reboot cells, erase their corrupted instruction files, and restore their proper function. What does this mean for you and me? By reversing the aging process in cells, we will one day be able to rejuvenate the body and halt diseases related to aging (Alzheimer's, heart disease, etc.). In one amazing example, Sinclair has successfully restored vision in blind mice by rejuvenating the nerves in their eyes through gene therapy. Next up? Testing in humans.

At the third annual "Human Genome Editing" conference, doctors shared incredible stories of people undergoing experimental treatments using CRISPR, a tool for editing or modifying genes. These patients had tried everything, and CRISPR was their last resort. Alyssa, a teenager in the UK who had an aggressive form of leukemia that did not respond to chemotherapy or a bone marrow transplant, was months from death when she decided to try CRISPR. Doctors were able to modify healthy T-cells from a donor so they would not be rejected by Alyssa's body and could freely attack her cancer. Ten months after the treatment her cancer was undetectable. She is back to living a normal teenage life.

While we could highlight countless other technologies, Tony recently published a *New York Times* bestseller titled **Life Force: How New Breakthroughs in Precision Medicine Can Transform the Quality of Your Life & Those You Love**. He interviewed more than 150 of the world's top medical minds about the latest research and amazing advancements in precision medicine. We highly recommend reading it, as it will greatly impact your health and that of your loved ones!

- Supersonic Travel—Although one can appreciate the expediency of modern air travel, sitting on a plane for hours on end can be a literal pain in the butt. Both of us are constantly on the road, so when someone declares New York to London in ninety minutes a realistic possibility, we get excited!

  This is the aim of Hermeus, a startup backed by the U.S. government and elite venture capital firms, including Khosla and Founders Fund, that is building a fleet of supersonic

aircraft not far from the world's busiest airport in Atlanta, Georgia. The company intends to build planes capable of Mach 5 (3,850 mph), a speed five times faster than any commercial aircraft today and twice as fast as the now-decommissioned Concorde. As an added bonus, the view will also be incredible, as the planes will fly at ninety thousand feet, the highest attainable altitude before crossing the threshold of space. Imagine looking out and seeing the curvature of the earth with barely enough time to enjoy a bag of peanuts before beginning your descent. Hermeus will be testing an autonomous plane in 2023 and hopes to have a passenger-ready plane by 2029!

- 3D Printing and Robotics—Owning a home is a wonderful privilege. Unfortunately, for 1.6 billion people, that is currently an unattainable goal. The solution? Affordable and durable 3D-printed homes. Much like toothpaste squeezed from a tube, these homes are created by a giant printer that squirts out layer upon layer of thin, specialized concrete to create flawless, fortified walls. The homes not only look very cool, they're also wind, water, mold, and termite resistant. This is a game changer for countries where hurricanes, typhoons, and floods quickly wipe out poorly constructed shacks at great peril to the families within. This profound technology is being pioneered by ICON, a company Tony personally partnered with to build nearly one hundred homes in a Mexican community. ICON is now building on a large scale, beginning with a master planned community in Texas that will feature a 3D-printed spa, pool, community center, and more. (Full disclosure: CAZ Investments was a seed investor in ICON.)

In construction and beyond, 3D printing will transform many aspects of manufacturing as we know it. One can now precision 3D print extremely complex objects using hundreds of different materials from titanium to carbon fiber. Researchers have even begun 3D printing human organs made of living human cells—equipped with blood vessels and all!

Like 3D printing, robotics has recently taken the world by storm, and Amazon is the perfect case study. Amazon's high-tech warehouses are staffed by a mixture of humans and robots working symbiotically. Robots self-navigate around warehouses to grab whatever you ordered so it can be packaged and shipped to your doorstep. These robots can pick and place over one thousand items per hour. **It is no wonder that Amazon now manufactures their own robots and currently has over 520,000 working 24/7.** We have seen estimates that the robotics sector could compound revenue at more than an 80 percent annual rate for the next decade.

FEARLESS FUEL

A true strength of capitalism is that venture investors are willing to take massive risks on visionaries that will improve the quality of life for everyone, not only in America but around the world. Karl Marx never sat in a self-driving car! We are lucky enough to be alive when the tempo of transformation is faster than at any other time in human history.

Venture is on the front lines of almost all technological progress. With billions in cash waiting to be deployed by venture firms, we can only imagine what advances will be funded and come to market in the years ahead.

Undoubtedly, there will be some big winners and big losers. **If you decide to invest in venture, *who* you invest with means everything.** The amount you invest should also be relatively minimal. As we mentioned earlier, even ultra-high-net-worth individuals are only willing to risk an average of 1–5 percent of their portfolios in this category. But whether you choose to invest in venture or not, we will all be the beneficiaries of its successes! For more information on venture investing, please visit www.WhyVentureNow.com.

KEEPING IT REAL

Wow, we have come a long way! We have now covered numerous alternative investing strategies, many of which could be a part of our personalized Holy Grail portfolio. But we cannot leave out the largest asset class of them all, one with a total value exceeding $300 trillion! Turn the page, and let's explore the world of real estate!

CHAPTER 8

REAL ESTATE

THE WORLD'S BIGGEST ASSET

"Buy land. They aren't making any more."
—Mark Twain

Real estate is the undisputed behemoth of alternative investments and is the oldest and largest asset class. It is likely a part of most Holy Grail portfolios whether it be a residential home, investment properties, or both.

With 7.9 billion people on earth, *residential* real estate is naturally the largest category, with a global value of $258 trillion!* Everyone needs a place to live regardless of the economy, interest rates, etc. And North America represents nearly 20 percent of the world's total real estate value despite holding just 7 percent of the world's population.

Agricultural land is the second largest category, with a total value exceeding $35 trillion. *Commercial* real estate runs a close third, with an estimated global value of $32.6 trillion.

There are numerous subcategories of real estate, from self-storage to hotels to life sciences to timber. On the whole, and over many decades, real estate performance has generated conservative mid-single-digit to low-double-digit returns. But the use of leverage has allowed for substantially higher returns—coupled with substantially higher risk! Of course, returns are very dependent on location, the local economy, the amount of leverage (loan-to-value levels), and numerous other factors.

*https://www.savills.com/impacts/market-trends/the-total-value-of-global-real-estate.html

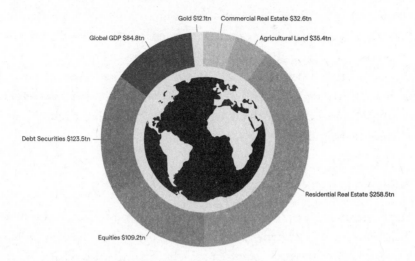

Gold $12.1tn   Commercial Real Estate $32.6tn

Global GDP $84.8tn   Agricultural Land $35.4tn

Debt Securities $123.5tn

Residential Real Estate $258.5tn

Equities $109.2tn

Real estate is the also an asset class that, for U.S. investors, offers government-sanctioned tax avoidance. As a refresher, taxpaying real estate investors receive the benefit of "depreciation," which means the cash flows from real estate income can often be sheltered from some or all taxation. Also, investors can avoid paying taxes on any increase in value when their property is sold by exercising the option of buying more property and rolling over the gains as equity in the new investment. This is called a 1031 exchange. Done over and over again, this can create a perpetual deferral of taxation.

To take it a step further, some investors can ultimately wipe out taxes on ALL their accumulated gains with some clever, and entirely legal, estate planning (particularly in the U.S.). Many of the preeminent real estate families know this tactic quite well. You should talk to your own tax advisor before using this strategy, but here is how it generally works . . .

As you buy and sell investment properties over your lifetime, you continually roll your appreciated equity gains into your next property purchase using a 1031 exchange. * Assuming current tax law holds, when you pass away, your heirs will inherit your property and receive a "step-up" in their cost basis. This means that the value of the property at the time of death

---

*This applies to U.S. taxpayers only and you should consult with a licensed tax practitioner.

becomes the new "floor" by which future gains will be calculated. Translation: All of the previous gains that compounded and accumulated over the course of your lifetime are eliminated, and your heirs can now choose to sell the appreciated properties with ZERO tax. **Tax-efficient income, potentially unlimited tax deferral, and tax avoidance of all capital gains (upon death) are precisely why many of the nation's wealthiest families are real estate dynasties.**

THE TIDE IS GOING OUT

For the past forty years, real estate investors have had tremendous wind at their backs. In 1981, the ten-year treasury was paying just under 16 percent interest. As interest rates fell for four straight decades, nearly all asset prices went up. Real estate was no exception (aside from the Global Financial Crisis, which had some unique dynamics that we will unpack in a bit).

In 2021, real estate was reaching a fever pitch as rates were flirting with darn near free. Unexpectedly, in the middle of the COVID pandemic, real estate produced the strongest returns since before the 2008 financial crisis (see figure on page 109). Residential real estate led the way as low inventory caused prospective homebuyers to literally form lines around the block. All cash offers, short time frames to close, no contingencies . . . these were the hallmarks of the buying frenzy.

Apartment investors were also gleeful as rents increased as fast as at any time in recent history. Industrial real estate came in a strong second, as consumer spending was fast and loose. **Self-storage facilities were sold out from the surge of people moving throughout the country. Real estate prices quickly became irrationally high, with disciplined investors left scratching their heads.**

But then, the tide turned.

The trillions of excess money printed by the government began to slosh around in the system. Inflation turned out to not be "transitory"—in fact, it was here to crash the party. The Fed began hiking rates and real estate has since felt the effects. **The lesson: While hard assets can be incredibly valuable, they can also turn quickly when their price is extremely sensitive to interest rates.**

REAL ESTATE VALUES SURGE (2021*)

Self-Storage	57.6%
Residential	45.8%
Industrial	45.4%
Retail	41.9%
Diversified	20.5%
Infrastructure	18.6%
Timber	16.4%
Office	13.4%
Retail	41.9%
Healthcare	7.7%
Lodging/Resorts	6.3%

Source: PREQUIN

As we write this, we are in the middle of a highly tumultuous real estate market, and charting a course in high seas is quite difficult. What we know for sure is that the long trend of sinking interest rates has reversed course, and as a result we are starting to see fractures within certain categories of real estate. Some segments of real estate are weathering the storm much better. **For this chapter, we will look at COMMERCIAL and RESIDENTIAL separately, as they are very different animals.**

COMMERCIAL REAL ESTATE

For decades, many have considered San Francisco the crown jewel of California, a once-gorgeous city, home to some of the world's most expensive real estate and finest restaurants. Buoyed by the explosive growth of tech companies, San Francisco was continuously ranked in the top ten most expensive cities in the world in which to live.

For companies that called San Francisco home, an office address on California Street was a coveted sign of success. As the *Wall Street Journal* reported, "The corridor runs through the heart of the city's financial district and is lined with offices for banks and other companies that help fuel the global tech economy." At 350 California Street stands a gorgeous twenty-two-story glass-and-stone tower that once housed hundreds of Union Bank employees. In 2019, the building was valued at $300 million. Today, less than four years later, the building is 70 percent vacant and droves of drug addicts and homeless loiter outside. **In early 2023, the building sold for roughly $60 million, an unprecedented 80 percent drop in value (and far less than it would cost to build today).**

According to the *San Francisco Chronicle*, the city has an "astounding 18.4 million square feet of vacant [office] space—enough to house 92,000 employees or the equivalent of 13 Salesforce towers." And it is not just San Francisco that is experiencing a commercial real estate crisis. Real estate firm Cushman and Wakefield reported that "as much as 330 million square feet of U.S. office space could become vacant and unused by 2030 due to remote and hybrid work. When added to another 740 million square feet of space that will become vacant from 'natural' causes, the total is around 1 billion square feet of unused office space building up over the next seven years."*

As we look to the future, there will be some pain and equity destruction, but like all market cycles, it will give way to some extraordinary investment opportunities. **That said, we can't treat this current downturn like those of the past.** The pandemic has introduced new risks and dynamics for us to consider when it comes to real estate investing.

RISKY BUSINESS

In decades past, we would look at commercial real estate through a standard economic lens. Real estate cycles typically coincided with the overall economy: A recession meant fewer jobs; fewer jobs meant less occupied office space; fewer jobs also meant less spending on shopping (retail) and less travel (hospitality). Historically, these downturns have predictably given way to a recovery and a new cycle begins. These traditional cycles will likely continue

---

*https:/www.cushmanwakefield.com/en/united-states/insights/obsolescence-equals
-opportunity

in a broad sense, but there are some new "post-pandemic" risks we must incorporate into our typical understanding of real estate cycles.

- Obsolescence Risk—During the pandemic, we all discovered that Zoom was pretty darn effective for keeping some companies running with remote employees. Many of those companies quickly did the math and realized that remote workers could create huge cost savings by reducing the need for expensive office space. **Hence, the recent phenomenon of empty urban skyscrapers dubbed "Zombie Towers."** This new dynamic of remote or hybrid work has also created what some experts are calling *obsolescence risk*. Commercial real estate buyers must ask themselves if the property they want to purchase is still viable. And beyond that, if it will be viable in ten years or fifteen years or twenty. Are traditional office buildings becoming obsolete? If so, will the surrounding retail and restaurants suffer as collateral damage? How will people choose to live, work, and shop five to ten years from now? Nobody yet knows

OFFICE VACANCIES CONTINUE TO CLIMB

Percentage of all office space that is vacant

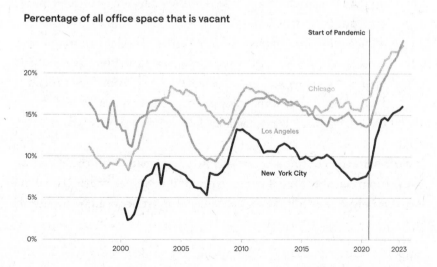

Source: JLL

the answers, but some commercial building owners refuse to sit on their hands while they wait to find out. In Boston, for example, *Fortune* magazine reported that the "housing market shortage is so acute, and the office glut is so big that [the city] will offer 75% tax breaks on office-to-residential conversions."* Some commercial buildings are converting to apartments; others are converting to data centers. All in hopes of staving off foreclosure.

Artificial intelligence is another new risk that could affect the value of commercial real estate as it makes certain jobs obsolete or, at minimum, reduces the number of people (and thus office space) required to get the job done. In May of 2023, the CEO of Chegg, an online tutoring and exam prep company, announced that Chat-GPT was having an impact on its ability to gain new customers. **Why pay for a tutor when AI can help you with your algebra homework for free? After his comments, Chegg's stock plummeted 49 percent in a single day due to fears that the company might be a canary in the coal mine of the knowledge economy.**

In fairness, some argue that AI will create a new genre of company and that a rising field of AI-based businesses will emerge to fill empty offices. This is indeed already happening to some degree, but these companies tend to have very low head counts and no need for large amounts of office space. Midjourney, the most popular AI image creation tool, has over 15 million users, nine figures in revenue, and a team of under twenty people![†] Our friend Peter Diamandis, a futurist, tweeted a prediction that with AI, "we will see the first 3 person, billion-dollar company in the next year!"

So what other obsolescence risks lie ahead? How will these disruptive trends play out when it comes to commercial real estate? The truth is, we simply do not fully know yet, thus we must proceed with caution.

---

*https:/fortune.com/2023/07/13/boston-housing-market-shortage-commerical-real-office-glut-pilot-program/
[†]https:/www.forbes.com/companies/midjourney/?sh=6d4292edf049

1. Geographic/Political Risk—As remote or hybrid work became a viable option for many, our country experienced a huge wave of internal migration. Large numbers of people fled expensive cities. **Not surprisingly, they chose states with lower tax rates, lower costs of living, and higher quality of life. California was the biggest loser in this reshuffling. Between April 2020 and July 2022, more than half a million people left California, taking with them more than $50 billion in total income. New York City lost 468,200 residents, nearly 5.7 percent of its population,* a loss reflected in high vacancy rates.** The billions lost in state income tax revenue has added to already steep deficits, raising conversation of even higher tax rates for those left behind. This vicious cycle could push even more people to pull the plug and move. California is so fearful of further exodus that they are discussing an "exit tax," which would confiscate a percentage of the total wealth of people leaving the state.† Reminds me of the classic Eagles song "Hotel California," where you can check out, but you can never leave.

   Like individuals, numerous companies have also relocated, to more business-friendly states with lower cost of employment. Stanford University reported that more than 352 major corporations have left California, including 11 Fortune 1000s. Charles Schwab, CBRE, and Oracle are just a few of the many titans that moved their headquarters from California to Texas.‡ This is bolstering the job markets of these more business-friendly states. **In 2023, the _Wall Street Journal_ named Nashville, Tennessee, the**

---

*https:/www.foxbusiness.com/lifestyle/new-york-city-lost-nearly-half-million-resi
dents-since-start-covid-pandemic
†https:/www.wsj.com/articles/the-hotel-california-wealth-tax-high-taxes-res
ident-flight-new-jersey-massachusetts-new-york-texas-florida-utah-tennessee
-cost-of-living-education-crime-silicon-valley-south-c39602ac?cx_testId=3&cx
_testVariant=cx_171&cx_artPos=3&mod=WTRN#cxrecs_s
‡https:/www.concordia.edu/blog/19-corporations-and-businesses-fleeing-california
-for-texas.html

#1 job market in the country.* **The income tax–free Music City has quickly become an economic powerhouse.** Florida and Texas have also seen explosive growth. So will these migratory trends continue? Only time will tell; however, we must take note as real estate values, both commercial and residential, are highly dependent on location as well as city and state level policies.

2. Interest Rates and Unintended Consequences—As we have mentioned, we've just lived through the fastest interest rate hike in history. This is going to have some harsh unintended consequences that will ripple through all the various categories of real estate, but none will take it on the chin like commercial real estate. While high vacancy is problematic, it is the trillions in loans on these buildings that could create a banking catastrophe. There is a fast-approaching debt wall. Approximately $2.5 trillion in commercial real estate loans will mature by 2028, with $1.5 trillion coming due by 2025. Barring some major government intervention, it's likely that many owners will be unable to refinance, or will be so underwater that it will be best to let the bank foreclose. This is happening already. According to *Bloomberg*, "In New York and London, owners of gleaming office towers are walking away from their debt rather than pouring good money after bad. The landlords of San Francisco's largest mall have abandoned it."[†] Banks will be left holding the proverbial bag, forced to sell these properties at deep discounts and write down the loans. To be fair, there are a few bright spots. When we interviewed Barry Sternlicht (Chapter 22), founder of real estate giant Starwood Capital, he explained that smaller, boutique buildings with world-class amenities are still filling up. They often house high-margin, low–head count firms like hedge funds, local law firms, AI companies, etc.

---

*https:/www.wsj.com/articles/sunbelt-cities-nashville-and-austin-are-nations-hottest-job-markets-5a454a53
†https:/www.bloomberg.com/news/articles/2023-06-23/commercial-real-estate-reset-is-causing-distress-from-san-francisco-to-hong-kong?srnd=premium

MASSIVE QUANTITY OF REAL ESTATE DEBT MATURING, NEEDING REFINANCING

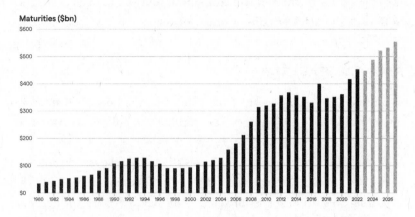

Maturities ($bn)

Source: TREPP Morgan Stanley Research Credit Daily Shot

As a result of the coming loan predicament for banks and tenants (see figure above), Morgan Stanley predicts a 40 percent drop in the value of retail and office space, which is unlike anything we have experienced in modern history.* As borrowers default, the banks will write down these loans, creating severe losses. This could ultimately lead to a banking crisis. **Even more concerning, 70 percent of commercial loans are held by regional banks, which have recently seen a string of failures, from Silicon Valley Bank to First Republic to Signature Bank.**

As values plummet, there is a tremendous amount of smart money chomping at the bit for deals. Several funds specializing in distressed real estate have recently been established and are on the prowl. Their thinking is in line with a principle made famous by the late Sir John Templeton (founder of Templeton Funds and brilliant contrarian investor): "Buy when there is blood in the streets." For investors, there will be a major opportunity to buy at deep discounts as this story unfolds.

*https:/www.bloomberg.com/news/articles/2023-04-08/a-1-5-trillion-wall-of-debt
-is-looming-for-us-commercial-properties

All things considered, a significant amount of commercial real estate seems headed for a cliff, but the residential real estate market is sending different signals. Let's dive a little deeper . . .

RESIDENTIAL REAL ESTATE

As we entered the second year of the pandemic, the housing market was redlining. It was early 2022, prices were surging and buyers were desperate to purchase something . . . anything!

At first glance, one might be quick to assume that we are flirting with another 2008 residential real estate bubble. The fear-mongering media has been beating this drum for quite some time. Below is a list of headlines from articles written by MSNBC's senior real estate correspondent; taken together, they demonstrate just how wrong one can be when attempting to predict the market.

"Housing Today: A bubble larger than 2006."—October 2015

"We're in a new housing bubble."—August 2016

"It's better to rent than to buy in today's housing market."—September 2018

"The housing market is about to shift in a bad way for home buyers."—July 2019

"Next year will be hard on the housing market, especially in big cities."—December 2019

"Housing boom is over as new home sales fall." —July 2021

In the years between the first and last of these headlines, the average home price swelled from $300,000 to $523,000, and buyers were able to lock in the lowest mortgage rates in history. Today, we have even more talking heads beating the "crash is coming" drum. And while prices are most certainly softening, the data seem to be telling a different story.

HOUSING PERFORMANCE THROUGH RECESSIONS

S&P Case-Shiller U.S. National House Price Index

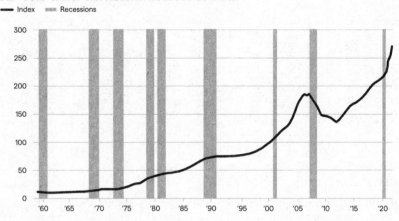

Looking at history, one would think that a recession would guarantee a decline in home prices. **However, since 1960, we have had nine recessions, and residential real estate prices only dropped during one of those—the Great Recession.** As I write this, we are flirting with another recession (the most recent being in 2020), and residential prices have indeed come down. The thirty-year mortgage rate is now above 8 percent, the highest rate seen in over twenty years. This has undoubtedly caused prices to soften. But will they keep dropping? Has demand completely dried up? Do we have too much inventory? Let's unpack the facts.

SUPPLY VS. DEMAND MATTERS

In a perfect world, the demand for new homes would line up exactly with the number of new houses being built (aka the number of "completions"). This would create a perfect supply-and-demand balance. Unfortunately, this is not how builders think. They simply make hay while the sun is shining.

Economics 101 tells us that when we have excess supply and low demand, prices will crash. For example, between 2004 and 2005, builders began building more homes than had ever been built in history. Nearly

Household Formations and New Home Completions

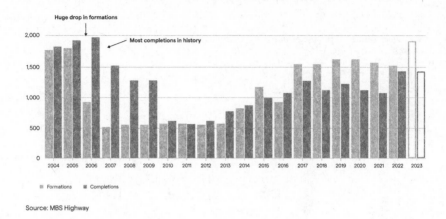

Source: MBS Highway

4 million new homes were built in just two years (see figure above). But after several years of incredible demand, the number of buyers began to dwindle. Even with all the speculators looking to flip homes for a quick buck, there still wasn't enough demand to balance the millions of excess homes for sale.

To make matters worse, we also know that during the period leading up the Great Recession, banks were being wildly irresponsible with their lending practices. No income verification, no down payment, no problem. If you could fog a mirror, you could get a loan. In the famous film *The Big Short*, a hedge fund manager visits Florida to try and decipher the insanity of the housing market. **He is introduced to a "dancer" who has five houses and a condo (with multiple loans on each house). And yes, it's a true story!**

So what's different about today? How do we know we aren't in for another collapse? It always goes back to Economics 101: supply and demand.

LOW ON INVENTORY

Home builders (and banks) learned some very painful lessons in the early 2000s. When you look at the figure below, which shows new housing inventory today, you'll see we are far below historical averages. **Consider this . . . peak inventory in 2007 was an eye-popping 4 million homes for sale.**

EXISTING HOME INVENTORY

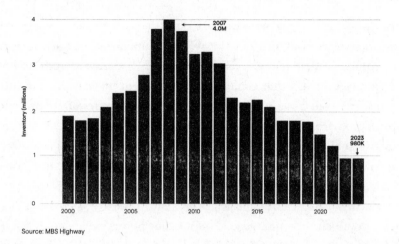

Source: MBS Highway

Today, 980,000 homes are for sale, a forty-year low.* Adding to the inventory challenge, nearly 40 percent of those are already under contract, meaning that the more accurate number of active listings, as of April 2023, is just 563,000.

That's barely more than half a million homes for sale across the entire United States—the lowest number since we began tracking this statistic back in the early eighties.[†] According to Realtor.com, in September 2022, the gap between formations (those needing homes) and completions (homes coming to market) stood at 5.8 million homes.[‡] Adding to the inventory challenge, builders are pumping the brakes on starting new homes as the cost of materials and labor has surged with inflation and rates have risen dramatically.

*https:/fred.stlouisfed.org/series/ACTLISCOUUS
[†]https:/tradingeconomics.com/united-states/total-housing-inventory#:
~:text=Total%20Housing%20Inventory%20in%20the%20United%20States%20
averaged%202287.13%20Thousands,United%20States%20Total%20Housing%20
Inventory.
[‡]https:/www.realtor.com/research/us-housing-supply-gap-nov-2022/#:
~:text=Between%20January%20and%20September%202022,single%2Dfamily%20
homes%20were%20completed.

AMERICAN HOMEOWNERS ARE EQUITY RICH

Another unique dynamic in today's market is the vast amount of equity the typical homeowner has. **In 2008, the average homeowner had just 19 percent equity in their home, making them highly leveraged and susceptible to price swings that could quickly put them underwater and into foreclosure. Today, as a result of larger down payment requirements and appreciation from years past, the average home buyer has 58 percent equity in their home!** Moreover, many of these buyers locked in a historically low rate, making them unlikely to move anytime soon, as a new home would require a higher payment. To be clear, it's not all unicorns and rainbows for residential real estate. Homeowners are now spending 40 percent of their gross income on their mortgage. **The median home mortgage payment is now at a record high of $2,322/month not including taxes, insurance etc. This "debt-to-income" ratio is alarmingly high and even higher than 2008.** Coupled with the fact that credit card debt is also at an all-time high, there are rough waters ahead. Will this confluence of factors result in a major price drop in residential real estate? Time will tell. With such low inventory, the market might surprise us with **somewhat steady housing prices or even moderate growth in higher demand areas, particularly if mortgage rates come down from here. Bottom line: investors proceed with caution.**

"I think you can really picture yourself stuggling to make payments here."

WHAT ABOUT APARTMENTS?

Although apartments (a.k.a. multifamily) are in the residential category, they are a very different animal than homes. Multifamily investing has had a great run over the past decade or so. Rents have been steadily rising for many years, making investors quite happy. That said, apartments are beginning to show signs of weakness in certain geographies, particularly where developers have overbuilt. **Meanwhile, a perfect storm of rising interest rates, falling rents, increased evictions, and rising insurance premiums and property taxes is brewing.** The severity of the storm is highly dependent on the local market.

Many apartment owners (which are often syndicated ownership groups) got greedy and chose not to fix their interest rate for a long period, opting instead for "floating rate" debt to maximize returns when rates were low. Not surprisingly, higher returns meant higher performance fees for the managers. **Now that rates are rising sharply, those owners/ operators undoubtedly regret their decision. The adjustable-rate loans have come back to bite them as their carrying costs have skyrocketed. In August of 2023, the _Wall Street Journal_ reported that** "the sudden surge in debt costs last year now threatens to wipe out many multifamily owners across the country. Apartment-building values fell 14% for the year ended in June after rising 25% the previous year."

Take Jay Gajavelli, for example. An Indian immigrant and former IT worker, Gajavelli made headlines in the _Wall Street Journal_ by selling extraordinary returns to investors.* **Over the past decade, Gajavelli accumulated over seven thousand apartment units across the sunbelt. He pitched "double your money" returns to potential investors in his YouTube videos, which raised millions from individuals.** It worked until it didn't. Gajavelli used floating rate loans to buy his inventory, and when interest rates began to rise rapidly, it was too late for him to refinance. Bank lending had all but dried up. **Eventually, he was unable to afford the increasing payments, and thus far, he has returned three thousand units to the**

*https:/www.wsj.com/articles/a-housing-bust-comes-for-thousands-of-small-time -investors-3934beb3

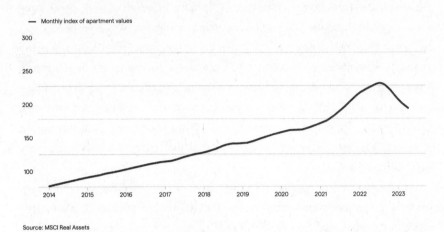

US MULTIFAMILY BUILDING VALUES DECLINE
Prices are down after a rapid climb in recent years, an index by MSCI shows

— Monthly index of apartment values

Source: MSCI Real Assets

bank in foreclosure. His investors, meanwhile, lost 100 percent of their investment—not because the apartments were bad properties, but because the owner/operator chose to take on more risk than necessary and unsophisticated investors were none the wiser.

It's not only the unsophisticated who are feeling the pain. Blackstone, one the world's largest institutions, opted to default on eleven Manhattan apartment buildings. The *Wall Street Journal* reported that "Veritas Investments, one of San Francisco's largest landlords, and partners defaulted on debt backing 95 rental buildings during the past year. It stands to lose more than one-third of its San Francisco portfolio as a result."*

IS OPPORTUNITY KNOCKING?

For those who like to buy things on sale, certain categories of real estate will become extremely attractive over the next few years. **We anticipate major discounts in commercial and multifamily real estate as sellers (and banks) are forced to unload their properties. Buyers will need to pick**

*https:/www.wsj.com/articles/a-real-estate-haven-turns-perilous-with-roughly -1-trillion-coming-due-74d20528?mod=hp_lead_pos2

their spots wisely and be able to answer the tough questions regarding viability. That said, experts we interviewed believe that there will be severe dislocations in the market that will create tremendous buying opportunities that we have not seen in nearly two decades.

Private credit is a different method through which individual investors can get exposure to real estate. Bank lending has all but evaporated, but both commercial and residential owners will still need access to capital, and in the absence of banks, many will turn to a subset of private credit (in some cases known as "hard money" lenders). These non-bank lenders will lend short-term capital against an equity position when a borrower needs quick cash. **This can generate very handsome returns for the lender, with very strong protections in place if the borrower defaults.** As an investor, real estate lending could be a great addition to a Holy Grail portfolio as a way to generate portfolio income.

We will leave you with a few words of wisdom for real estate investors in today's landscape . . .

1. Seek Out the Experts—Investing in real estate is best done by sophisticated professional investors who understand the nuances of geographies and leverage and have a long-term track record of successfully navigating down-market cycles. History is littered with stories of unsophisticated real estate investors who got too far over their skis and tumbled into bankruptcy.
2. Diversify—Investing with a top-tier manager can give you a diversified portfolio of numerous properties versus betting on one or two. The same is true with private credit, so that you can invest in a portfolio of loans versus just lending to one or two borrowers.
3. Be Patient—We will see tremendous deal flow and many discounted opportunities in the years to come. Pick your spots carefully and don't jump at the first thing you see.

EVERYONE LOVES A DEAL!

Everyone loves a deal! So what happens when an investor in a private equity fund decides that they would like get their cash out early? Well, since private equity (and venture capital, for that matter) is generally illiquid, the investor is left with one choice: sell their position in the fund to another investor. **This is known as a "secondary" transaction, and for a savvy investor, it can represent an opportunity to get a great asset at a discount with a shortened timeline to getting their money back.** Let's explore!

CHAPTER 9

SECONDARIES

EVERYONE LOVES A SALE!

*"Anyone who tells you that money can't buy
happiness, doesn't know where to shop."*
—Bo Derek

We sure have come a long way and with just one strategy left to cover! So far, we have done a deep dive on six alternative investment strategies that one could consider as part of a Holy Grail portfolio design.

As we now know, Dalio's approach is to utilize eight to twelve uncorrelated investment strategies. When coupled with traditional stocks, bonds, and other more liquid investments, there are plenty of options for one to consider. That's a good thing, of course, as it goes without saying that not all strategies are right for everyone, and it's always a good idea to consult a professional advisor.

In truth, there is an entire universe of alternative investments that our research team continuously monitors and tracks.

In this final "mini-chapter," we will visit a small corner of the world of alternative investments where there are opportunities to get great discounts on high-quality investment assets. After all, who doesn't love a good deal?

THE GREAT DISCOUNT

The new, highly sought-after Ferrari F8 has a window sticker of $350,000. The cars are scarce and nearly impossible to find unless you are willing to pay more than sticker! Now imagine walking by a showroom and a sparkling red brand-new one was discounted by 25–50 percent off. **Would you pull the trigger? I sure hope so!** Everyone loves a good deal. Funny enough, this phenomenon seems to apply to everything but investments. **When stocks are 10 percent, 20 percent, or even 50 percent off their high, typical investors avoid them like the plague, and if they own them, they are likely willing to sell them to avoid further pain.**

But not everyone who sells when the market is down is having an emotional breakdown. In fact, some of the most disciplined investors in the world, the smart institutional money, are at certain times *required* to sell some of their investment holdings. Why in the world would they be "required" to sell quality investments?

Let's dive in and explore how these unique situations can give us investors (the buyers) a significant advantage . . .

OUT OF BALANCE

The most disciplined investors typically have a clear asset allocation plan: a fixed percentage they want to maintain in each type of investment (e.g., 30 percent in stocks, 20 percent in bonds, 40 percent in private equity, and so on). However, because markets fluctuate, the value of their holdings is never static, making their asset allocation target a moving one.

In 2022, the public markets took a tumble and nearly everyone felt the pain. Stocks, bonds, and real estate fell in unison, so there were very few places to hide. The biggest institutional investors in the world (endowments, sovereign wealth funds, pension plans, etc.) were left shell-shocked as their portfolios experienced their worst performance since the Great Recession. Pile on the invasion of Ukraine, rapid inflation, and persistent supply chain issues, and the world of institutional portfolio management was left battered, bruised, and confused. **How did these massive institutional investors respond? They took significant steps to get back into balance. Let me explain . . .**

First, let's talk Portfolio Management 101 for a quick second. Say you have $1 million invested in stocks and bonds, with a target allocation of 60 percent stocks and 40 percent bonds. You would strive to maintain that industry standard 60-40 allocation. If your stocks go up in value and your bonds drop

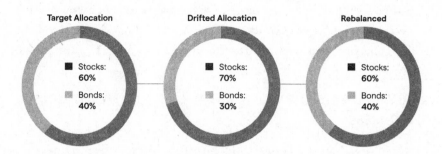

Target Allocation	Drifted Allocation	Rebalanced
Stocks: 60%	Stocks: 70%	Stocks: 60%
Bonds: 40%	Bonds: 30%	Bonds: 40%

or stay flat, your percentages have now "drifted" from their intended target. You may end up with 70 percent in stocks and only 30 percent in bonds, for instance, as illustrated by the figure above. In such cases, it's time to rebalance, like replacing an unevenly worn tire that's causing your car to vibrate. For a disciplined investor in the above situation, **this would mean selling some stocks and buying some bonds in order to get back to their 60-40 target.**

In 2022, almost every institutional portfolio on the planet experienced the equivalent of three unbalanced tires that nearly shook the doors off. While stocks and bonds both dropped significantly, many of these portfolios' alternative investments (private equity, private credit, etc.) fared much better. **This meant their alternatives now represented a MUCH higher percentage of the portfolios' intended—and often required— asset allocation target.** For portfolio managers, this is less than ideal and *requires* them to take action.

ONE MAN'S TIMING IS ANOTHER MAN'S TREASURE

In today's current landscape, we know that there are hundreds of billions of dollars invested in high-quality *private equity, private credit, and private real estate* assets, many of which have significantly grown in value in recent years. Now they will have to be sold to help these institutions rebalance their portfolios. This is because most major institutions have a self-governing mandate to course correct and rebalance when necessary. **And if the people running those portfolios do not take action to get back in balance, they get . . . fired!** Therefore, it is not an option they might pursue; it is a move of self-preservation that they MUST pursue.

But now the obvious questions . . . **What happens when you are invested in something** *illiquid* **like private equity?** How does one go about selling an *illiquid* investment? **Enter the world of secondary transactions.**

EARLY BIRD GETS THE WORM BUT THE SECOND MOUSE GETS THE CHEESE

In a traditional private equity fund, investors will wait five to ten years before the fund is liquidated and their capital is returned. So if an investor wants or needs to liquidate their position early, the only way they can achieve this is by selling their position to another interested investor who would simply take their spot. This is called an *"LP-led secondary,"* as it's initiated by the limited partner.

In today's world, finding another interested investor to whom you can sell your position is quite easy. There are numerous investment funds whose sole purpose is to buy secondaries from existing investors (limited partners). **In fact, in 2021, the secondary market transaction volume totaled an incredible $134 billion (up from $60 billion in 2020).** Many experts believe this category will grow to $500 billion in short order.

So why have secondaries become increasingly popular as an "asset class within an asset class"? We can break the appeal down into three major benefits . . .

And why is liquidity so important to you?

1. A Discount—In a private equity investment, there is an existing quarterly valuation of your investment (sometimes called the net asset value, or "mark" for short). If an investor wants to sell their position, they are often going to have to sell their position at a discount relative to its current value. This means the buyer is already "in the money" and has a buffer by which the portfolio would have to drop in order to lose money. For example, if the current value is $100, the buyer and seller might agree on a price somewhere between 70 to 90 cents on the dollar. **The seller gets their needed liquidity, and the buyer gets a deal. Win-win.**

2. Shorter Timelines—Since it typically takes five to ten years before investors in a private equity fund get all their money back, including the profits, buying a secondary position can drastically cut down on the time it takes to return your capital. **For example, if the seller is already five years into a ten-year fund, the buyer may be cutting their "wait" time in half.** This helps eliminate the J-Curve, which we spoke about earlier. The J-Curve (shown in figure below) simply shows how investors in a private equity fund are deploying their capital into investment assets for the first many years, and once those dollars are fully deployed, only then do they start to grow. Much like planting seeds for a future harvest, it takes time for growth.

3. Visibility—When a private equity manager starts a fund and you invest right away, you are betting on their experience and track record. **This is often called "blank check" risk.** On day 1, you do not yet know what companies they will purchase in the fund, how they will perform, etc. However, by the time you're buying a secondary, the fund will usually have invested its capital, so you can see exactly what investments are owned, how they are performing, and so on. . . . This *"information edge"* **is key for experienced secondary investors who can pick and choose which secondary investments they want to buy, managed by which managers, and so forth . . .**

WHY DO INVESTORS LIKE INVESTING IN SECONDARIES?

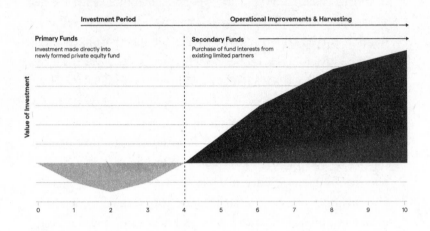

Source: CAZ Investments. This chart is for illustrative purposes only and does not represent past or projected performance of an actual investment. There is no guarantee any future performance will match this illustration

THAT'S A KEEPER

Following the global financial crisis, private equity managers found themselves in an interesting position. As mentioned, most private equity funds are set up as ten-year "closed end" funds that are required to wind down, which simply means they sell the companies and send the money back to the investors. But at the time, the managers had portfolios of some great companies that, as the economy recovered, were starting to really hit their stride. The managers knew it would be foolish to sell such great companies at that point even though the fund effectively mandated that they do so. It was time for an innovative solution.

This created a large wave of what we call "GP-led secondaries." Instead of selling all of the companies in their fund at the end of the ten-year fund cycle, managers instead created the equivalent of an "overtime" period, in which they hand-selected one or more companies they wanted to hang on to and moved them into a new fund called a *"continuation vehicle."* Then, they gave their investors (the LPs) two options:

1. The LP can choose to cash out at the current value and NOT participate in the overtime period. If someone chooses to cash out, this creates room for a new investor to come aboard.

2. The LP can choose to stay on board and "roll" their existing investment into the new *continuation vehicle*, which allows them to participate in the ongoing upside potential. **This is presented as an option but not an obligation.** The fund manager (GP) will typically create an alignment of interests by rolling over their personal investment and performance fees to the assets that are continuing. **They are ultimately showing their investors that they have such strong conviction in the underlying companies that they want more time to maximize the value for all parties.**

It is no surprise that "GP-led secondaries" have grown to be nearly half of the entire secondary market. The typical ten-year timeline of closed-end funds is somewhat arbitrary, and it rarely lines up to the optimal business life cycles of the underlying companies. The GP-led secondary has evolved into a valued portfolio management tool with the goal of maximizing everyone's returns. **Bottom line: Nobody wants to sell great companies too early.**

So where is the opportunity for investors like us? The good news is, for the foreseeable future, we are going to be in a buyer's market. **There simply is not enough capital to buy the number of available secondaries. Thus, sellers will likely entertain higher discounts, and we can be more discriminating in picking only the highest quality holdings.**

One can also surmise that buying secondaries requires immense sophistication. The buyer needs to be able to fully understand the asset they are buying, which requires substantial due diligence. Therefore, we would recommend the following . . .

1. Select a manager/fund that has a proven track record of successfully buying and exiting secondary positions. They should have strong relationships with the fund managers, so they are on a short list of buyers that the fund managers want to work with.

2. Invest in a fund that has numerous secondaries so that you get

diversification across a variety of managers and their underlying portfolios. Ideally, the fund is also invested in secondaries across various asset classes (e.g., private equity secondaries, energy secondaries, real estate secondaries, etc.).

3. Invest with a manager that has their own personal capital at stake to achieve maximum alignment!

For more information on investing in secondaries and to watch key interviews with experts in the space, visit **www.WhySecondaries.com.**

TIME FOR THE TITANS

Wow, we have covered some serious ground so far! Our hope is that you now feel empowered to consider how the strategies we've discussed can become part of your personal Holy Grail strategy. **Next, we have the incredible opportunity to hear directly from the "masters of the financial universe."** These are some of the most brilliant minds in the world of private equity, private credit, real estate, venture capital, and beyond. Although past performance is no guarantee of the future, many of those we will hear from have generated compounded returns of north of 20 percent annually. These titans, many of whom are self-made billionaires, have tremendous insight, and it was a privilege to be able to extract as much of their wisdom as possible to bring to these pages. Part 2 of this book contains the "boiled down" versions of these interviews, many of which ran two to three hours in length!

You can find additional insights and resources on our website:
www.TheHolyGrailofInvesting.com.

PART 2

AT THE TABLE OF
TITANS

CHAPTER 10

ROBERT F. SMITH

FOUNDER AND CEO OF VISTA EQUITY PARTNERS

Accolades: Listed by *Forbes* as one of the Top 100 Greatest Living Business Minds. Member of the philanthropic Giving Pledge. The wealthiest African American in the U.S.

Total Asset Under Management (as of August 2023): $100 billion+

Area of Focus: Enterprise software

HIGHLIGHTS

- Completed over six hundred private equity transactions, representing nearly $300 billion in transaction value since inception.
- Vista's ecosystem spans more than eighty companies with more than ninety thousand employees active in over 180 countries.
- Named as a Top Founder-Friendly Investor by *Inc.* magazine four years in a row.
- In 2017, Robert was named one of the 100 Greatest Living Business Minds by *Forbes*.
- *Time* magazine 100 Most Influential People 2020.

ROBERT:

Good to meet you, Tony! I was just telling Christopher that I get to talk to very interesting people all the time. And I shared with my wife (that I was having this interview) and this was the only one she was actually excited about! She said, "Oh my god, he is the best person you can talk to." So she's a fan.

TONY:

I'm glad to hear that! Also, I'd love to meet you in person if there's ever a chance to do that. But I want to be respectful of your time, so thank you for joining us. We really appreciate it.

ROBERT:

Thank you. Happy to be a part of this journey with you guys.

TONY:

Robert, you're a legend in this business, but I don't know if many people know your origin story. Would you mind sharing a little about that with us? How did you end up in this position?

ROBERT:

I come at this as a child of two schoolteachers in Denver, Colorado. While it was a segregated community, I always felt loved and cared for by the members of my community, which extended beyond my parents. And I think what this does is give you a sense of security and an ability to wonder—have an intellectual curiosity that you can indulge in. So, an important part of my origin story is having a regular chance to explore and learn. My father educated me in opera and classical music. My mother took us to the library every Saturday morning. We'd check out eight to ten books and she'd check out fifteen and we'd read them that week. And then we'd do it again the next week. The music and the books created a sense of wonder about the world outside the little community that I grew up in. And a curiosity about solving problems.

Fast-forward to high school and we were being introduced to computers.

My generation were digital immigrants, not digital natives. But I had this learned curiosity. I said to my teacher, "How does this thing work?"

And my teacher said, "Well, it runs on this thing called a microprocessor."

I said, "Well, how does a microprocessor work?"

My teacher said, "It's run by things called transistors."

And I said, "Who invented that?"

And my teacher said, "It's this place called Bell Laboratories."

So, I went down to our little career center and asked if there was a Bell Laboratories here in Colorado. This nice woman told me there is one in Brighton. I picked up the phone and called them, and said, "I'm interested in an internship working on computers," and the human resources person just kind of chuckled. She told me that they have internships for students who are between their junior and senior year of college. She told me to call when I was a junior in college. So, I called her the next day and the next, and she stopped taking my calls. For two weeks, I called every day and left a message. And then every Monday. I did this from about February until June. She called me back in June and said, "A student from MIT didn't show up. We have a space in the program." Then she told me I'd just need to come down for an interview.

I had one Sunday suit and I put that thing on the next day and put $2 of gas in my '69 Plymouth Satellite. I drove out there and I got a job at Bell Laboratories. I worked there basically throughout college, and the beautiful thing about that was that I discovered the joy of solving problems. Today, I like to say my real role is creating elegant solutions to complex problems. That's what Vista is. So, a lot of my origin story has to do with people who excited my imagination. People who sparked my curiosity, gave me some freedom to explore, expand, make mistakes, and ask questions. But who also took the time to unpack solution sets and help me become learned in specific technologies and sciences and mathematics that inform the way that I now invest and the way that I've built Vista.

So, a lot of my origin story has to do with people who excited my imagination. People who sparked my curiosity, gave me some freedom to explore, expand, make mistakes, and ask questions.

TONY:

As you recall that path, who are some of the most important people that shaped you? And how did you go from Bell to Vista Equity Partners?

ROBERT:

I watched my dad form a civics association in Denver. We used to get a lot of snow during the year. And of course, as a kid you celebrated because you had snow days. Well, what I eventually realized was that those were the same days my parents could not go to work because, in the black neighborhood, they didn't plow the street. So, it'd be three, four days, and then the city would put one stripe down the middle of the road, and my dad would make my brother and me dig out a path from the car to that one stripe so he could get to work. And then the bus would eventually come down and we'd get on the bus and go to school. We'd get to the white neighborhood, and guess what? The streets were not only plowed, they were also dry, which means they were plowed days ago. I saw my dad take initiative and say, we need to help people understand that if our community can't get to work, we can't feed our families. And this diminishes the standard of the whole city. He eventually got the city to plow our community's streets.

My parents leaned into their positions and used them to make positive civic changes. They helped launch the Head Start program in Colorado. And my mother wrote a $25 check to the United Negro College Fund every month for over fifty years.

Besides my parents, I was really impacted by a guy by the name of Vic Hauser, who was my first mentor at Bell Labs. I walked into Bell Labs as a teenager, all excited, and he pulls out this semiconductor to an operational amplifier. He says, "This thing is failing in our Merlin systems. Your job is to figure out why it's failing. And that's going to be your summer project. You have the full resources of Bell Labs at your disposal. Library's down the hall. I'm here. You can ask me any question you want. Good luck."

And then he turns his chair around. So, I'm thinking, man, that's pretty rude. But I walked myself down to the library to look up what an operational amplifier is. I studied the description and then I went back to Vic's office and said, okay, here's what I understand about operational amplifiers. And he turned his chair around, and for the next two hours, he started unpacking how it all works, what it is, what it's supposed to do, and what it isn't currently doing. We did that every day.

TONY:

That's beautiful.

ROBERT:

And so, what he did was he helped me discover the joy of figuring things out. He didn't give me the answer. He forced me to ask the questions and to do the research. In doing so he was reinforcing what my parents had been teaching me all along.

And so, what he did was he helped me discover the joy of figuring things out. He didn't give me the answer. He forced me to ask the questions and to do the research. In doing so he was reinforcing what my parents had been teaching me all along.

TONY:

Robert, what an incredible family you have. I honor them so much, and so many people in the world have benefited from the foundation they gave you and that you expanded on. If you don't mind, what made you finally decide to go out on your own? And what made you decide to focus on enterprise software?

ROBERT:

I'll tell you the funny story about that. So, I worked for six years as a chemical engineer. I loved it, Tony. I didn't think there was a more noble pursuit than to come up with an idea that no one else in the history of humankind had ever come up with. I was working at Goodyear Tire and Rubber, and thoroughly enjoying what I was doing, and then we had a takeover attempt by this guy, Sir James Goldsmith. So, I'm like, what's that all about? It ultimately inspired me to go get an advanced degree.

I did well—top student after the first year. And then I was asked to come back for the summer graduation to receive a first-year award. There was a keynote speaker, a guy by the name of John Utendahl. Six-foot-eight, big, tall, handsome investment banker. So, they gave me my award and he gave his keynote address and afterward he called me over and asked me if I'd ever thought about a career in investment banking. I said, I don't really understand what investment bankers do. So, he invited me to his office for a thirty-minute lunch and we went two hours. At the end of that, he picked up the phone and called all these black guys on Wall Street and tells them they should really meet me. I'm a scientist at heart, so I ended up talking to not only those guys, but to over a hundred people. I needed to understand. Eventually, I figured out that the only part of the business I liked was mergers and acquisitions. Building sustainable infrastructure through a process that's long living and that you can tune. At the time, there were six firms that did it. Goldman Sachs was the only one that had a teamwork structure.

Eventually, I got asked to be what's called the business unit manager, working for a guy by the name of Mac Hill. Brilliant M&A guy. But then Gene [Sykes] calls me to see if I'd like to work with him, and he is the only partner I hadn't worked with. I tell Mac, and he says, "Robert, let me tell you. I'm really, really good. Gene is out-of-this-world good. If you have a chance, go work with Gene."

So, Gene tells me he's thinking about starting a tech group. I said, "Only if you commit to spending time mentoring me in San Francisco." He said, "Deal." And in spring 1997, I became Goldman's first M&A banker on the ground, focused on technology.

TONY:

Wow.

ROBERT:

Now I was there in the hinterlands, i.e., away from New York City. You have nobody really helping you. So, I had to build a team and a plan. And the good news is you don't have a whole bunch of people over you. If you get on a deal in New York, you had four to five partners, who you never met, who were signing their name to your deal. But out in San Francisco, I didn't have that. So now, all of a sudden, I get to be one of the principal people working on these deals with little oversight. I had Apple. I had a little company called Microsoft. Little company called Texas Instruments. Little company called eBay. Little company called Hewlett Packard. Little company called Yahoo. This is '97, '98, '99.

Now, here's what got interesting. I started looking at these companies and the landscape of technology and I said, you know what? There is no one doing private equity in enterprise software. Why is that? If you think about it, it's the most productive tool introduced in the business economy in the last fifty years. As an engineer, I really started to understand the impact of introducing computing power to a business environment. It has an exponential return. When I was an engineer and I got done implementing what was called a programmable logic controller, Honeywell TDC 3000, into a plant for Goodyear Tire and Rubber, there was a considerable increase in productivity. This is from a plant that was built in the forties. So, with computing power, your waste goes down, your productivity goes up. That's just by putting in digital control systems. That's what enterprise software does.

Now, go put that dynamic in an insurance company and process an insurance claim. Go put it in at a bank and process a transaction. Go put it in an automobile dealership or mortgage company and process a loan. This is the level of productivity that enterprise software has infused into the entire world.

This level of productivity makes enterprise software extremely sticky for its customers. So now you have a long-term sustainable relationship with thousands of customers. Relationships that aren't measured in quarters or years; they're measured in decades. With a 95 percent gross margin product that you build once and sell as many times as you want. Negative working capital, no inventory. That's the elegant solution to a complex problem.

With a 95 percent gross margin product that you build once and sell as many times as you want. Negative working capital, no inventory. That's the elegant solution to a complex problem.

TONY:

Marc Benioff is one of my dearest friends, and he left Oracle after going to five of my events in a row. He'd be in the front row every day. I love the man so much. I'll never forget, he came up to me after an event and he said, "You've convinced me."

I said, "Well, I've not even talked to you."

He says, "No, but I've been to five events in a row. You've convinced me that I'm leaving Oracle. I'm going to start this thing called Salesforce. Tony, we're going to change business. We're going to do a hundred million in business."

Salesforce does what . . . $33 billion now? So, I've been on that figuring-it-out journey with him, watching that business take off, and it's just been incredible to see. It's so interesting to me the correlation between his path and yours. The shared intellectual curiosity and drive to find solutions to problems. I feel the same hunger in you today that you had as a young boy. Tell me this: What was the day like when you said, okay, I'm going on my own?

ROBERT:

At this stage, I'd been working with technology companies and enterprise software companies for years. I'd seen hundreds of these software companies and guess what? They all were making it up. I'm serious. How do you price software? Back then, you made it up. Somebody was sitting there and saying, "Well, okay, I've got about two years of R&D in this, and I got a bunch of computer programmers and computer hardware so I should probably sell this to that client for, I don't know, $80,000. Sure. Why not?" Seemed like a lot of money for something with a value you didn't really comprehend. But when I thought about this software, I thought, you might have one client that it saves $3 million a year and another client that saves $30 million. There was much greater value, and few people saw it.

So, what happened was, in advising and making recommendations for my clients, I realized the commonality and I said to myself, if you don't do this, someone will figure this out.

So Tony, what you do is you help inspire people to become their best selves using best practices. Marc Benioff internalized it his way and went out and did that. Similarly, we have built and continuously refine a whole set of best practices that help to accelerate the corporate maturity of the companies we buy. Since founding Vista, we have completed over six hundred transactions.

The other piece is that most software businesses are still founder-led. And most of these founders are running the biggest business that they've ever run. So, most of them are trying to figure it out, because they've never done this before, right? What do I do tomorrow to take this business that's

$100 million to $200 million, or $200 million to $400 million? So, part of our magic at Vista is that we have built an ecosystem where these executives and their direct reports can get together and learn from each other. It's kind of like Young Presidents Organization on steroids. **So, if you're a CTO of a $30 million software company, you're sitting next to a CTO of a $300 million software company being taught by a CTO of a $3 billion software company. We're creating a shared learning ecosystem where these executives can operate in a penalty-free environment.**

CHRISTOPHER:

Robert, you're talking about something Tony talks about extensively, which is that proximity is power. You share and help implement all of these best practices into these companies, but then you provide proximity to other entrepreneurs implementing the same best practices.

ROBERT:

Right, and the big advantage is that you can help them, in many cases, prevent mistakes that they would otherwise make, without that support.

TONY:

You can feel it vibrate from you, Robert. You emanate all of that, which is so beautiful. Tell me, where is the greatest opportunity for investors today in this sector in your mind? And where does AI play a role?

ROBERT:

Great, great question. I believe the best opportunity to invest is of course with Vista. No question. Hands down. And I sincerely mean it.

Why? Because we know how to bring institutionalization to the operation of these enterprise software companies. I am better off rolling as much as I can with you and then giving you and your team the tools to make the changes. As I mentioned, we accelerate the corporate maturity of enterprise software companies through sustainable infrastructure so these businesses can grow at scale, profitably. If you build infrastructure in these businesses, your CEOs get quiet time. They don't have to deal with the contract administration process. They don't have to deal with the services process because you have built systems that self-correct and self-tune and reduce noise. And so now your CEOs can think about what it is that they can go do to advance the business.

TONY:

They get to work *on* the business instead of *in* the business, which is what makes you CEO in the first place. So, tell me about what you see as the opportunity investing in this category now. We've seen the SaaS development; now we're seeing AI enter the picture. Tell us where you think the greatest opportunity is today from your perspective.

ROBERT:

So, 2010 through, call it 2013 or 2014, only about 15 percent of companies were what I call cloud native. SaaS being the business model. Today we're probably closer to 40 to 50 percent.

TONY:

Really? There's still that much growth in the market?

ROBERT:

Yes. There's a whole lot you have to convert and tune. Remember, there's a hundred thousand software companies and you probably recognize 250 of them. But the newer companies are now cloud native, so they're coming up from the bottom. But there's a middle with a whole bunch of clients that are either on-premises or hybrid and are trying to become cloud native.

The U.S. has always been the bellwether of opportunity in computing. But we distributed computing power throughout the 2000s. So now this computing power sits everywhere. And so, every economy, every industry is digitizing in one shape, form, or another. In many cases they buy U.S. source software, UK source software, but in some cases, they're trying to figure it out on their own. In fact, five of the largest economies don't have an enterprise software layer.

TONY:

Really? Who doesn't have one?

ROBERT:

China doesn't have an enterprise software layer. All their software sits in state-owned enterprises or private-owned enterprises. Japan, all the software sits in the *keiretsus* for the most part. Korea, all of it sits in the *chaebols* or the family-run businesses. India, same deal. So, there's a massive opportunity to establish enterprise software layers.

Still, the best opportunities for enterprise software are in the U.S. And what we can do is implement all forms of catalytic technologies across our platform because of our ecosystem—things like machine learning, robotic process automation, and a little thing called artificial intelligence. So, I still believe that enterprise software, on a risk-adjusted basis, is the best place to invest any form of capital, either equity or debt. You just have to put it in a place that makes sure it is evolving in utilizing these catalytic activities.

CHRISTOPHER:

Robert, when we look at enterprise software itself, we saw this massive increase in valuations. We've seen a significant correction in valuations back to more of a normal average, if you will. When you think about this, what has happened over the last couple of years that you did not expect?

ROBERT:

What I did not expect is that people would just flood that market and believe that trees would grow to the sky. You guys remember . . . '97, '98, '99, 2000, NASDAQ is going to 10,000, dotcoms, all that stuff. There was no real infrastructure to support those valuations and, of course, sure enough it didn't last. So, when you start flooding the market with free money, I thought people would be a little more thoughtful about it and wait for these valuations to come down, as opposed to paying a premium off a fifty-two-week high to take these companies private that are growing 3 to 5 percent at 30 percent or 40 percent EBITDA margins. There's not much further to go with that business unless you believe there's always a greater fool who will take you out of it.

CHRISTOPHER:

What's fascinating about that, Robert, is that many of the same people who were so excited and enthusiastic about paying those exceedingly high multiples now think enterprise software is a bad investment. Now that multiples have come down by 50 to 70 percent, they don't want any. The psychology is just fascinating to watch. Many people cannot accept the fact that there were great businesses just trading at wrong valuations.

ROBERT:

Fear begets opportunity. We continue to believe investing in enterprise software companies is the best use of capital anywhere in the financial markets.

CHRISTOPHER:

When you think about how investors are not seeing the opportunity set the way that they used to, how would you coach investors to look at enterprise software differently today, if at all, then they did in the past?

ROBERT:

It's a great question. If you look at it domestically, there's a couple macroeconomic factors that are going to influence this. First of all, in the U.S. you actually have, call it, a wage inflationary environment. So, employers have to figure out ways to drive efficiencies. Enterprise software is the most productive tool to do that. So, the consumption dynamic of enterprise software is going to continue to be robust.

If you add up all the Vista companies, it's over $25 billion in revenues. Sometimes a little bigger than Benioff, sometimes a little smaller. Across the entire enterprise, I'm looking at high teens growth rates. Even in this economy. That's the resiliency of it. We actually measure the ROI of the products that we sell to the customers. It's 640 percent. I don't know of any investment in the world that you get a 640 percent return on except software. So whatever business you're in . . . if you're in automobile repair, if you're in fast food, if you're in hotel management, your next best dollar is probably spent buying more software. The key is to figure out what software is going to be consumed in that environment.

TONY:

What are most investors getting wrong when they look at the industry?

ROBERT:

Some people will say, Robert, if you're not investing in software, what would you look at? If you are a long-term investor, you have to really understand what businesses are going to be sustainable in the context of sustaining human life. Right? And sustaining human prosperity.

CHRISTOPHER:

That's a good pivot there. Let's give you the opportunity to talk to the world for five minutes. What would you want the world to know today?

ROBERT:

I would like the world to know that there really is value in liberating the human spirit. And what I mean by that is providing the substratum of opportunity to all people. That doesn't mean everybody's entitled to a house. The substratum of opportunity is education, nutrition, and access to opportunity. Now, if people choose not to take it, that's fine. But to exclude people for different reasons, I think is a fallacy of mankind.

TONY:

Robert, I know we're kindred spirits in our value systems, that's for sure. The concept of this book is related to an interview I did years ago with Ray Dalio. I asked, what is the single most important investing principle if you had to give only one? The Holy Grail for him is finding eight to twelve uncorrelated investments because that guarantees an 80 percent risk reduction and an increase in return. Part of why we did this book was to show the general public that alternative investments are so important. High-net-worth people usually have 45 percent of their assets in alternatives. They're in private credit. They're in private equity. They're in private real estate. What would be the Holy Grail of Investing from your perspective?

ROBERT:

I'm going to first say that Ray has it exactly right—if you are a portfolio manager, managing a portfolio of a group of assets. I have the unique task to manage a portfolio of assets in alternatives and private equity. My answer for that is make sure the critical factors for success are under your control.

TONY:

Give us an example, if you don't mind.

ROBERT:

So, a critical factor for success in enterprise software is something like talent and talent development. Do I just run around and try to find a bunch of headhunters who can find talent? No. I've got a whole talent management system that we juxtapose against the top performers for over thirty years across our enterprise to say, this is what a profile of a really good entry-level developer looks like. This is the profile of a great services person. This is a profile of a top salesperson. So, we can interview 450,000 people a year to find 25,000 that fit. That is a critical factor for success. That's under our control.

Another critical factor for success under our control is pricing dynamics. Understanding what is the ROI of the product that we are selling to our customers. And how can we capture that economic rent? How can we do it systemically? Well, you have to create a deal desk so that your salespeople aren't just running around with the sales sheets, saying, "Oh, they have forty-five employees. Here's the price. Oh, they have five hundred employees, here's the price." No, you sit down, and you build these ROI calculators and say, here's the value of that product to that customer. Sell it to them at that price. That's a critical factor of success. That's under our control.

Managing your cost, managing your go-to market, managing your most important resource, which is your people, your contract administration processes, all those. You can control those.

I can't control what the multiples are in the marketplace. But I can control if I want to make these companies grow and be more profitable. Even if I just make them grow and be more profitable, I can return capital through cash flows because I don't have capital expenditures in the world of software. So worst case, I'm making money on cash flow.

CHRISTOPHER:

You had a great group of mentors, you had a great construct before you started the firm, but what are a few things that you wish somebody would've told you before you started your firm?

ROBERT:

That's a good question. So, at the highest level, it would be to create a construct where I would have the ability to keep companies longer.

The way the world of private equity is constructed is that you have to buy a company, you have to, in our case, improve it, and then you have to sell it. Benioff picked one industry, in essence, and can hold it forever. And it can just grow. We have done over 130 transactions in the past two years because part of what I have to do is return capital. I wish I had figured out a construct where I could keep companies longer in the ecosystem.

CHRISTOPHER:

The private equity world is shortsighted in that regard. And it's actually in their best interest to just compound money and value and growth over decades. Not just over quarters.

ROBERT:

Exactly. So, it's the nature of the U.S. pension plan system to need money back. I get that. But there should be certain exceptions, certain businesses, where you sell the company and the LPs come back and say, okay Robert, now put it back to work. I've built some beautiful recycle models with certain clients and now they automatically recycle a certain amount. If you need the money back, you have it back. If not, we'll recycle it.

CHRISTOPHER:

I think the industry will continue to try to do that.

One of the amazing things I've witnessed in the time we've worked together, is the amount of growth that you've had as a business. Very few private equity firms, or even private alternative asset management firms in general, are able to scale the way that Vista has scaled. Why is it that some firms just cannot get from $3 billion to $30 billion or, like you, over a hundred billion AUM? What holds them back?

ROBERT:

I will give you three reasons. And I'm going to give you a contrast of what I know enables us to scale. First is a model. The model of the investment team, the value creation team, and the management teams and how we work together in that construct. Why is that important? I don't like any single point of failure. I'm an engineer, right?

So many of these firms, they build their firms based on the personality of a person or the "talented investor." And you look at many of those talented investors, they've got loss ratios that are well higher, but they just had some bigger wins. To me, investing isn't, I made a bunch of money on a couple things, I lost some on others, and I bring it together and it's pretty good on average. I look at the loss ratio. That's what I think about. So why [else] do some people not scale? Because they end up in the moral hazard problem, where they have bifurcated returns and some years it's great and some years it isn't. And some of them have built their organizations as a second point. Their organizations are too centric on one person as opposed to a system.

And I guess the third thing is the culture of the organization. We have a 95 percent retention rate of VPs and above. We have only two managing directors or above who didn't start as an analyst or an associate. This way you can build culture. And by the way, we have a gender parity firm and nearly 40 percent people of color too. What that does is give you the ability to build people and train and teach and mentor and develop and make sure they have a place where they can be their unique and authentic best self in the construct of an organization. That is going to enable them to be successful. I don't know what everybody else is doing, but that's what we do.

CHRISTOPHER:

It's a unique thing that you should be very proud of. There's no one that's going to be perfect, but it's best to try to find the people that are as close to perfect as possible. They have an edge, if you will.

ROBERT:

And part of that edge is evaluating. Is it . . . they've just got one big slugger out there and they're living and dying by that slugger? Or are they building teams, farm teams, and giving them experience and places to grow? I tell my teams all the time: There are two management styles, two ways to grow you. You can create constructs for people to grow in and you can create vacuums for them to fill. You, as a manager, have to decide what a person needs. Sometimes it's a construct where you need to be informed and learn. [Or] there's a vacuum that I need you to fill with your best self and what you've learned. It takes a lot of management overhead to do that. But if you don't consciously do that, then you have an organization that can't make decisions and can't grow without the leader.

CHRISTOPHER:

I think that's exactly what I see more than anything else. We now have GP stakes in over sixty different firms. We've gotten to know that all of them are really good at what they do, otherwise we wouldn't be there. But when we look at the differences, what I see more than anything else is talent-driven shops versus management-led shops. Neither one is a totally right or wrong answer, right? But the scalability comes from having that level of management that enables the talent to be talent and allows management to be management and allows everybody to, as you put it, become their best version of their best self.

ROBERT:

Perfectly said. That's exactly right.

TONY:

To finish that thought up, I'd like to know when you're looking at that management—which is really leadership if it's effective, right—what do you think are the most important qualities? What are the most important ingredients that you're looking for in an individual to be a true leader in your organization who can produce results and continue to grow to those higher levels?

ROBERT:

That's a great question. The majority of investors at Vista come in as analysts and associates, and part of what I'm looking for is are they naturally curious? Do they have an open mind to learn? You know this, Tony. We're in the transformation business. We have to find people who are nimble in their thinking, open-minded in their approach to life, and actually have intellectual curiosity that, you have seen from their past, they will really run things down. They're going to go figure it all the way out and say: Here's the source code to why this is the way it is. I guess you could say, I look for what I learned at the very beginning of my career at Bell Labs, what I was taught by my parents—the joy of figuring things out.

CHAPTER 11

RAMZI MUSALLAM

CEO OF VERITAS CAPITAL

Accolades: #280 on the *Forbes* 400 World's Wealthiest
Total Asset Under Management (as of August 2023): $45 Billion
Area of Focus: Veritas Capital specializes in acquiring companies in heavily regulated industries such as healthcare, national security, and education.

HIGHLIGHTS

- Veritas's portfolio companies are generating over $25 billion of annual revenue as of June 2023.
- Portfolio companies are employing over 120,000 people as of June 2023.
- In June 2023, Veritas was 2023 winner of the North America Top Performing Buyout Fund Manager Award from Preqin.
- 2022 marked Veritas's tenth consecutive year among Preqin's Most Consistent Top Performing Fund Managers.
- In February 2023, Veritas ranked #2 worldwide "in terms of aggregate performance based on all buyout funds raised between 2009 and 2018" by HEC Paris and Dow Jones.

- In August 2023, Ramzi Musallam was named one of the 21 Private Equity Power Players by *Fortune*.

TONY:

Ramzi, I know you don't do very many interviews, so we're really honored to have you. You've got an unbelievable track record. Many people know that. I don't think most people know the story of what you've gone through. You've been in the business twenty-six years. In 1997, as I understand it, you joined Veritas. Five years later, you lose your friend and partner, and you could have lost the entire business. And not a single investor left the firm. You've taken [Veritas] from $2 billion to $45 billion and have generated extraordinary returns. I'd really love it if you wouldn't mind sharing with us just a little bit about your origin story.

RAMZI:

Well, I'll give you the high level and then please interrupt with any questions. The background in terms of how we started it all is while I was at business school, I got an amazing opportunity. At the time, Jay Pritzker was the patriarch of the Pritzker family. It wasn't fifteen different fiefdoms as it is today; it was controlled entirely by him. And I basically, through a lot of perseverance at getting to know his assistant pretty well, finally connected with him. After a short conversation, he said, "Look, I have an opportunity I want you to take a look at. This is potentially of interest for me. Meet with the management team and then come back and tell me what you think."

Long story short, I came back, I sat down with him and his two right-hand people, and I provided them with my perspective on the potential investment opportunity. He hired me then and there. My mindset has always been entrepreneurial. My father came to this country and built a business. My brother's now on his third startup. So, I have that entrepreneurial mindset of being an owner, so to speak.

But the reason I bring all that up is that [while working for Jay] I was introduced to Bob McKeon, the gentleman you referred to who passed away. He was investing at the time with a group of former executives, the CEOs of Fortune 500 companies who provided a little bit of capital doing relatively small generalist deals. He and I got to know each other, and we decided to raise a fund. That's when I decided to come back to New York. I left Jay after an amazing eighteen-month experience working for him while I was in grad school. Truly transformational as it relates to my professional life.

Bob and I started to raise our fund and it was a generalist fund, no focus. And it was a small fund, $175 million. It took us eighteen months. And what happened, is that there were three transactions, three investments that Bob had been invested in prior to the fund that morphed into fund investments—a steel manufacturer, an auto components manufacturer, and a ship repair business. So, nothing to do with what we're doing today. I always say it's better to be lucky than good. I was fortunate enough, I was lucky. And the firm took advantage of the next opportunity to come.

A friend had introduced us to an opportunity down in Huntsville, Alabama. It was a defense technology business, at one time a part of Chrysler. We had never invested in that ecosystem. I went down there, and I started to learn a lot about that opportunity and the ecosystem they were a part of. Long story short, that became the cornerstone to our first investment in what we call today the intersection of technology and government—in that case, defense. That company was Integrated Defense Technologies. We built it, we repositioned it, we grew it, took it public, and then sold it. **That is the genesis of the focus today—investing in technology and technology-enabled businesses in government-influenced markets.** The three most active areas for us are national security/defense, healthcare, and education. [Early on] it became apparent to me that we were rudderless as an investment firm. We were a generalist and didn't have any raison d'être. We needed to focus. We were an investor, but without any specialized knowledge or strategic position in a marketplace. So, in October of 1998, we bought that company and consummated that deal. And since that point, we've focused strictly on this overarching technology market.

Carlyle started off in the defense world in the late 1980s, under Frank Carlucci. But by the late 1990s, [they] had moved into what they are today—a very large, successful, overarching investment firm. So, we were the only ones, and we feel like we're still the only ones with this unique focus. That really was the genesis of the track record that we have today, which we're very proud of. We're investing out of Fund VIII right now and the thrust really is that performance volatility has been almost nonexistent. Our loss ratio is less than one-half of 1 percent over the last quarter century.

TONY:

If I did my homework right, I saw there was only one deal you lost money on over these last ten to twelve years.

RAMZI:

We learned a lot more from that one than any other. We learned a lot about what we could have done better. Even in the context of the overarching returns, we don't want [our investors] up at night worrying about the returns and the volatility therein.

Going back to what happened because you highlighted it. [Bob] and I were key persons in the fund. He passed away. Very tragic for me personally. I obviously was close to him. But from a professional standpoint, our LPs (limited partners) understood how the deals were getting done since inception and what we were doing to add value to our portfolio companies. So, when we did go through that, we had 100 percent of our LPs decide that they wanted to continue with us. That was unprecedented but, from my perspective, expected. That was my mindset.

TONY:

That's incredible. Did you personally go out and talk to them?

RAMZI:

I and my partners did. We went out and met with everybody. And we did this under, quite frankly, a very difficult circumstance. I actually had our first meeting the day after he had passed away. And he had unfortunately taken his own life so it was very sudden. It was very difficult. But I felt I had a responsibility not only to our firm, but to the portfolio companies, the employees, and our investors to make sure that we could optimize their returns over the long term. So, I and two other partners from the firm started meeting with everybody right away.

TONY:

Several people have said that some of your LPs were most impressed that, in the middle of this—you were personally shaken by it obviously—you somehow found the center to stay focused. That made them believe that whatever you'd face financially in the future, you'd be able to do that as well. It says so much about your character.

RAMZI:

Well, thank you. I think one of the things that you have to be able to do in the world we live in is compartmentalize. There is a greater good. I felt as if I had the sense of responsibility to everybody to make sure that we could continue doing what we were doing and do it at the best and optimal level. There was a clear modus operandi to achieve the greater good.

From a day-to-day standpoint, people internally didn't see a difference because I had been effectively running the business anyway. So, it wasn't something that they noticed as being different. But obviously, there was a big difference. And from an LP standpoint, as I said, he was one of the key people. So, it was challenging. Fortunately, we have an amazing team. Culture really is everything. You don't differentiate yourself in the world we live in by the widgets you make. It's by the people and how you define who you are and how you maintain that culture as you grow. We have the right people in the right places and a culture of openness and collaboration. From my perspective, unlike any other. That is what I'm most proud of—this is everlasting.

We've gone from $2 billion to $45 billion over the course of the last ten years, yet our culture is the same. And that's something I take a lot of pride in. It ties to that entrepreneurial mindset that I feel like I have, that I was brought up with. A number of the other partners have similar backgrounds, very entrepreneurial, which is not typical in private equity. We are truly strategic in the markets we engage in. It's very rare that we don't know more than the management teams that we work with relative to the markets that we're focused in, whether it's healthcare technology, education technology, or a national security and defense technology. We've immersed ourselves in these markets for more than a quarter of a century. I believe we understand the levers of value better than anybody. And we continue to build on that IP. That's what we make. We generate IP and build on it. Now for over twenty-five years.

When you think about government and technology, government is at the forefront of all the complexities that we face, technology-driven and otherwise. So, if you can actually stay close to what government is seeing—what issues we are being confronted with, what complexities, what challenges, and how can technology and technology-oriented businesses help face those challenges. I call it tip of the spear internally. We have maintained that position, being at the tip of the spear. We are viewed as a custodian of national assets, quite frankly, whether it is in healthcare, education, or national security. I have the highest-level security clearance any individual can have. It's an onerous process sitting through polygraphs in intelligence agency bunkers and being vetted regularly, relative to your activities. But it's a function of being strategic in the marketplace and being able to bring that perspective to add value to what our portfolio companies care most about—our customers. That thrust has been consistent for us. It hasn't changed or wavered. And that's very important as you grow in private equity. Our first fund was $175 million. Our second fund was only $150 million. Our most recent fund was $11 billion. Now we have $45 billion of assets under management.

TONY:

That's really amazing. You've certainly aligned yourself with the biggest buyer of tech in the world, as you've said, at the forefront of the world economy. It's so smart. I'm surprised no one else has done that, but you own it at this stage.

RAMZI:

If you look at the mix of our portfolio, about 60 to 65 percent is sales to government agencies. A third to 40 percent is revenue from commercial entities. The element that's so important, which I found out during our first investment, is that the government is the largest investor in technology by multiples, relative to the VC community or otherwise. What I've learned and appreciated, which we've now really focused in on, is that the government would invest in these companies through what's called customer-funded R&D programs. Yet, these companies would retain the IP and have the ability to utilize that IP to drive opportunities not only in core markets they're engaged in, but especially into ancillary and adjacencies that they target in both commercial and government marketplaces.

So, a large part of what's on your iPhone has been developed through collaboration with the government, from Siri on. The algorithms which serve as the backbone for Google, developed by the government. Tesla technology, self-automation technology, developed by the government. It's not only the funding, which, again, represents hundreds of billions of dollars a year, but it's also the collaboration with folks within government to drive and develop those technologies. We gleaned on to that early and we utilized and leveraged that to the benefit of our customers for our portfolio companies.

TONY:

You mentioned earlier that culture is everything. And that's been consistent with every single person we've interviewed who's been the best in the business, like yourself. I'd love to hear, if you don't mind sharing, a little bit about your upbringing and how that has affected your way of developing relationships and the culture that you've built at Veritas.

RAMZI:

It is really so important to me personally and I think to the firm as well. I was born in Jordan. And I am Middle Eastern by descent. I have a Palestinian and a Lebanese background. My father had immigrated to this country to go to college. First person in his family to do so, did it on his own, didn't know anybody here. Took a boat from Italy to the United States. First night in the United States, stayed at the YMCA, went to take a shower, and everything he owned was stolen. And no cell phones back then. So, he didn't have anybody here. He still found himself a way to get to University of Missouri to ultimately get a Civil Engineering degree. And from there, he had various jobs—including the Department of Transportation and the Army Corps of Engineers.

He was working in various parts around the world when I was born in Jordan. And then, we moved to Jeddah, Saudi Arabia, first and then we went to Mbeya, Tanzania, where I was homeschooled because we were in the middle of a rural area. We then went back to Riyadh, Saudi Arabia, where I was in grade school. I think that is so important from a couple standpoints. Immersing myself in different cultures at such an early age was eye-opening to me. Living in rural Mbeya, and then living in, at the time, a very different environment in Riyadh than it is today. It allowed me to see how others live and be more empathetic to issues that we face across the globe. After that, my dad decided he wanted to start his own business, and he felt there was no better place to start his own business than the United States of America. So, we came to the United States. This gave me a firsthand view of someone who is very entrepreneurial, who said, "Look, I've learned a lot. I've developed skill sets and I'm going to now take a risk and do something that we all dream about doing in terms of starting my own company." And he obviously risked everything to do that.

That had a very significant impact on how I think about things and how I am as a person. Our culture here, as I mentioned a little bit earlier, is very entrepreneurial. So, when I talk to our team, I say, "Each one of you is an owner." You can leverage all the resources we have, all the knowledge we have, all the IP we have, and it's incumbent upon you to think like that. Take initiatives, take risks. I'm all for taking risks as long as you think through the parameters of those risks and drive opportunities for the firm therein.

So, the people that we attract are people who are very entrepreneurial in the way they think about things. And that culture is critical. We all are aligned in the same way, obviously, in the way we work in terms of the incentives and strategic objectives. But importantly, we also are aligned in the way we think and operate with one another to get to the end goal of making something bigger and better. And that I think comes from the ability to see things early on, building businesses and being part of different environments in Africa and the Middle East.

TONY:

What did you learn from your father or from your upbringing about dealing with disappointment or dealing with failure?

RAMZI:

We have a class of interns who are finishing up the summer here. **I tell them the most important [thing] is to learn from failures, because if you don't have failures, you won't succeed.** I firmly believe that. If you don't go through the hardships, you won't understand what success even means. How do you do that? You learn from your mistakes. We sit down after successful investments, and we talk about how we could have done things better. Where did we miss? What did we miss? Because even when you have a successful investment outcome for our investors, you could have done better.

There are certain things that you've missed. I always think about optimizing that intellectual property, and so, we've codified that. It's important that we institutionalize it for future folks who join Veritas and understand the playbook [on] what mistakes we made and how we could have done things better.

And here's something very unique, digressing a little bit, but important to the point that we're trying to make in terms of differentiating ourselves. This may sound unorthodox to an investor in our fund, [but] first and foremost, I don't look at the financial results of our businesses first. I look at the strategic transformation of those businesses first. So, for the first two years after every investment we make, we think about these core technologies and where we can invest in additional research and development, additional sales and marketing, to not only further penetrate the core markets we're in with this capability, but also move them into adjacencies that can drive their presence in new markets that they weren't engaged in when we acquired the businesses. How do we make them more strategic in the ecosystem? Move them up the proverbial food chain? We gauge that success, and that happens over the first two years.

So, when you look at some of the investments we make, a lot of times, expenditures are going through the roof. We're making a lot of changes relative to management teams, executives, bringing in new talent, trying to open the aperture, so to speak. So, there's a lot of, in some cases, volatility in that regard. But then, what you see is these companies become very disruptive in their ecosystems. They become very agile, so that they can actually take those capabilities, that technology, and move into targeted adjacencies that we ourselves identify as strategic. And that's a very important part of the reason that we're able to generate the types of returns over that twenty-five-year period. It's by no accident that close to seven out of ten of our exits are sales to strategics.

I always say the litmus test, if we are truly making our companies more important in those ecosystems, is that we should open the eyes of strategics in those markets.

CHRISTOPHER:

What you're talking about there is something that's such a common theme that Tony and I have had the blessing to hear from so many fantastic investors. It's consistent application of a playbook to a particular area, to a particular sector, and making a repeatable process.

When you think about investment today in government technology, what are the greatest opportunities you're seeing?

RAMZI:

That's a great question. Look, there's a reason that we're focused in the areas we're focused. It is somewhat personal for me too, at least from the context that we're making a difference for citizens, not only in the United States, but across the world. I can't think of three more important areas to focus in on, relative to our daily lives, than our own education, our own healthcare, and protection of citizens across the globe. Those are the three areas that we are focused on, and we'll continue to focus on that. And these are multitrillion-dollar markets. There's ample opportunity to find clear-cut opportunities for outsize returns as we do what we say we're going to do, making our companies more important to their customers, which is the target for each and every one of our investments.

I'll give you an example. Shortly after 9/11, many, many, many of us experienced a personal loss. One of my best friends from college was on the first plane from Boston to LA that hit the World Trade Center. It changed all of our lives. At that point, we had invested in that defense technology business that I mentioned, but we were looking at a lot of different areas. That really, quite frankly, left an imprint on me, and it became very personal for me to really try to understand how the private sector could support initiatives to help protect people across the globe.

So, I started meeting with a number of folks within the intelligence apparatus, senior-level folks. And it became apparent after sitting down with a number of those, and one of whom was the head of the CIA and NSA—the only person in our country's history to run both. And it became apparent that one of the biggest vulnerabilities we faced globally was what they referred to back then as DPIA, data protection/information assurance. And the vulnerability was strategic in nature. Back in '01 and '02, there were sensitivities to what we were engaged in at a government level. But the vulnerabilities also transcended into the private sector and the commercial markets. So, as an investor, that led us to really think about opportunities in cybersecurity way before anyone started thinking about it from a private equity standpoint.

And that market itself is significant. It's very, very large. Today, the topic du jour is artificial intelligence, ChatGPT, etc. The government's been at the forefront of artificial intelligence.

We started investing in AI businesses in 2010. For example, one of our companies back then was taking exabytes of unstructured data and satellite imagery, in real time, providing analytics to high-level cabinet members, including the president of the United States, upon which critical decisions were made.

When we think about our three core areas, I don't want to stray. One of the things that some firms have done in the private equity world is stray from what they do best. When they want to grow, they move into new areas. If you asked me how to build a retail operation or a consumer products business or a transportation company, I have no idea. I mean, throw a dart against the wall. But if you tell us to build a business in the ecosystems I've highlighted, we have a good sense of what matters, where to invest, and what markets to engage in. So, when we think about the future, I can't think of more important areas than healthcare, tech, education tech, and obviously global security technology.

CHRISTOPHER:

It's fascinating because the world obviously has changed so much in the last twenty-four to thirty-six months from a technology standpoint. Because of the volatility that we've had over the last couple of years in technology in general, and all over the general marketplace, what's happened that you did expect to occur and what has happened that you didn't expect to occur?

RAMZI:

I think volatility lends itself to opportunity, but I also think it lends itself to, quite frankly, separating the cream from the rest. Challenging environments are important from that standpoint. We have a fiduciary obligation to provide the best returns to our investors—the pensioners, the family offices, the insurance companies, whoever they may be. That's the Holy Grail for us.

We've worked through wars across the globe, the Great Recession, government shutdowns, sequestrations, continuing resolutions, a lot of chaos in the White House, however you want to qualify that. And what we've been experiencing now in the broader economy is something that everybody should have anticipated based on the environment, at least the macroeconomic environment that we had been experiencing prior to the rates and the volatility. So, I anticipate, again, the dispersion between the best performers, those who have a raison d'être, and the rest to become larger. I think that's what you're going to see.

There's a lot more focus on top performers. And there's a lot of demand for access to managers that are top performers based on the uniqueness of their strategy and application of that strategy over a long period of time.

CHRISTOPHER:

Because your strategy is very unique, I'm curious what investors get wrong when they look at technology that is engaged with the government. I have to assume people just really don't get the story until you explain it to them.

RAMZI:

Yeah, we've got the scars to prove it. It's not easy. It's a very unique marketplace. [But] this is not a monolithic entity. There are over a thousand different government agencies. But the way that the government procures products, goods, and services is very different than the commercial market. Unfortunately, while I have a lot of respect for a lot of very successful private equity firms, some have tried to come in and come out of these markets. Unless you immerse yourself full-time, especially in an area like this, it's very difficult to do so, unless you've built that IP. The IP is critical because it's not only to help understand what the businesses are. It's to help you know how to grow a business selling to government agencies. How do you grow it organically at double-digit rates? Well, you've got to make sure that you hear what the customers say, and you understand how to sell to those customers and make sure that you're satisfying each and every one of their objectives. And, quite frankly, working with them to think about the next five, ten years in terms of where things will be so that you can satisfy even those future requirements.

TONY:

You mentioned the Holy Grail of Investing for you. The book title is *The Holy Grail of Investing*. And it came from ten, fifteen years ago when I met with Ray Dalio. I interviewed Warren Buffett, Ray Dalio, the cadre there—more macro investors and so forth. And Ray and I became good friends. One of the early questions I asked him was, "If you had to codify the single most important principle of your investing, do you know what it would be?" And he said the Holy Grail of Investing is having eight to twelve uncorrelated investments. For you, there's a different way of looking at things, obviously. What's the Holy Grail of Investing for you with Veritas?

RAMZI:

What I would say, especially in the world that we live in, [is that] data is coming at us from all angles. We look at over a thousand investment opportunities every year. And we have a concentrated approach. What are the ones that we want to move forward with? And what are we going to do to transform and reposition those companies?

That's not driven by attractiveness of company. That's not driven by value. It's driven by [whether] our playbook applies to the opportunity that we see in front of us. We pass on a lot of great companies. We pass on great companies that are actually valued appropriately. But if one doesn't tie into that strategic level of immersion that I mentioned and reorientation and repositioning, we're going to pass. We see a lot of data. [But] out of all that you see, take the three most important things, and understand those to the nth degree and how you can apply them relative to strategic investment. That's much harder done than said.

It's really being able to discern what are the three or four most important things, simplistically. And then, expounding on those to drive value for us, in our model, strategically reorienting these companies so that they can move up the food chain, become more important to their customers, and take their core and move it into new adjacencies. If we can do that right, we have a high chance of getting the types of returns that we've been able to generate.

TONY:

Growing large investment firms is obviously a lot more than just great performance. What do you think has been the primary reason for your success? You exploded. So, there's a fulcrum point in which your business was good, and then it went to great. What was the fulcrum point? What is that factor that has caused this explosion of growth and results?

RAMZI:

I'd say the first one was when we made that first investment in that company in 1998 and integrated and decided that we needed to focus. We also have continuity. There are folks here who have been with us since the beginning, and that continuity is very important. The ability for us to chart our own course, so to speak, and go after things that maybe we couldn't or wouldn't have been able to prior, just opened up the opportunity.

As I said earlier, one of the biggest things is I firmly believe that you'll have opportunities over the course of your lifetime; you've just got to be very prepared and eager, anxious, aggressive, relative to tackling and taking advantage of the opportunity. I'd say that was a clear opportunity that, from a market standpoint, surprised a lot of people. But I'd say [to them], stay tuned because there's a lot more to come. But it isn't only the growth in AUM.

I don't look at that. Yes, AUM has gone from $2 billion to $45 billion. Our returns, which defy the "laws" of private equity, have generally increased as our funds have gotten larger. So, fund six, as an example, which is a 2018 vintage, is the top performing fund according to Preqin. I know it sounds simple, but when you are strategic, you build on that IP. We're smarter today than we were last year. We should get better. That's our collective mindset.

That's the expectation. That's part of the culture. When I talk to people here, we talk about [how] the next fund, which we'll start raising shortly, should be our best performing fund. That's the expectation.

CHRISTOPHER:

You obviously took over under very difficult circumstances. What are a few things that you wish somebody would've told you before you took over the reins?

RAMZI:

I'd say, day-to-day it was no different for me. I and the team in place were running the investments prior and post. At the end of the day, no one could predict what's going to happen. **There are two words I live by: compassion and passion. Obviously, be compassionate, as I mentioned earlier in the background that I have. But also, passion. I love building businesses, whether it's our own or portfolio companies. You got to have that passion because ultimately that's the true test.** It's not about anything other than that. They are by-products of your success, but it's really about what you really love to do. And I can't think about anything more interesting from a day-to-day standpoint than the areas we invest in and the people we interact with within Washington. But I don't think there's anything specific that has surprised me, negatively, at least.

CHRISTOPHER:

Is there anything that, with the benefit of hindsight, you would've liked to have done differently in the business?

RAMZI:

There are always some things. People are everything for us. We take a lot of pride in developing people because, first and foremost, we are fiduciaries to our investors. We need to be the best and therefore our people need to be the best. So, can we do a better job in developing people, and mentoring people, which we look at all the time. And in some cases, you've got to make those harder decisions sooner rather than later.

One of the biggest failures comes when you hang on to someone longer than you should have. When the decision was obviously already made, but you just, for whatever reason, don't make those changes, whether it's internal of Veritas or executives or whatever the case may be. You learn from those. You want to give people ample opportunity, but you should also act when you know for a fact that things aren't going as they should.

TONY:

Building on that, when you think about the universe of investment talent, what do you believe are the most important key traits that separate the highest performers from good performers?

RAMZI:

We have our own analytics to assess that. But I'd say it's an art in terms of what we do, more than a science. For me, there's the capability side, the IQ side, which you can easily assess. But more important is the EQ side. We are in a people business. We're talking to owners. We're talking to investors. We're talking to management teams. We're working internally amongst different folks. The ability to assimilate across those levels, the ability to articulate and really understand the person you're speaking to, that art of listening, the ability to assess and judge—how do you really assess all that?

Ultimately, you don't until they're within the firm. But we look for those type of traits and those type of experiences to help us make those decisions. Because if you're coming to Veritas, you're not going to have your hand held. You're going to leverage a great platform. You're going to work with tremendously successful people, exciting people. But at the end of the day, we're looking for people who have that [entrepreneurial] mindset. And then, ultimately, passion. I mean, this is a hard business. People work long hours. You've got to understand that and appreciate that. And you've got to be in it for the right reasons. The right reason is you want to make a difference.

TONY:

The work feeds their psyche then, because it's a deeper meaning, as you said. It's not just the surface meaning.

RAMZI:

Exactly.

TONY:

And you lead by example in that area.

RAMZI:

I try.

TONY:

We really have enormous respect for what you've built here and you're just a delightful human being as well. Your father must—I know he's passed—be so damn proud.

RAMZI:

He's watching over me.

CHAPTER 12

VINOD KHOSLA

FOUNDER OF KHOSLA VENTURES

Accolades: Turned a $4 million investment in Juniper Networks into $7 billion in profits. Early investor in Open AI. Member of the philanthropic Giving Pledge.

Total Asset Under Management (as of August 2023): $15 billion

Area of Focus: Disruptive technologies in healthcare, sustainability, fintech, and AI

HIGHLIGHTS

- Vinod Khosla cofounded Sun Microsystems in 1982, which created the Java programming language, and was later acquired by Oracle for $7.4 billion.
- Through his career, Mr. Khosla has been an early investor in Google, LinkedIn, Nest, DeepMind, Instacart, DoorDash, Impossible Foods, Affirm, among many others.
- Among his many honors, Mr. Khosla has been named as one of the top tech investors in 2023 by *Forbes*, the world's greenest billionaire, and has won the National Medal of Technology.

TONY:

Vinod, I don't know if you remember but we met once when I spoke at TED back in the days when it was still down there in Monterey. I had that little interaction with the vice president, and you and a group from Kleiner Perkins invited me to dinner that night to discuss what had happened that day. I've been a fan of yours ever since, to say the least.

VINOD:

Yes! TED is of these places that has the right kinds of people. I hate to admit it, but I've gone to every main TED since 1986.

TONY:

Holy cow. You've seen a lot during that time. You're extraordinary. I'd just love if you'd share with us a little bit of your origin story about how you went from living in India with the excitement of what was happening in Silicon Valley, to being turned down multiple times by Stanford, to getting $300,000 in seed capital and building Sun Microsystems to a billion in a few years, to making those investments we know about, like the $3 million investment in Juniper that brought almost $7 billion to Kleiner Perkins. How do you go from starting there in India to one of the most respected and most successful VCs in the world?

VINOD:

I grew up in an extremely conservative household. My dad was orphaned when he was three. He lived with various other families and then at fifteen or sixteen he got recruited into the British Army. At sixteen, he was fighting in Egypt. So, the best thing that ever happened to him growing up was being a part of the army. He was never going to have to worry about a job. So, he wanted me to join the Indian Army at sixteen. That was his vision for me. I was the exact opposite. I wanted to take risks.

TONY:

Is that the way you were wired or was there something that helped to trigger that? What created the contrast?

VINOD:

I did get wired that way. [My dad] didn't think doing engineering and going to college was a good idea. **I was more focused on, what are the problems I see and are there creative ways to solve them?** By the way, I didn't know a single person in business. We always only lived in army areas. So, the equivalent of an army base. They were called containments, which were areas where only army people lived. So, I'd never known anybody in business or anybody in technology, never ran into anybody, but was curious. And when I read about Andy Grove starting Intel, I said, that'd be cool to start your own company and do something technically hard. That's why after my graduate degree in biomedical engineering, I decided I'd come to Silicon Valley. **And even though Stanford turned me down twice, I had to fight my way back in. I kept telling them they were making a mistake.**

TONY:

Third time's the charm. That's awesome.

VINOD:

Well, the real story is that I'm always looking for creative solutions. They turned me down the first time, and I was unhappy. So, I argued with them, and they said, you have to have at least two years of work experience, which means you sort of go away. So, what I did is I got two full-time jobs the next year. And I had two years of work experience in one year, and I applied again. And they turned me down again, and I argued with them. I said I had two years of experience. So, just to not have me bother them, they actually moved me from rejected to the wait list. And then I kept bugging them. They only admitted me three or four days before classes started in the business school because somebody else had canceled.

As the story goes, I was friends with everybody in the admissions office—other than the admissions director, who just hated my guts. One of the women in the office called me three or four days before classes started and said, somebody's dropping out of the class. I called the admissions director and said, "Hey, you have a slot. I'm available." I was three weeks into the business school at Carnegie Mellon already. This woman [in admissions] put me up in her living room because I had no place to go. I left Pittsburgh on twenty-four hours' notice because I didn't see why not.

CHRISTOPHER:

Persistence is an amazing thing.

TONY:

Every person we've interviewed in this context has something in their story where their level of persistence was crazy. And that's part of why they are where they are. So how did you go to Sun Microsystems? And then tell us a little about Kleiner Perkins and how that came about.

VINOD:

When I was in business school, I'd already decided I'd start a company. The story is that I was going to get married, and I had no job. So, I was going to do a startup. Then I ran into some guy who knew somebody who was thinking of starting something, and I contacted him. I said, "You can keep your job at Intel. I'll be the first full-time employee, so I'll take the risk."

Two years into it, I realized that what we were building, which was a CAD tool for electrical engineers, needed a platform company. I immediately decided Sun (Microsystems) was the platform company we needed to start. And that's how Sun started as the platform company on which the Daisy application was to be built. That's how I got going. And then Kleiner Perkins was my investor.

TONY:

They gave you $300,000? Is that true? And you turned it into a billion-dollar business in five years?

VINOD:

So, the first $300,000 came from a guy who I was working with to fund my first company, Daisy Systems. When I left Daisy to start Sun Microsystems, literally on one paragraph, he wrote me a $300,000 check because I'd tried to support him during the Daisy thing. He got screwed by one of the founders, but we kept a good relationship. Right after that, Kleiner Perkins invested in

Sun, and John Doerr came on my board. That's how I ended up working at Kleiner Perkins.

TONY:

Unbelievable success there. Tell us a little bit about why you made that move [to start Khosla Ventures] and what it's meant to you at this stage.

VINOD:

I like small groups and KPCB got too big for me. In forty years, I've never called myself a venture capitalist. I always say I'm a venture assistant. This idea you work with the founders to help them realize their dreams is what I enjoy doing and why most of my peers have retired because they were doing a job and then they retired. I'm doing a passion. So, I don't see retiring until my health doesn't allow me to continue.

In forty years, I've never called myself a venture capitalist. I always say I'm a venture assistant. This idea you work with the founders to help them realize their dreams is what I enjoy doing.

TONY:

That's beautiful. Who has been the most important person that helped to shape your success?

VINOD:

I would say I've never really had a mentor. I would say the person who's influenced me the most is John Doer, because I argued with him the most. We worked together for twenty years. We worked together at Sun, then we worked for twenty years at Kleiner Perkins. Most people would say we never agreed. **So, people always thought we would never keep working together because we always argued about everything. But what I learned from him was a critical thing. We'd always argue about what the questions were that were important. We developed a really great mutual respect, which was based on vigorous debate.**

TONY:

Finding the right questions, even though you might have different views of them, to uncover what's really needed.

VINOD:

My view was it hurts the entrepreneur if you're too polite with them. Frankly, if you say all the good things, but don't say things you're concerned about, the entrepreneur likes you more. But they don't get helped as much because they're not focusing on the weak links in their chain.

CHRISTOPHER:

It's interesting because I've heard from a number of people that what changed from 2019 to 2021 was that entrepreneurs were so courted by those in the venture space that they were told whatever they wanted to hear. And so there were not enough critical questions being asked to allow these businesses to be run in a more productive way.

VINOD:

Capital efficiency went through the window because a lot of money was available, and everybody was saying polite things.

CHRISTOPHER:

Where's the greatest opportunity for investors—as a venture assistant, as you put it?

VINOD:

Our focus is on much deeper technology that makes a large difference. Our view is if you do that then the returns will be a good side effect of building a large business as opposed to focusing on the return. I don't think I've seen an IRR calculation in our firm in the last fifteen years. We just don't do it. We're probably the only investment firm that never does an IRR calculation. **The focus is: Can we build something substantial? And if you do, then everything sort of takes care of itself. It's a very different philosophy than optimizing the transaction.**

CHRISTOPHER:

With that in mind, and knowing that you've seen so many different cycles of technology and biotechnology, is the greatest opportunity today artificial intelligence?

VINOD:

I think I've long believed in AI as a game changer. I just didn't know when it would explode. **We invested in OpenAI four or five years ago because that was the thesis I first wrote about in 2012.** There are some famous blogs that I got criticized for. Almost everybody agrees with me ten years later. So, AI is definitely one of those opportunities. But my view is, and I always look at the contrarian view, I actually believe if you look at twenty, twenty-five years from now, and look back at the early 2020s, as sad as they were, the two best things that happened to the planet were Ukraine and COVID. Why? Ukraine started a path to energy independence. There was no chance Germany was going to say, we are not going to use Russian gas. They didn't even think that was possible. And literally a year and a half later, they have now declared they have no Russian gas being used in Germany. So, what I'm leading to is that the energy transition will now happen because of Ukraine. And because of that, all of the climate technologies have become much more important and much more invigorated. We did the IRA Act, which has a lot of incentives for these climate transition technologies and infrastructure technologies. The Europeans had to compete with us, so they have their own act, which is equally impressive. All that really opens up a new era of climate-related investing.

And then what COVID did was two things. First, it proved we can develop a vaccine ten times faster than we thought we could. There were new models like remote work in enterprises. There was new consumer entertainment. There were all new sets of assumptions. But the biggest thing was not only every government, but every company is now committed to getting out of China from a single point of dependence. The world's labor was in China. The world's steel was in China. The world's rare materials were in China. **So, all supply chains and all material concentration will move out of China. That opens up a whole set of new opportunities.** So, I would say COVID started this sort of independence from China, which will mostly develop on technologies that can be cost-effective without needing to be in China. And so, the COVID axis, which is what I call the supply chain axis, and the Ukraine axis, which is the energy axis, and then AI for everything else. Those three things dramatically changed venture capital for the next fifteen years. There'll still be enterprise apps and internet apps and progress in bio technologies. We do a lot of that, and we feel like we are uniquely positioned to have an advantage in those areas because we have such a deep technical bench.

CHRISTOPHER:

What has happened over the last couple years in the world of venture that you did expect to happen and that you did not expect to happen?

VINOD:

I would say mostly that these swings, I expected them to be more moderated. It's more euphoria about AI than is warranted. Not in the impact it's going to have, but in the valuations. They make no sense at all. We've looked at almost all the billion-dollar valuations [and they] make no sense to us. You have to have real revenue to get to a return on a billion-dollar initial valuation ten years later. So, I would say we are seeing that swing in AI without enough diligence to say what will have a differentiated advantage. I jokingly say the batch of Y Combinator companies that started in January, most of them, like 60 percent were doing AI. Half of them were obsoleted by developments in the three months of the launch because ChatGPT came in. **It took TikTok almost a year to get to a hundred million users. That was the fastest ever. It took ChatGPT sixty days to get to a hundred million users. Nobody in their remote mind would've assumed revenue can grow this fast on anything, anywhere.** That was a phenomenon—how fast it happened—that surprised me.

TONY:

The title of the book we're working on is *The Holy Grail of Investing*, which sounds over the top, but it's really about finding the Holy Grail—the most important investment principle—of each of the greatest leaders that we've talked with. What's the Holy Grail of Investing for you in?

VINOD:

I would put it this way. You can have different Holy Grails for different people or, I like to say, different styles of investing. You have to know what you want to do and what you're good at, and then stay true to that. To me that's the basic principle. There are many ways to do venture well, and being conservative and shooting for lots of two-to-three-times returns results in really good IRR. We focus much more on the fundamentals. So, when the crypto thing happened, we just couldn't figure out where the meat was. We said, the blockchain is really valuable, but speculating in crypto is just not a long-term sustainable strategy. If you want to get money out of China, it makes a lot of sense to be on the blockchain. If you want to not be in Argentinian pesos, it makes a lot of sense. But what we did is a company like Helium, which uses the blockchain to build a real communications network. Now they're building a 5G cellular network using the blockchain. So, we always focused on real applications of blockchain. It doesn't happen overnight. But our focus is: Where can technology play a large role and where can it have large economic impact? If that's true, then we get the right team, and it builds a company, and if you build a big company, then you'll get fine returns. That's a very different principle than optimizing IRRs. I'd rather have solid ten-year returns than high two-year returns.

TONY:

So, you're looking for the long term. You're looking for not the two-times or three-times return; you're looking for the ten-, twenty-, or a hundred-times return by building something that has lasting value, that you see will really shift the world in some way.

VINOD:

You got it. So, when Pinterest went public, the *Wall Street Journal* did an article on the all-time best venture returns. And Juniper came up. It was a 2,500-times return. I was at Kleiner then, on a $4 million investment or something—I forget the exact numbers. We made $7 billion as distributed. Like, off the charts. But here's the thing . . . we believed in making that change happen. I actually consider this one of the most significant business achievements in my life. We made the change happen. It wasn't the return, even though it was $7 billion. I wanted the world to be TCP/IP, and no telecom carrier in the U.S. or in Europe was planning on TCP/IP as the public network. Every telecom carrier has that today, but there were zero that planned on that. If you look in 1996, every Goldman Sachs report only talked about ATM as the backbone of the internet. And I believed in TCP/IP. **I said, I don't care what the customers think; we'll build the right thing, and they will come. And that's what happened.** I don't believe TCP/IP would've happened if we hadn't done it. As weird as that sounds.

CHRISTOPHER:

It's consistent with what Henry Ford talked about. If you asked his customers, they wanted a faster horse instead of actually creating something that they absolutely needed. They just didn't realize it.

VINOD:

Right. Look at the press in 1996, every single plan for every telco was based on ATM technology. You take somebody like Cisco, which was the dominant player in TCP/IP; they bought StrataCom in 1995, because every customer wanted ATM. And their CTO told me they'd never do TCP/IP for the public network. Never. I said, fine, we'll do it. And that's why we got the return. We just built what we thought would be valuable to the world. It's very much our style.

Same thing happened when we did Impossible [Foods]. We said plant proteins, it saves the planet; it can taste better than meat. Nobody believed it. So, we took the long view and it's the only plant protein company that's growing today.

CHRISTOPHER:

Vinod, you obviously you think differently than the vast majority of the venture community. What do you look for the most in the people that you're going to hire at Khosla, that allows you to know that they're different than the average person that you might consider?

VINOD:

Both in our entrepreneurs and who we hire, the single most important factor is not what they know, but their rate of learning. What rate can they learn at, which is a very hard thing to judge when you're interviewing somebody. But the rate of learning is way more important than what you know, or what experience you have.

CHAPTER 13

MICHAEL B. KIM

FOUNDER AND CHAIRMAN OF MBK PARTNERS

Accolades: The Godfather of Asian Private Equity and wealthiest man in South Korea

Total Asset Under Management (as of August 2023): $25.6 billion

Area of Focus: North Asia markets: China, Japan, and Korea. Financial services, consumer media, and telecommunications.

HIGHLIGHTS

- MBK Partners is the largest private equity manager in North Asia, with $25.6 billion in assets under management.
- Top-decile returns performance for every active fund—"The Most Consistently Top-Performing Buyout Fund Manager(s)," 2019, by *Institutional Investor*.
- Michael B. Kim was ranked as one of "The 50 Most Influential People in the World" in 2015 by *Bloomberg*.

TONY:

Michael, as I understand it, you wanted to be a writer to start with and, somehow, you went from that to becoming the "Godfather of Asian private equity" and the richest person in Korea—the one who kind of rescued the country during tough economic times. How did that all come about? Would you mind sharing with us a little bit of your origin story?

MICHAEL:

I'm a bit of an accidental investor, but I think you'll find many of the people in my field are. I grew up in in Seoul, South Korea, thinking I'd be a writer or maybe a professor. I went to junior high school in the U.S. Didn't speak a word of English. My father was kind of old-fashioned. He said, "If you want to learn English, read." So that's what I did. I started learning English by reading books. When I told him I needed help with my oral English, his response, of course, was, "Read books out loud . . ." But reading books really is at the heart of my formative education. I fell in love with books, novels especially but also history, philosophy, science books. I went on to major in English at a liberal arts college—Haverford. Upon graduation, I was set to go to graduate school when I saw all the whip-smart kids around me applying to something called Wall Street. I had no idea what that was, but it sounded cool, so I thought I'd try it. One of the Goldman Sachs co-chairmen, John Whitehead, was a Haverford alum, and while Haverford is not a clubby place, there are so few of us in that sector that I think he took a flyer on me.

So I started as a banker at Goldman Sachs, back in '86. Worked like crazy for two years and then went back to get my MBA at Harvard Business School. I swore I'd never go back to Wall Street, and of course, upon graduation, went right back to Goldman Sachs.

TONY:

And how did you go from that to going back home to be a part of the Asian crisis? What was that transition like?

MICHAEL:

That was an inflection point in my career. I was sent out by Goldman to its Hong Kong office. It was a tiny team back then, trying to cover one-third of the world's population in Asia. I got recruited to be Salomon Brothers' COO for Asia at a young age. Then in '97 the Asia Financial Crisis hit. Korea was one of the hardest hit countries. I helped to lead the sovereign rescue not because I had any experience in sovereign restructurings—I just happened to be one of the few senior Asians in the company around at that time. People in the West probably have only faint memories of this crisis in '97–'98. But it was cataclysmic. Half of Asia was ready to collapse—Thailand, Indonesia, and, most urgently, Korea. We led the restructuring of Korea's balance sheet. We led the sovereign bond offering to get $4 billion in much needed new dollars into the country. And I guess this, in hindsight, helped me make a name for myself. From there I got recruited by David Rubenstein at Carlyle, who just wouldn't take no for an answer. And so, just as I went to Wall Street on a lark, I decided to try out this thing called private equity. I joined as president of Carlyle Asia in 1999, based in Hong Kong. And I was there for a very constructive and educational six and a half years before branching out on my own.

TONY:

What made you finally decide to branch out on your own at that stage?

MICHAEL:

I had this vision of creating an Asian private equity group owned and operated by Asians. Some people called it a hallucination. My view was that all the players in Asia at that time were global PE firms with a flag in Asia, and they were doing "pan-Asia" coverage. I will tell you pan-Asia is a false concept. It's some Western cartographer's imagination of Asia. Asia is much too large and its markets much too fragmented to treat as one monolithic market, and to try to scale. So, our concept, our strategic insight, was to focus on a sub-region. For us: China, Japan, Korea—North Asia, whose three countries constitute one of the largest economic blocs in the world. In terms of GDP, numbers two, three, and ten. That's larger than the EU and larger than the U.S. And importantly, we thought these three countries were scalable because of several millennia of shared history, some of it not so friendly, and shared culture, customs, and, today, economic trade flows and business practices.

CHRISTOPHER:

Michael, you obviously have a different perspective because of where your company is based. What is it that investors are missing right now, and what is the greatest opportunity for investors in North Asia?

MICHAEL:

I don't think investors are "missing" Asia. They understand China is big. They understand India is a big opportunity. Three billion in population between the two countries. **But I think the pitfall that many Western investors have when they're seeking to invest in Asia is looking through a Western-centric lens.** Yes, Asia is getting "Americanized," and a lot of the finance, including alternative investments, driving the development of the Asian markets was developed in the U.S. But the American way is not the only way; the American financial model is not "the end of history," as Francis Fukuyama said of the U.S. liberal democracy–free market capitalist system. This way of thinking is false, it's immoral, and it's dangerous.

You have to accept that Asia is different. Asia is also not monolithic. You need to treat each market, at least the subregions, differently from the rest of this vast area. American capital is smart, it's sharp, but it's also inward looking, thinking things should be done the American way. That the American way of finance is transferred well. There's a lot of culture sharing between America and Europe. Asia is not another Europe.

TONY:

What differences stand out most that Americans are probably missing?

MICHAEL:

It starts with the big things—the infrastructure, the regulatory environment, policy-making imperatives. Governments play an important role in in North Asia, and you have to accept that. I was trained at Harvard Business School and Goldman Sachs, so I'm a believer in laissez-faire, a free market system with as little regulation as possible. For anyone with that kind of education and training, Asia is a culture shock. Asia has a very strong and active, some would say intrusive, ministry of finance or ministry of industry and trade. You can tie back the role of these ministries to the Confucian tradition of civil servants, who assumed the role of guides and guards of society. These ministries see themselves as performing the same role. I've heard a policy-maker, a government official, refer to himself as the invisible hand that Adam Smith talked about in free markets. Yes, I have a slightly different take on that. But that's the role they play. And you have to work with them if you're going to do business in Asia.

So, it starts from those things and goes to the way business groups are structured. In Korea and Japan, they have these large conglomerates. In Korea, the family-owned conglomerates control 80 percent of Korean industry. So, you have to learn to deal with these family-owned conglomerates who are now on their third generation in succession of ownership.

I mentioned the small things. **The business customs in Asia are different. The tips I was given when I was going for my Goldman interview— give 'em a firm handshake, smile, look 'em straight at the eye—all those things are considered disrespectful in Asia.** You want to be humble, and you want to keep a respectful distance while conveying your character to the person you're engaging with. I know that's maybe a difficult lesson to impart, but you start with the premise: Things in Asia are just different. If you can keep your mind open to that, you'll gain much more traction in your dealings with Asians.

TONY:

With your proximity to the leaders that you've grown up with, and with your understanding of the East and West, what do you think are the greatest opportunities for investors in Asia right now? And what is the focus of MBK Partners?

MICHAEL:

The answers to the two-part question converge. Because we practice what we preach, we think the biggest opportunity in Asia is in alternative assets. And we think it's in North Asia because of the scale I talked about, but also because of demographics. **Demographics really is destiny.** If you look at our markets, particularly Japan and Korea, which are the most bona fide buy-out markets in Asia today, and sizeable, what you see is not just large economies with ready-to-play buyout candidates; you also see huge consumption markets. People think of Japan as an export-oriented country. But over two-thirds of its GDP comes from domestic consumption. **People tend to forget that Japan had been the second wealthiest country in the world after the U.S. for four decades before being surpassed by China. And its GDP per capita income is still much higher than any other Asian country. So, there's a country of vast wealth.**

Another demographic theme I'd point out is the rapidly graying population. Japan is the world's grayest population. Thirty-five percent of its population is over sixty-five years old. Guess which country is number two in silver quotient. It's Korea. And China, unbelievably, is catching up rapidly, after six decades of a one-child policy. So, this rapidly aging population has important implications for our investment strategy. We do a lot of healthcare. We went through a period where we did a lot of investing into leisure and entertainment. We owned Universal Studios in Japan. We used to own Accordia Golf, the largest chain of public golf courses in Japan. We still own the largest chain of public golf courses in Korea, called GolfZon. But we have moved from entertainment and leisure to healthcare and, in particular, elderly healthcare. We are now the owner of the largest elderly nursing care franchise in Japan. In Korea, we own a company called Osstem Implant, which is the largest dental implant provider in the world. So, we play demographic themes along with the growth that is inherent and, I think, the most attractive part of Asia.

One last statistic: The rise of China is the economic/financial story of our generation. I won't go into all the statistics you're probably already familiar with, but I'll cite you a couple. **McKinsey estimated, I think it was three years ago, that a billion Chinese would be joining the middle class in the next ten years. So, in seven years, we're going to have a billion new consumers. That's unprecedented in human history.** You may be surprised to learn that the portion of China's GDP attributable to domestic consumption is now larger than that portion attributable to exports. So, it's become a domestic consumption giant in its own right.

On the domestic consumption point, we own the number one and number two rental car operators in China. And our thesis boils down to this pair of statistics. There are 450 million driver's licenses in China but only 270 million license plates. And issuance of license plates is slowing down even further as the government tries to control emissions. So, there are 180 million drivers who are looking for cars. That's the kind of scale you just don't see. That's the booming consumption opportunity for managers like us.

TONY:

You're getting in front of a tidal wave of consumption, looking to improve the companies that you purchase, and then let it move from there. It's wild.

CHRISTOPHER:

You know, we talk a lot as a firm about investing with tailwinds. Those are tsunamis of epic proportion! What has happened that you didn't expect in the China market?

MICHAEL:

The political turn that the Chinese leadership has taken over the last couple years has taken a lot of investors, including me, by surprise. I saw China's rise from the ground up. I've been in Asia now for thirty years. I saw the way it developed. When I first came out to Asia back in '93, China and India were at about the same level of economic development. If you look at what's happened, China has done none of it by accident. They have the smartest, strategic-thinking leadership, the invisible hand, the ministries I referred to earlier. You're talking about the best and brightest out of a talent pool of 1.4 billion.

My view, watching all this happen in real time, was that the market growth will continue unabated because the Chinese leadership has brought economic prosperity to its 1.4 billion people for the first time in one and a half centuries. Why do anything to jeopardize that? But what you saw the last couple years showed the growing pains of a country and an economy that is going through an experiment unprecedented in history. And we're so used to the China boom story that we're surprised when it takes a step back, right? They're trying to pair a Communist-based political system with a command economy with important elements of a U.S. free market system. No one's ever done that, at least not successfully. China had been successful in doing that, in executing on that experiment for over two decades, and while I always advised our investors that it would not be a linear trajectory, I expect it to return to that path of success.

I think the leadership in China felt compelled to project China's emerging power and show the rest of the world that it is now not an American hegemony, but a bipolar world where China and the U.S. coexist somewhat as peers, but also as rivals ideologically, militarily, and economically. What we witnessed over the last year and a half, two years, I think, are the by-products of that projection of China's emerging power. And so, you've had this unfortunate stalemate. It's not good for anyone: not for the citizens of the two countries, and certainly not for the rest of the global economy, which has seen the adverse impacts of this kind of ongoing trade war. **My conviction—and I bet my career on it—is that China will resume its economic and financial market liberalization drive.** Once you open the doors to market liberalization, you can't close them.

TONY:

The driving force then is really the consumers of the country, meaning the citizens themselves, as long as they're prosperous. And if they're not, that creates instability. Is that the essence of it?

MICHAEL:

Exactly. I think you nailed it. Something that wasn't reported widely in the West is that when president Xi implemented this zero COVID lockdown for the second half of last year, it engendered a great deal of resistance from the people. It was the first time I saw my friends and colleagues in China very anxious and some angry, not so much about the curtailed individual freedoms but about the inability to just feed their family. They couldn't go out to the local grocery to buy food for dinner. To President Xi's credit, he sensed the growing anger among his people, and he made the extraordinary step of reversing his decision and lifting the lockdown. That's been a boon for the economy, but I think it's also an important gesture to his people, that he has their interests at heart. So the social-political covenant is restored. I think he and the leadership of China will resume its drive for economic prosperity and financial liberalization. **To summarize: Economics will trump politics.**

TONY:

Yes, and economics comes down to the quality of the life of your people, right? And you have a very large population there. If they're not happy, the politics will change.

Ray Dalio's a dear friend of mine and when I first interviewed him about a decade ago, I asked him, What is the single most important investment principle of your life? And he said, Tony, I can tell you very clearly. He said the Holy Grail of Investing is finding eight to twelve uncorrelated investments that you can bet on. I know that he's a macro investor. Obviously, private equity is a different type of investment, but what would you say is your idea of the Holy Grail of Investing?

MICHAEL:

Ray Dalio is not only a macro guy; he's a hedge fund manager. So, yes, I think his way of looking at things is a little bit different from ours. It's a bit of an oversimplification, but hedge funds seek alpha. **In private equity, we create alpha. And the way we create alpha after buying a company is by rolling up our sleeves to do the hard work to create value.** So, the Holy Grail is value creation. At MBK Partners, we buy good companies, and we make them better. So, fundamentals of the business are absolutely critical. I think every GP in our space will agree with that. The U.S. model of value creation is the blueprint. But in Asia, you have to adapt to the local conditions and the local way of doing things. The senior prime minister of Singapore, Lee Kwan Yew, was famous for saying that we in Asia need to adopt our own Asian form of democracy. You can't just take the American form of liberal democracy and transplant it to Singapore or Korea or Japan and expect it to flourish.

Conditions are different, right? You can't pluck a plant from California and expect it to flourish in Singapore, where you have different soil conditions, different sunlight—even the water is different. You have to adapt it to local conditions. And in the same way, I think you have to do your value creation in a localized Asian way.

One of the tools in a private equity manager's toolbox for value creation is cost savings. And there are many different ways to do that. What I used to do at my former firm was to cut wages. There are a lot of companies, if not almost all companies, that have fat, right? Layoffs in Asia are anywhere from discouraged, to prohibited in Korea. It's illegal to fire people. You can't have layoffs in Japan. It's discouraged. If you're a manager and you have to lay off your employees, you haven't managed very well, you haven't done your job well. So, through both cultural discouragement and some legal restrictions, we have to find other ways to capture cost savings. And we do that by getting better at procurement or consolidating back office and doing a lot of synergistic things with our sister portfolio companies. It's harder work, but we think it's the right way to do it because it's the Asian way to do it. So, there are different ways to get at value creation, but I think the Holy Grail is creating value in your business after you acquire it.

TONY:

So, there's more focus on, I assume, top line growth as well, not just the cost cutting?

MICHAEL:

Of course. Each market is different, but in the case of China and Korea, which are high-growth GDPs, the top line growth is a little bit easier. Japan is more like the U.S.—even more challenging than the U.S. Its GDP is going to grow one and a half percent, and that's cause for a celebration this year. So, the easy top line growth is a little bit different in Japan, but it's doable because of what a great fundamentals market Japan is—the best pool of mid-cap companies in the world, after the U.S. It has, I think, the most talented managerial pool in the world. And of course, it's a borrowers' paradise. You can get five-to-seven-year senior debt to support your equity in an acquisition at 2.5 percent to 3 percent, all in cost. If you can't make returns with that kind of leverage, you shouldn't be investing.

TONY:

I love your answer because in, in my own life, I'm fortunate enough to have about 111 companies of my own. We do about $7 billion in business across the different companies. Everything we do in every industry is find a way to do more for others than anybody else—add more value. And that is what I love about private equity. So, a big factor, I assume, would be having a certain amount of control over who's the CEO over a variety of factors. Is that true for you? How important is control for your organization to be able to add that value?

MICHAEL:

Control is not just helpful, but, in my experience, vital to value creation. And we can define control for you. It's control over, exactly as you pointed out, the CEO. We have to have the flexibility to hire the best CEO in her field and the ability to replace her if we're wrong. So, the CEO and top management. We have to control the board. We have to have control over the business plan, dividend policy, capital expenditure policy, capital raising, and M&A. **If we have control over those seven factors, that constitutes control, and that enables us to do real value creation.** You have to have those levers of control post investment.

TONY:

You're managing about $30 billion, if I understand correctly. As the businesses get bigger, keeping [your own company's] culture alive becomes more difficult. Tell us a little bit about how you've made your decisions. You're the biggest in all of Asia. You're the "Godfather of Private Equity in Asia." It's an amazing title to have associated to you. But when it happens, people tend to throw money at you. So how have you decided about taking money versus not? How do you manage that in your mind so that you can still be as effective as you guys have been?

MICHAEL:

We want to be right-sized. On your last point, we have always left money on the table during our fundraises. I'm focused on moving the needle on returns. The reality is—not many managers like to admit this—but the reality is that the larger your fund, the tougher it is to really generate outsized returns. So, we have been focused on returns and that has served us well over the long term.

My first day of orientation at Goldman Sachs, this guy, I think he was one of the partners, came up on the stage and told us to be "long-term greedy." There's a lot packed into that simple statement. You don't want to go for the biggest bang or the largest bucks, short-term. You want to build long-term relationships. Of course, we're about returns and of course we're about wealth creation for our investors. But you do it over the long term on the basis of long-term relationships. So, we have grown steadily. Yes, we are the largest independent manager in Asia, but we have done that in the right way over the last eighteen years. I think that's the only way you build the franchise.

A vital point, one of the key contributors to that steady growth, is culture building. We have been blessed with extraordinary stability on the staff. We have the lowest turnover in Asia. Of course, we compensate our people well. But a bigger part of it is, I like to think, the cultural ethos we built. I mentioned our mission of being the preeminent Asian GP, owned and operated by Asians. And our shared vision of being an agent of change in Asia. So, there's a sense of shared mission. Everyone at our firm has bought into that mission. That sense of shared mission is tied together by culture. Culture is everything. That was one of the great takeaways from my years at Goldman Sachs. **It's a little bit corny, but we have this thing called the "TIE" ethos: Teamwork, Integrity, and Excellence. Those are the three themes that bind the firm together.** And for us, it's important to have the sense of one firm, because we operate across three different markets, three different countries, and three different cultures. I think that sense of culture, that we're doing something special and that we're all in it together as a team, is what has sustained us and led to some great stability.

TONY:

That's beautiful. Every business has a point in which it's doing well. If the business is truly extraordinary, if it goes from good to great, there's some fulcrum point. Can you pinpoint that in your own business? What was the trigger that really took it to another level?

MICHAEL:

I'm not sure there was one inflection point or fulcrum. When I started MBK Partners, I had done private equity investing at a global firm, as I mentioned. And that was a very valuable trial and error. We tried everything in Asia. We tried different products. Every country and market in Asia, I traveled to and tried. So, that gave me a good sense of what's doable and what's not doable. I had the benefit of that experience, particularly the unsuccessful experiences, to calibrate our strategy.

TONY:

That makes sense.

CHRISTOPHER:

We started our firm in 2001, and I always think about all the things that I wish somebody would've told me before I started the firm that I had to learn the hard way. What are some of the things that you wish somebody would've told you before you started your firm in 2005?

MICHAEL:

In my case, the demands of leadership. **Leadership demands sacrifice. People think if you're born a leader, people will just follow. My experience is kind of the opposite. People follow leaders who take care of others and who are seen to be making sacrifices.** The Koreans have this concept called *jeong*, which means, literally, giving a piece of your heart. And I think that's what comes across. Words are cheap. If you can embody that concept of *jeong* and share a piece of your heart with your employees, that's the way they're going to follow you.

TONY:

What do you believe separates the highest peak performers from their peers? And, as a subset of that question, I'd like to bring it back to the very beginning and say: Why did [Goldman Sachs] pick you when you didn't even know what Wall Street was?

MICHAEL:

The first answer is that when I hire, I look for people with different perspectives, people who can bring a fresh perspective on how to approach a problem. Our business is solving problems with an unrelenting focus on excellence. Yes, a high IQ is a prerequisite. But that's what sociologists would call a necessary-but-not-sufficient condition. There are a lot of bright people in our field. And many of them have a strong work ethic. I think the sufficient condition is a willingness to learn and improve. If I look at the people among the senior ranks in our firm, they're not the ones who were the highest performers as associates. They're the ones who improved with time and effort.

The Japanese refer to something called *kaizen*, meaning continual innovation—a commitment to continual improvement. I think the highest performers have that sense of *kaizen*, and in case they forget it, we remind them through continual training.

In my case, I'm not sure what the Goldman Sachs interviewer saw in me. I'd like to think he saw that even though I didn't know finance, he recognized that knowledge is interdisciplinary. It's all related. And he saw that I was different in my perspective but got a sense of my willingness to learn and maybe a little bit of a spark that aspired to excellence. And I guess he was right about my being different. I published my novel, *Offerings*, in 2001, after working on it, on and off, for over eighteen years—thanks to my day job. I gather there aren't many novels out there written by a Wall Street insider.

TONY:

Michael, I'm most struck obviously by who you are as a man, as a leader, the quality of your values. But one of them that really comes across and you can't fake is your humility. And a big part of that, I think, comes from someone who has great gratitude in their life. I know it's a part of the culture that you're in, but I think it's such an admirable quality that so rarely is seen, unfortunately, in people that are very successful in financial terms. I'm curious, how do you cultivate that humility, that depth of caring, that depth of appreciation?

MICHAEL:

I do feel blessed. I think you inculcate in your colleagues the sense of humility or gratitude by living it and showing it. I'd like to think that the people around me in the office every day see the humility, which comes from a sense of gratitude, which comes from this recognition that there are a lot of smart people out there, there are a lot of hardworking people, and I happened to be in the right place at the right time. Call it luck, call it strategic positioning, but I happened to be someone with a little bit of international finance experience right at the peak of the Asia financial crisis. I happen to be Korean. If all those things didn't fall together, I don't know where my career would be. If I were born on a farm in North Korea, I'm pretty sure I wouldn't be where I am today.

TONY:

We're privileged to be right alongside you as general partners, investors with you. But to get a chance to meet you personally and to hear your entire philosophy, the level of humility, and yet the level of strength that you bring to the table has been a true privilege. You've shared so much solid information here that can help shape the quality of someone's life and the quality of their investing. And I think those two go together.

MICHAEL:

Couldn't agree more. **There's a lot of discussion these days about finding the right work-life balance. What I seek is not so much a balance, which implies a trade-off, as a *work-life harmony*. You can harmonize work with your personal life for mutual benefit to both sides.** Having a good, rewarding experience at work enhances, not detracts from, a good personal life.

TONY:

You talked about failure as one of the biggest keys to investing because nothing replaces experience. What was the phrase you gave about investing?

MICHAEL:

Investors are born; great investors are *made*.

CHAPTER 14

WIL VANLOH

FOUNDER AND CEO OF QUANTUM CAPITAL GROUP

Accolades: One of the largest and most successful private equity firms focused on energy investing, including both oil and gas as well as renewable energy and climate tech

Total Asset Under Management (as of August 2023): $22 billion

Area of Focus: Sustainable energy solutions for the modern world

HIGHLIGHTS

- Founded in 1998, Quantum Capital Group ("Quantum") is one of the leading and largest providers of capital to the global energy and climate tech industries, managing in excess of $22 billion across its various private equity, structured capital, private credit, and venture capital platforms.
- Quantum has differentiated itself by fully integrating technical, operational, and digital expertise into its investment decision-making and operational value-add, hands-on partnership with the companies in which it invests.

TONY:

You've got a storied career to say the least—twenty-five years in business. You've been able to be incredibly successful and take care of your investors through all that time. Would you mind sharing with us how this all came about, to build this extraordinary organization that you've built today?

WIL:

I grew up in a small town in central Texas, and both my parents had very lower-middle-income jobs. As I grew up, I didn't know I was poor, but I was poor. I wanted to play football in college, and Texas Christian University had a great football program back in the mid 1980s, when I was starting to look at colleges. I was fortunate enough to have an opportunity to go play there, but I got injured in the summer after my freshman year and my dad told me the only way I could stay is if I got a job and paid for most of my tuition and expenses. So, I started three or four businesses in college and made enough money to graduate almost debt-free from a private school.

While I was at TCU, I took a fascinating course on value investing that was based on Benjamin Graham and David Dodd's seminal book on that topic, *Security Analysis*, and I fell in love with the idea of becoming an investor. As I started exploring different career paths, **I realized that there are two types of investors: those that buy public stocks, and they are generally people that keep their heads down and crunch numbers, and those that buy private companies, and they are people that get involved with those companies they buy and help them improve their businesses.** Given that I was an entrepreneur at heart, and I loved to solve problems and interact with people, the latter sounded much better to me.

During my senior year, I was invited to join the Educational Investment Fund, an actual pool of about $1 million in capital that was set up for students to be able to make investments in the stock market. We researched stocks and then made investment recommendation to a student-led investment committee. And if the committee approved your investment recommendation, the fund would buy the stock. This experience further solidified my passion for investing and identifying companies that have a competitive advantage. A couple of my professors, Dr. Chuck Becker and Dr. Stan Block, suggested that I could further my investing skill set by going to Wall Street and working in investment banking.

I was fortunate to ultimately secure an analyst position with Kidder Peabody in their energy investment banking group, but after a few years of working ninety to a hundred hours per week, I made the decision that if I am going to work that hard, I am going to start my own investment bank. And so, when I was twenty-four, I launched Windrock Capital with Toby Neugebauer, one of my analyst colleagues from Kidder. What we really wanted to do was be principal investors, but we needed to build a track record as investors, so our strategy was to find great companies and go raise capital for them and re-invest most of our fees back into the companies for which we raised the capital.

I figured two years of working for a Wall Street investment bank made me an expert on financing oil and gas and midstream companies—right? Wrong. What I did know was how to create a financial model in Excel and how to put a pitchbook and an offering memorandum together, and I had pretty good sales skills from all those businesses that I started and marketed back in college. This was back in the early 1990s when the energy industry had been decimated from the price crash in the mid 1980s. I think 90 percent of the companies in business in 1984 were out of business by 1994, when we started Windrock Capital. And the ones that were left, they were left for a reason—because they were exceptional at something; they had some competitive advantage. The launch of our investment bank benefited from a combination of a solid foundational skillset we learned on Wall Street, the hard work ethic of a couple young and hungry entrepreneurs, and good timing. Getting into energy in the early 1990s proved to be exceptional timing, because the entrepreneurs that were still in business were still alive because they were great at what they did, and there wasn't very much money, and we had a skill set for finding capital for those great entrepreneurs. You put those things together and you can make some exceptional returns.

We spent the next five years raising money for companies, getting paid fees for doing so, and then reinvesting 75 to 80 percent of our fees back into the companies for which we raised money. After we built an investment track record, we approached A.V. Jones, a "legendary oil man turned venture capitalist" as people affectionately called him, to partner with us in raising a private equity fund. He had the experience, credibility, and capital, and we had the vision, budding private equity skills, and lots of passion and drive. Fundraising went really slow for the first year as LPs were skeptical about investing in a first-time fund raised by two guys that had not turned thirty yet, and a sixty-year-old oil man that had no formal experience in private equity. Fortunately, we met Vic Romley and Alan Hsia at Union Bank of Switzerland and they wrapped their credibility around us and introduced us to some of their LP clients in the energy private capital space. They helped us land General Motors' pension fund as our lead investor, and within a few months six other blue chip institutional LPs followed their lead and gave us $100 million to start Quantum Energy Partners in 1998.

TONY:

The first billionaire I ever met, when I was twenty years old, I asked him what the secret to his success was, and he said, I overserve underserviced markets. And I said, what does that mean? Because he sold bolts and screws and things that really didn't have much of a differentiation. He said, well, I sell them in Africa. I sell them in parts of Asia where no one goes. If I go to New York, I go to the bowels of the hospital, and I find the guy that orders everything that nobody services. And I overservice him. If I remember correctly, you went to Midland, you went to the places New York bankers weren't going to in those days. Is that true?

WIL:

That's exactly right. We went to the places that were one extra stop on Southwest Airlines. Southwest Airlines flew from Dallas to Houston and maybe to New Orleans. But they didn't go to Midland, Tulsa, or Shreveport directly. As you said, we found underserviced markets and overserviced them—we went to the places that were hard to get to, where the Wall Street banks wouldn't often go. And in those markets, we found some great entrepreneurs who had not been called on by many bankers offering them capital in a very long time.

TONY:

I'm curious to know, who is one of the most important people in your life that really helped to shape your business success and who you are today?

WIL:

It's hard to put my finger on exactly one person. I am a big believer in learning everything you can from other people's mistakes, so I am a voracious reader, which means I have learned a lot of things from a lot of people. **That said, the two people that I give most credit to making me who I am today are my mom and my dad. I am grateful for the hard work ethic they taught me and the value system they instilled in me: that you treat people like you want to be treated, and that no matter how much you want something, you always put other people's interests before your own.**

My dad was a civil servant for the U.S. government, and my mom was a schoolteacher who tried to become an entrepreneur. She failed miserably. My parents had very little savings. What little they had, they used for my mom to open a clothing store so she could literally put clothes on her four kids' backs. This was a bad reason to start a business, and after a few years, it drained all their savings and they nearly had to declare bankruptcy. But my family got through it, and despite the outcome of the clothing business failure, I always admired my mom's ambition and willingness to bet on herself. The example she set by taking a chance and starting a business inspired me and gave me the confidence to go out and try something on my own.

TONY:

Tell us a little bit about A.V. Jones. What role did he play in your life?

WIL:

A.V. was a mentor to me, but he was much more than just a mentor. He was a friend, a business partner, and most importantly, an encourager. He was the most positive person I've ever known and one of the few people that I've met in my business career that you literally could not find one person that would say something bad about him. He was humble and treated everyone with kindness and respect even though he was also a larger-than-life guy who achieved extraordinary business success. He gave us credibility by putting his name, reputation, and capital behind us and helped us build valuable relationships in the industry, given his outstanding reputation.

I remember A.V. telling me many times that "everybody thinks I was an amazing entrepreneur, and while I was a good entrepreneur, where I made my real money was picking the right people to back in business and then supporting them any way I could." That was why A.V. never tried to tell us how to run the business or what investments to make or not to make, but rather he asked some questions, offered to make introductions when he could, and encouraged us to go figure things out ourselves. **He was an amazing partner and Quantum wouldn't be the firm it is today without A.V.'s vision and generosity to back two young guys who had an insatiable curiosity and desire to learn and just didn't know how to take no for an answer.**

TONY:

So interesting because so many people as investors, when they start out, they think, I have to be the entrepreneur. But as you said, you can find somebody who's a greater entrepreneur and earn a great return if you can provide the capital for them. Let's make the shift now to where you see the greatest opportunities in this energy evolution. I'd love to hear where you see the greatest opportunity for investors. And can you give us a sense of how your business has done over the years?

WIL:

We currently manage more than $22 billion of capital and have been in business for twenty-five years. Despite tremendous volatility in commodity prices and capital markets over that time period, we are proud that **every fund we've ever raised has made money for investors and that our returns have been consistent and surpassed our expectations.**

I'm big on identifying risks that you can manage and areas where you can remove volatility. Supply and demand of energy fluctuates quite a bit over time which creates volatility in commodity prices. When you have an industry that's very volatile and you mix that volatility with financial leverage, it's a perfect formula for losing money eventually. Therefore, commodity price volatility and financial leverage are two risks that we are fixated on actively managing by aggressively hedging commodity prices in the futures markets and using modest financial leverage in the capital structures of the companies we build. If you do these two things consistently, then you can really focus on making your money through margin expansion—meaning driving down capital and operating costs and increasing revenues—which is the best way to make money in any industry.

So, what we try to do is isolate and mitigate the variables that can take us out in a down market. **Being unhedged and using lots of debt may make you look really smart in an up market, but sooner or later prices will fall, and like that proverbial poker player that stayed too long at the table, you're going to lose all your money.** The problem with the oil and gas sector is that it attracts very optimistic people. You must be optimistic to spend billions of dollars drilling wells ten thousand to fifteen thousand feet below the earth's surface and another ten thousand or fifteen thousand feet horizontally. We know that to be successful in this business, Quantum must not only be a risk taker, but also a risk mitigator.

TONY:

I've had the privilege of interviewing fifty of the wealthiest investors in history, the Ray Dalios, Carl Icahns, the Warren Buffetts, etc. They all have very different investment strategies, but the one thing they all seem to push for is asymmetrical risk-reward. Tell us about the industry right now as a whole. What is the greatest opportunity today and what's causing that opportunity to show up from your perspective?

WIL:

I think the greatest investment opportunity at scale in the world today is in the energy industry, specifically in the oil and gas sector, and to a lesser extent, the energy transition sector. I don't think there's a close second to oil and gas. It's not the most popular answer. Over the past two or three years many investors have been very fixated, for good reasons, on the climate. We need to be very focused on that, and we need to be doing everything we can to address changes in the climate and support efforts to achieve net-zero emissions. **But we also must be very focused on making sure the world has reliable, affordable, and abundant energy, because without it, the modern world doesn't work, and poor countries won't be able to raise their people out of poverty.**

A group of first world countries such as most of the countries in Europe, the U.S., Australia, Japan, South Korea, and a few others have become very focused on the energy transition. Christopher, you refer to it as the energy evolution and I like to think of it as the emissions transition. Energy evolution or emissions transition are much better names than energy transition because when most people think of the word "transition," they think of moving away from one thing and towards another thing; however, the truth is, the world has never displaced any form of energy, rather it has developed new sources of energy which were added to the existing energy mix in order to supply growing energy demand. **Unfortunately, most of what we hear about in the media is how renewables and EVs will take over the world and we won't need oil, gas, or coal in the not-to-distant future. Nothing could be further from the truth. Even with the massive investment going into wind and solar over the past decade, the world still only gets about 4 percent of its energy from wind and solar and 80 percent from fossil fuels.**

TONY:

The oil and gas sector was the best returning sector in the stock market last year. The S&P was down about 20 percent while the oil and gas sector was up.

WIL:

Exactly. **The public oil and gas sector was up about 86 percent in 2021 and 48 percent in 2022, which compares very favorably to the approximately positive 27 percent and negative 20 percent returns delivered by the S&P 500 in the corresponding time periods.**

TONY:

And yet the financing for oil and gas has really shrunk. So, is that part of the opportunity? Because we are going to have another 2 billion people in the next twenty to thirty years on the planet. We're going to need 50 percent more energy by 2050 than today if I understand correctly.

WIL:

Let's start by looking back to Thanksgiving 2014, when oil prices had been moving between $85 and $100 a barrel for several years. At the time, demand was falling but OPEC made the decision not to cut production. The price of oil then started to fall, and it ultimately bottomed at around $20. So, it went from roughly $85 to $100 dollars a barrel down to about $20 a barrel over about three years and created a massive financial shock to the balance sheets and income statements of oil and gas companies. Up until that time, investors had been throwing money at oil and gas companies focused on the shale revolution. The industry was spending hundreds of billions of dollars per year trying to figure out the technology to economically unlock the shales, where to drill, and how to drill and complete shale wells—all of which required a tremendous amount of experimentation and capital to figure out. During the decade between 2010 and 2020, the oil and gas sector wrote off about $350 billion of capital. To put that in context, that was approximately 55 percent of all the write-downs and write-offs in the S&P 500 in that decade. Public investors finally realized that the industry was solely focused on growing production and adding reserves, but it was not focused on making money. And that was true, but public investors didn't appreciate that finding and producing this massive shale resource required a wave of capital destruction to figure it out—no different than the destruction of capital that happened during the dotcom boom and bust, which birthed companies like Google, Amazon, and Facebook several decades ago.

There is however a silver lining to the massive capital destruction that happened in the oil and gas sector—during the decade of the 2010s, the U.S. grew oil production by about 180 percent and natural gas production by about 100 percent, which resulted in the U.S. going from being the biggest importer of oil in the world to being a net exporter of oil and becoming one of the largest global exporters of natural gas. We became energy independent, and what that did geopolitically and economically for the United States of America is nothing short of one of the greatest success stories in American history.

When the party finally ended, many public investors decided the oil and gas space was not investable because oil and gas companies were not responsible stewards of capital, and thus they decided to sell their positions and exit the sector. There was however a much smaller number of public investors that were still willing to consider investing in oil and gas and they forced a new model upon the industry that looked something like the following—companies should spend 30 percent to 50 percent of their cash flow to reinvest in their businesses and send the other 50 percent to 70 percent back to investors through share buybacks and dividends, companies should limit their production growth to low, single-digit percentages, and companies should deleverage their balance sheets.

The same destruction of capital was happening with private companies too, and thus LPs started materially slowing their commitments to private equity and private debt funds. Five years ago, there was probably $90 to $100 billion of dry powder in the oil and gas private equity and private debt space. Today there is more like $15 to $20 billion. More than half of all GPs that were active in the space five years ago are either out of business or can't raise a new fund because their returns were so poor. Banks have also meaningfully reduced their lending to the oil and gas sector.

In summary, the amount of public and private capital available to the oil and gas sector has shrunk dramatically from just a few years ago. Oil and gas are a depleting resource, so they need constant reinvestment to replace produced reserves. That investment over the past eight or nine years has averaged about 50 percent of what it should have been to replace that production. Global population will grow meaningfully as will the number of people entering the middle class between now and 2050, thus materially increasing the demand for all forms of energy, including oil and gas. **There is a huge mismatch between future global demand for oil and gas and the world's ability to supply that oil and gas, and this mismatch will likely result in meaningfully higher oil and gas prices over the next decade.**

CHRISTOPHER:

Talk about what people are not expecting over the next three years. And what should they be expecting? And then, for investors who are willing to be involved in all aspects of energy, where are we at over the next ten years?

WIL:

I think a lot of people expect that we're going to wake up in a few years and we won't need hydrocarbons anymore, that wind and solar will create all the energy we need, and all cars will be powered by batteries. This could not be further from the truth. Quite frankly, it's an incredibly dangerous way of thinking, not only because it is not possible, but also because it would jeopardize America's energy independence and put many Western countries in a disadvantaged geopolitical and financial position relative to China.

J.P. Morgan's CEO Jamie Dimon periodically comes to Houston to visit with their energy clients, of which Quantum is one of their largest credit exposures. A few years ago, I asked Jamie about how committed J.P. Morgan was to continue lending to the oil and gas sector, and I think his response pretty well sums up why the world needs to be very careful about starving the oil and gas sector of capital. He responded, and I paraphrase, that the price of energy affects almost every other sector in the economy, so **if energy prices are low, that creates tailwinds for most other sectors, and if energy prices are high, that creates headwinds for most other sectors.**

If we care about economic prosperity, if we care about the environment, we must have affordable and abundant energy so that we have the profits to reinvest in making this energy evolution happen.

If we care about economic prosperity, if we care about the environment, we must have affordable and abundant energy so that we have the profits to reinvest in making this energy evolution happen.

It is my strong belief that oil and gas is going to be used in very significant quantities, probably greater quantities than it's used today, a decade from now. I will go even further and say that I expect oil and gas will continue to be used in quantities close to that which it's used today, even two or three decades from now. So, we're going to need a lot of oil and gas to support demand and we're not investing enough in it.

Fortunately, wind and solar will continue to become an increasingly larger share of the overall energy mix, but the world needs to recognize that energy additions take a long time. The greatest market share penetration that any energy addition has ever made in its first fifty years was coal, which got to 35 percent market after its first half a century of use. For context, wind and solar are at only 4 percent after a little over ten years since the massive investments in this space began. We expect the world is going to invest more in wind and solar power, battery storage, and electrification of transportation, than it has in any sector in the history of the world, and probably by multiples. And that's going to create unbelievable opportunities to make investments.

But anytime the opportunity set increases at an incredibly rapid pace, and you have managers who haven't invested in that space before investing capital, and management teams who have never run these kinds of businesses before receiving capital, it's also a formula to destroy a lot of money. On one hand, it may be the single greatest investment opportunity, in terms of capital deployment, the world has ever seen, and on the other hand, there may be more capital destroyed in the energy transition than in any other industry in the history of capitalism.

CHRISTOPHER:

The opportunity is certainly there, as are the risks that we have to navigate through. In recent years, what has happened that you expected to happen, and what has happened that you didn't expect to happen?

WIL:

We certainly did not expect Russia to go into Ukraine. That event refocused the Western world back on the facts, instead of feelings and desires, regarding the energy transition. Before Russia went into Ukraine it was challenging to get certain institutions to sit down and talk to us about investing in oil and gas because they were either against investing in the sector for ESG reasons or they were afraid the world would not be using much oil and gas in a few years and thus the oil and gas assets we bought would have no terminal value. Most of those institutions are now engaging in discussions with us because the facts are overwhelmingly in favor of oil and gas having a long runway and being a great place to generate strong investment returns over the next decade. We didn't expect that conversation to shift so rapidly.

I also didn't expect the U.S. government to pass a landmark piece of legislation like the Inflation Reduction Act (IRA), which earmarks almost $400 billion of federal funding and tax credits to stimulate investment in the energy transition. The IRA is much bigger than its nameplate amount because it automatically keeps renewing until certain targets are achieved.

The IRA does a lot to completely change the economics not only for re-newable energy, battery storage, electric vehicles, hydrogen, and nuclear, but also for carbon capture and storage (CCS). CCS is essentially decarbonizing hydrocarbons, meaning the CO_2 created when oil, gas, or coal is burned to generate energy is captured and then permanently stored or sequestered in underground reservoirs. **Natural gas turbines can turn on in a matter of minutes, which means they are baseload energy, and with a carbon capture device hooked up to that gas turbine, it turns what is considered by many to be dirty energy into baseload clean energy.** This is very different than solar and wind energy which are not baseload, because the sun doesn't always shine and the wind doesn't always blow. The world must primarily use baseload energy to run smoothly as energy demand fluctuates materially at different times during the day and night, and the world needs energy when it needs energy, not when the energy is available.

TONY:

What's different about nuclear today? Would you just take a moment and share that and what the opportunity might be there as well?

WIL:

The new generation nuclear power plants use a very different reactor tech-nology than what was used in Three Mile Island, Fukushima, and Cher-nobyl, which were three nuclear power plants where accidents occurred that turned much of the world against nuclear power. The new reactors are much safer, and are generally not prone to having the reactor core meltdown that people are so worried about. Additionally, we now have what are called SMRs, or small modular reactors, which are nuclear power plants that are much smaller than utility scale nuclear power plants, so they can be built in a factory instead of onsite. SMRs can thus be built much quicker and cheaper than the old utility scale nuclear power plants. SMRs can also be built on a much smaller scale which means they can be used in a lot more applications. And the icing on the cake is that some of the SMR designs use the spent fuel from the existing nuclear reactor fleet as their fuel source which means they are essentially providing a solution regarding what to do with the nuclear waste generated from our existing fleet of nuclear power plants. Historically, one of the other big knocks on nuclear power is that it is very expensive. SMRs will likely defy this trend as they can be built in factories, and next generation utility scale power plants can defy this trend if we can remove the bureaucracy from the regulatory approval process and deploy them at scale.

TONY:

So, what are most investors getting wrong right now in the energy sector, from your perspective?

WIL:

One big thing that most investors are getting wrong is assuming this energy evolution is going to happen a lot faster than it likely will. Additionally, many investors are convincing themselves that they can make high returns in the energy transition space, when in fact, many companies operating in the energy transition sector don't make any money today and have no real apparent path to getting to profitability. And for the companies that are making money today, most of them are generating very low returns. Lastly, many investors are also underestimating the amount of risk they are accepting. As a result, the risk-adjusted returns on many opportunities in the energy transition space are very unfavorable to investors.

CHRISTOPHER:

If you had the attention of the world and you could tell them one thing to take away, what would it be?

WIL:

That is a very profound question. If I could grab the attention of the ten most important leaders in the free world, I would tell them this—be very careful what you ask for. The energy evolution is an amazingly important and noble cause, and humanity must pursue it. The prosperity we've achieved in the West over the last forty years has been made possible by two primary things: offshoring manufacturing to the country that can do it the cheapest and reducing the cost of capital to the lowest levels in history. Both these trends are likely to reverse over the next decade and that is going to create immense challenges for the West.

Part of the offshoring megatrend has included offshoring the essential components of the renewable energy transition. Essentially, in order to make wind turbines, solar panels, lithium ion batteries and electric vehicles, you have to mine minerals (like copper, lithium, cobalt, silicon, zinc, and a number of other critical minerals and rare earths), then you have to refine and process those minerals, and then you have to use those minerals to manufacture the turbines, panels and batteries. The West has offshored most of the mining, refining, and processing, and manufacturing of these essential inputs for the energy transition, to many countries around the world. The country that's taken the biggest advantage of this offshoring trend is China, as they started strategically thinking about this renewable energy transition that was coming more than a decade ago. **China has a stranglehold on all key inputs for the energy transition—their market share ranges from 30 percent to 60 percent on mining for various critical minerals, from 40 percent to 70 percent for refining and processing for various critical minerals, and from 60 percent to 80 percent for the manufacturing capacity for wind, solar, and lithium-ion batters.**

Think about the power that Saudi Arabia was able to exercise over oil prices over the last thirty or forty years and they only controlled 10 percent of the world supply. OPEC, which comprised thirteen countries, in total controlled about 30 percent of global oil supply. When they acted in concert, they could bring the world to its knees. Today, China controls four to eight times the amount of market share in each of the key areas necessary for the energy transition than Saudi controls in oil. Russia's war on Ukraine was a wake-up call to the West regarding the overwhelming importance of energy security, and for the U.S., Europe, and our allies to have energy security we must control our own supply chains.

Building our own supply chains for the energy transition in mining, refining and processing, and manufacturing will take decades, not years, and will require trillions of dollars of investment and a massively streamlined regulatory environment. On one hand, this represents the single greatest opportunity to bring high-paying jobs back to the U.S., but on the other hand, this represents the single greatest vulnerability to the United States from an economic and national security perspective if we fail to get our act together and execute.

TONY:

I want to come back to one thing before we talk about your business a little bit. I want to really emphasize these investments, because you've got this scarcity of capital and demand that's growing even more with the larger population in third world countries wanting more of this energy. A lot of us have had the mindset of, okay, we're going to embrace ESG. You look at Europe and they've reduced their domestic production of natural gas by 30 percent or 35 percent, and all that supply shortfall was being made up by Russia before they invaded Ukraine. We know what the challenge is there. Can you just comment a little further about that aspect of things and is it really as true as it seems that in order to have sustainability, hydrocarbons are the real answer—carbon capture for them—so that we have that baseload power available throughout the world and we still protect the environment? Is that the case? And what do you see as the political impact of pushing things offshore to other countries?

WIL:

It's the classic tale of two cities right here, or a tale of two continents. Europe went down the path that wind and solar should replace everything and hydrocarbons are bad. And, as I mentioned earlier, the U.S. went just the opposite direction. We went from being the largest importer to one of the largest exporters. And in doing so, not only did we become energy independent, but also, just think about the jobs, the taxes, the national security benefits of that.

I think there are a lot of good things that come with ESG. This is where I try to work as a bipartisan statesman, if you will, to bring people together on progressing toward sustainability, because I think the right and the left really get this issue wrong. Many people on the left think renewables, batteries and EVs are the answer, but they haven't taken the time to put the enormity of this transformation into perspective and understand the herculean challenges and obstacles that must be overcome to get there. They essentially have blind faith and think somehow it will just miraculously happen.

Many people on the right deny that the climate is changing, and that mankind might have something to do with the changes. Many also believe that the ESG movement is nothing more than liberal values being pushed down our throats, and so they just summarily reject both climate change and the ESG movement without considering the implications of doing so. And the truth is, like most things in life, when you really peel the onion back a few layers and you ask enough questions, you realize the truth is probably somewhere in between. I think that's the case here.

Do we have a climate issue going on right now? Yes. We can debate how much of that is caused by man and how much is just nature being nature. It doesn't really matter; it's not a risk we can afford to ignore. And oh, by the way, there's a lot of good that comes out of cleaning up hydrocarbons. We get much cleaner air. People are a lot healthier. They live longer lives. It smells better. That's what I say to my friends on the right.

And to my friends on the left I point out that energy transitions take decades, not years, and that there are many structural challenges to the energy transition that we must contend with and that if what they really want is clean energy, that we can provide that through a process known as carbon capture and storage. I also point out that we have an entire infrastructure system built out in the U.S. and globally to supply this energy, transport and store it, and then use it, so all we have to do is add on the CCS technology and build out the infrastructure to store the CO_2. **In summary, natural gas and coal, combined with CCS technology, can deliver baseload (remember, wind and solar are intermittent energy) power that is as clean or cleaner than wind and solar power, and the U.S. has a massive domestic supply of both.**

Many don't realize that more people die every day in third world countries from breathing carcinogens released from burning dung and wood to cook food in their homes than have died in the history of mankind from all the nuclear power plant accidents which have ever happened. Many people have an irrational fear of nuclear, but nuclear must be a significant part of the solution if we are serious about providing clean, baseload energy. China has plans to build at least 150 new nuclear reactors in the next fifteen years, which is almost double the number of reactors in operation in the U.S. today. Even our friends in the Middle East are embracing nuclear. They have hundreds of years of oil and gas supply and yet they want to build nuclear power plants because they want to get to net-zero and export another kind of energy. **Nuclear is going to become increasingly relevant, and it's** not dangerous. Hydrocarbons can be decarbonized, and wind and solar are really good forms of energy. We need as much of them as we can get. And for the math to add up, we must have all the above. And, if we don't, it's a dark, dire future for humanity.

One more important point I'd like to make—my family foundation does a lot of work in the southern part of Africa, where I have seen the horrible implications of energy poverty. **There's probably a billion people on the continent of Africa who live in abject energy poverty. They don't have energy, and it takes energy, lots of it, to move up the economic prosperity ladder. They cook with wood or cow dung, and the carcinogens they breath in from doing so kill millions of people a year. That's not fair— those people deserve access to energy and thus we're going to need all forms of energy to supply the modern world with the energy it needs to sustain itself and the developing world with the energy it needs to improve its quality of life.**

TONY:

And it's got to be at a price people can afford, because, in those countries, that's an even bigger issue. So, carbon capture and storage sounds like it's one of the ultimate solutions. We need all these forms of energy, as you said, but that one would allow us to use hydrocarbons in a way that wouldn't have a negative impact on the environment. Let me shift a little bit for a moment to your firm because the size and growth of your firm is pretty historic and growing a large investment firm takes a lot more than just having great investments. Aside from strong performance, what will you say is the primary reason for the success of your business?

WIL:

I'd say two things. Our people and our culture. In any industry, any business, people are your most valuable asset. Humans are the only aspects of any business that can cause the future to change. They can come up with innovative ideas. They can out hustle the competition. They can do things in new ways that haven't been done before. So, we are and have always been focused on hiring the absolute best people in all the different disciplines necessary to run a world-class energy investment firm.

We also focus on maintaining a strong culture. Unfortunately, Wall Street investment firms in general are known to be sharp elbowed places that attract very talented, successful people, but a lot of times, also very individualistic people. It's an industry where, if you're really good, you can make a lot of money and achieve a lot of fame for yourself. And the problem is that you can have teams that become dominated by one or two franchise players. But individuals don't win championships, teams do. The best investment firms are very collegial. Teamwork is at the core of what we do because it takes a lot of people with many different areas of expertise, working in concert, to execute our business well.

My background was in finance, so when we started the firm, I knew we needed to go out and partner with operating and technical experts. And, twenty-five years later, we have a firm where more than one-third of our investment team has either technical, operating, or digital backgrounds, and they are all fully integrated members of the overall investment team. Every person on our team understands the unique value or skill set that every other member on our team brings to the team. We have this philosophy that we win as a team and we lose as a team, but we're always a team first. I think it's made us an enduring franchise.

TONY:

As you look at the history in your company, what would you say was the real fulcrum point that allowed you to go from good to great?

WIL:

I think for us it was a confluence of two things. In the beginning, we had all the ingredients, but we didn't have the scale. And without the scale, it was truly impossible to attract the world-class talent in some of the critical skill sets we needed. Our firm was founded in 1998, but when the shale industry took off about a decade later, I realized the world had really changed. The capital intensity of the companies we were backing increased by literally adding a zero. We used to write $10, $20, $30 million checks—all of a sudden, we needed write a $100, $200, $300 million checks. This was because shale wells cost about ten times more to drill than a conventional well. Shale wells also have about ten to twenty times more recoverable hydrocarbons. So, the scale changed. And when that happened, the fund sizes that we were raising increased a lot, providing us with the revenue to then go out and hire more of the best, world-class people. That was the inflection point for Quantum.

It's a dynamic world we live in. The only constant is change. No matter how well you think you have planned, things change, often very materially. Thus, it is important to be quick on your feet and able to realize that something has changed, and then have the will and courage to make mid-course corrections and adjustments to end up getting to where you're trying to go.

CHRISTOPHER:

You and I have something in common in that we both started our businesses at very young ages. What are a few things that you wish somebody would've told you before you started your business in your late twenties?

WIL:

Starting a business is the most exciting thing you'll probably ever do, and the most terrifying thing you'll ever do. So, do it while you're young. Also, don't be afraid of failure. You are going to fail, so fail quickly, learn from your mistakes, make adjustments, and try again. Most people are afraid to admit they've failed because they think it makes them look weak or bad, so they cover up their failure or don't admit they failed and keep doing the wrong thing over and over. I call that pride, and it is the single largest contributor to most people's inability to achieve greatness. You have to put failure in its proper perspective—most people see it as a negative—I see it as a positive, meaning, failure is successfully figuring out another way not to do something and puts me one step closer to figuring out the right way to do something.

The other thing I'd say is have fun. Life is so short. We're here for a very short period of time. Do it with people that you love being around. Buffett says he does business with people he likes, admires, and trusts. That may be the sagest advice I ever got—to do business with people that you like, admire, and trust.

CHRISTOPHER:

Indeed. When you think about Quantum's history, what is something that you would've done differently if you had it to do over again?

WIL:

In the early days, we were probably too conservative, too afraid of failure. I think being young, we were very fearful that if we made a big mistake, we might not ever raise another fund. You know the old saying that a master tailor measures three times and cuts once? We probably measured eight or nine times before we cut. We may have made the most perfectly tailored suit, but by the time we finished it, our suit size had changed—so in hindsight, I wish I would have been a little more willing to take the advice I now give on appropriately embracing failure.

CHRISTOPHER:

What do you think are the biggest difference makers for why firms are able to scale and why they're not?

WIL:

It goes back to the people in your organization. As you scale and you do bigger deals, the complexity increases, the managing of those businesses and operations increases, and it requires a different skillset. **Therefore, you must hire curious people, who have high integrity, a voracious work ethic, and an insatiable desire to keep learning. They may be really good at what they do today, but they have to also want to keep getting better and be committed to being lifelong learners.**

What I look for is people that have above average intelligence, that are hungry and have a strong work ethic, and are honest. And when I find those three things, I know we can teach those kinds of people everything they need to know.

One big mistake I see a lot of founders and senior partners of investment firms making is they hog too much of the economics for themselves. And that's the best way to ensure that your best people go somewhere else. We have a program at Quantum where every single employee across the firm participates in the carried interest we earn as the general partner of our funds, either directly or through an employee pool. Everybody therefore thinks like an owner. And the only way you can foster this mindset is by compensating your team and treating them well.

TONY:

There are levels of intelligence and there are different types of intelligence, right? Musical intelligence, book intelligence, street intelligence. What separates those highest performers from the peers? Is there anything we've not mentioned?

WIL:

Self-awareness, humility, and great communication skills would be three attributes that separate those highest performers from their peers. We were built to interact with other human beings. Getting along, building relationships, and communicating are skillsets that are critical to being a great private equity or private credit investor. I think that to be good at doing these things you must be self-aware and humble. You also must have a reasonably high EQ. And so, we look very hard for that. **Emotional intelligence is often much more important to being a successful investor than being smarter than everyone else.** The relationships we make and the people's lives we touch and influence are what continue to effectively live on after we are gone. When you build an organization with people that possess these skills, you will not only have an amazing culture, but you will also generate great returns for your investors.

TONY:

Yes. When I was interviewing Warren Buffett, I asked him what was the best investment he ever made. I thought he was going to say Coca-Cola or Geico. He said it was Dale Carnegie, because if he hadn't learned to communicate, everything else wouldn't have happened.

CHAPTER 15

IAN CHARLES

FOUNDER OF ARCTOS SPORTS PARTNERS

Accolades: A pioneer in creating the industry's first sell-side advisor for private equity secondaries
Total Asset Under Management (as of August 2023): $6 billion
Area of focus: Professional sports (MLB, NBA, MLS, NHL, Premier League)

HIGHLIGHTS

- In 2002, Ian Charles cofounded Cogent Partners, the first secondary market sell-side advisory firm, which was later sold for nearly $100 million. Cogent is widely recognized for transforming the private equity secondary market by providing institutional-grade advisory services while providing unprecedented deal flow.
- Mr. Charles later went on to cofound Arctos Partners, the first institutional platform to pursue a global, multi-league, multi-franchise sports investment strategy.
- Arctos was the first firm to be approved to purchase multiple franchises across all eligible U.S. sports leagues, and their 2020 equity

investment into the Fenway Sports Group marked the first ever fund investment into a professional sports team by a private equity firm.

• Arctos's debut fund was the largest first-time private equity fund ever raised at close to $2.9 billion, and the firm was included in the 2023 *Sports Illustrated* Power List, which marks the fifty most influential figures in sports.

TONY:

Ian, what you've built is amazing. I understand you're not a sports fan, and yet you've put together the most amazing thing I've ever seen in sports. So, can you give us a little bit of background of how this all came together?

IAN:

If I go back to where it started. First and foremost, I've been an entrepreneur since I was probably thirteen or fourteen years old. I'm also a nerd and my first job just happened to be at a private equity fund of funds, learning the asset class at a very high level making primary fund investments and equity co-investments. Back then private equity was much more illiquid than it is today. If you were invested in a private equity fund, you were kind of stuck there for ten to fifteen years. If you needed or wanted to get out, there were only four or five firms in the world that would give the option to buy you out, and they would take a significant pound of flesh to provide you with liquidity. The market for private equity fund liquidity is known as the secondaries market.

The discounts in private equity secondaries used to be substantial. I was really young and really naïve, and I had a couple of colleagues who were also young, and we were all a bit naïve, I guess. We thought we could help these sellers, and our idea was to start the industry's very first advisor in the secondaries market, helping institutional investors sell their funds. That business was hugely successful and really transformed liquidity for private equity globally and created all the infrastructure that powers the global secondaries market today. Helping start that firm and my role there really launched my professional opportunity as an entrepreneur in illiquidity.

From there, I joined one of the original buyers in the secondary industry, and for fifteen years I helped them create competitive advantages, hone their strategy, and create other products to unlock liquidity in other illiquid markets. One of the markets I spent some time looking at was the professional sports market in North America.

North American sports assets, like Major League Baseball and the National Basketball Association, was a big, growing market, with a lot of minority ownership and no access to institutional capital. The sports market looked a lot like private equity twenty years ago. But when I started to study the sports industry, we realized none of the North American leagues allowed institutional capital. It was prohibited by the leagues, which are, in effect, the regulators. Sports was a really interesting asset class, because it was mathematically very difficult to replicate the risk/return characteristics of predominantly North American sports. These are very unique businesses. But if the regulator doesn't allow you to invest, you're not allowed to invest. That prohibition on institutional capital changed in 2019. Major League Baseball was the first North American league to open up its ownership architecture for institutional investment, but only to a very specific kind of fund that requires unique architecture, an onerous approval process, and there are a bunch of investing conflicts that have to be managed by any new entrant. But we identified the opportunity to be the first mover in this space. **I knew enough about this market to know that a bunch of finance geeks weren't going to be successful on their own. You really needed to partner with people that were accepted by this industry, had strong reputations in this industry and operating experience in sports.** So, our founding team has a blend of backgrounds that look like mine, or they look like my partner David O'Connor's—everybody calls him Doc—where they have decades building, running, and leading important parts of the sports and live entertainment ecosystem. Together with our founding colleagues, we built the first firm designed to provide value-added growth capital and liquidity solutions to North American sports teams and ownership groups. It has been an unbelievable experience. But, for me, the origin really started twenty-five years ago, helping create liquidity solutions in other illiquid markets and understanding kind of repeatable patterns that appear in illiquid investments and in building businesses in alternative assets. When you marry that up with Doc's experience as an operator and entrepreneur in sports and live entertainment, that gave us an opportunity to build something pretty special, and since our founding we've tried really hard not to blow that opportunity.

TONY:

Give us of a feeling of what came out of that, because you guys didn't enter in with just capital. You really have this massive added value that you bring to these sports entities that are now really media companies. Maybe you can give a little bit of what the benefit of that is and how it is that you serve them.

IAN:

What's really interesting is that when we started the firm, if you had asked me that question, I would've said, look, to be honest, I don't know. I don't know what we're going to be allowed to do in that area. Because the leagues hadn't really set the rules. We didn't know what the leagues would allow, or what owners were going to be receptive to [or] where they were going to want or need help. Over the last three years, as our firm has grown its reputation, scale, asset portfolio, and data, we have continued to invest in our own capabilities, our team, and in our data systems to build a proprietary data science and applied research business, which we call Arctos Insights, and a value creation program, which we call the Arctos Operating Platform. What we've done is we've built a whole suite of services around data, analytics, and value-add. I guarantee you, if you ask me this question in six months, the answer will be a little bit different. And in a year, better be a lot different. We're constantly evaluating our customers' needs. Because we have two sets of customers, the owners that we've partnered with and the investors who have entrusted us with their capital. The feedback loop we have with the owners, leagues, and club executives is a constant part of our process. **So today we help them with acquisitions, buying other franchises, real estate, live entertainment complexes, investing in technology, and improving their venues. We're helping them in areas like digital engagement, data science, and machine learning.** We're a huge data shop. We've built an applied research business where we provide really important business content and analytics to the owners in our portfolio. International expansion is a really important topic for owners as they want to take these brands and grow them to a global audience and fan base. Some of them have no idea how to do that. We just opened our London office because our teams want to grow internationally. We want to have boots on the ground, resources, and a playbook that they can just grab and tap into in order to accelerate the growth of their business and grow their brand internationally.

So, it's a constantly evolving, deep set of capabilities, and this is an industry that really hasn't had a chance to partner with an institutional resource like us. So, there's a lot of low-hanging fruit. There's a lot of repeatable pattern recognition. **What one team needs, probably fifteen other teams in the same league need. We are able to invest centrally in these capabilities because we know that we can spread the cost of that investment across six, seven, sometimes twenty platforms.**

TONY:

Peter Guber is one of my dearest friends, and I know you've done multiple deals with him, obviously between the Warriors and the Dodgers. But what about the investors themselves? What advantages are there? This idea of this legal monopoly, the impact on inflation, and the fact that these teams, like in the NBA, own one-thirtieth of all the revenues. I mean, most of these things, investors have no clue about.

IAN:

Peter is incredible. He sees just about everything a little earlier than the rest of us, but you are right. What you're hitting on is a very unique feature of North American sports assets. This isn't true in European football or other kinds of sports ecosystem opportunities. Every North American team owns an equal share of the global business that is their league, and the league is a global intellectual property and a kind of brand management business. The leagues sell media rights, data rights, and sponsorship at the national and international level. The leagues have their own overhead and cost structure, but then they generate dividends, and they pay them out annually in equal proportions to their owners. So, it doesn't matter if you're in the smallest market or the biggest market, you get the same dividend distribution. It also doesn't matter if you finish in last place or first place, you get the same payment. The ownership stake in the league and the aggregate revenue that comes from long-term, diversified contracts with annual payment escalators create this really stable, durable asset that everyone in the league owns.

The leagues and owners don't like to call the local license a monopoly, but it functions like one. A sports franchise owner has a protected geographic region, just like the franchisor of a restaurant chain—no one is allowed to compete with you in your geographic zone for revenue around your sport. **The fandom around these brands is generational and these are important assets in their communities, so your customer acquisition cost is essentially zero. These businesses are communal, they're shared experiences across generations, across political parties—they are the only asset that has those characteristics today.** Owners can then use that local license to expand into real estate and build a live entertainment complex, digital distribution, and marketing direct to your consumer. We find that local platform activity interesting. **If you are doing it right, this is a platform for you to be a civic leader, but also compound your wealth in an uncorrelated way with very little leverage, very little geopolitical risk, no currency risk.** When you combine the ownership stake in the league with the local license, a North American club provides a nice "portfolio effect," has all of these really unique attributes that are hard to find and replicate. For our fund, because we provide liquidity to minority owners when they want out, and provide growth capital to owners that have a big vision, we're able to come into partnership with great owners in great markets who have unbelievable brands and ideas, and do that at a really attractive entry point.

TONY:

And you've done so much to add value. Then you've got this inflation hedge with both the real estate and also the pricing power because as you said, these people are fanatics; they're tried-and-true in that area. Tell us a little bit more about you for a moment. Who's been the most important person or one of the most important people in your life that shaped your growth, your success, and your career or life path?

IAN:

This is going to be super cheesy, and Christopher might make fun of me down the road, but it's true. I always tell people I met my wife when I was thirteen years old. She didn't know I existed until I was probably sixteen; she was too cool and too beautiful to pay attention to me! We grew up in the same small town. We made a bet on each other. Despite both of our parents forbidding us from going to college together, we outfoxed them a little bit and ended up going to school together. If it wasn't for my wife, Jamie, I never would've taken that first risk as an entrepreneur starting the secondary advisory business. She was a special education teacher, and I was working as an analyst at this fund of funds business. If not for her paycheck, her faith in me, and her encouragement, I wouldn't have had the courage to leave my job and try to start the business.

TONY:

Wow.

IAN:

Fast-forward almost twenty years later, and she knew that I was longing for something different professionally. She knew that I had this itch to be an entrepreneur again. **I think we all probably put way too much of our career into our self-worth and personal identity. I know I certainly have many, many times. The idea of leaving a great job and an important role, you have a bit of an identity crisis, right? It's scary.** But Jamie knew me better than I knew myself. She knew I have this drive to try and build something. She also knew if I ever made that leap, I wanted to use the name Arctos and that the name had connectivity to our roots in Alaska and to the bear. She knew those things. My Christmas gift from Jamie in 2018 was a crystal bear and a note that just said: "I think it's time." Five months later Major League Baseball changed their ownership rules. She's always believed in me. She's always encouraged me. She's lifted me up and supported me when I didn't even know I needed it. So, she would, without a doubt, be the answer to that question.

CHRISTOPHER:

The thing that's so amazing for a lot of us men is, if we would do more of what our wife thinks we should do, we would be much better off and much happier.

IAN:

We'd be happier. No doubt.

CHRISTOPHER:

Let's talk about sports a little bit. So obviously we talked about the attributes of sports that are very different than most of the other investments that are out there. As you know, but for the benefit of everyone else, it took about eighteen months for us to have a good conversation and for us to understand the business model before we did our partnership together. And it's something that just, candidly, took me a long time to figure out. When you think about the opportunity set, what do you feel like the opportunity is? What are the real interesting opportunities for investors in the world of professional sports or sports in general?

IAN:

We are laser-focused on helping North American owners unlock all of the potential of the assets that they have right in front of them. Sometimes it's that simple. Sometimes you've got something so special in front of you that has so many growth nodes and opportunities to unlock that the best thing to do is just focus and help them. So, over the next three or four years, it's all about live entertainment, improving the fan experience, media rights becoming more valuable as you go from a linear system to a streaming system. It's about helping these brands grow internationally. And it's about creating that direct connectivity with the customer.

As an example, if you're a season ticket owner with the Astros and you can't go to the game, you may decide to sell that ticket on one of these ticket exchanges. Let's say I buy it, but then Jamie (my wife) reminds me we have a scheduling conflict (which happens a lot by the way). I can then choose to put that ticket up on another exchange and Tony may buy it from me.

Right now, the team doesn't know who I am (the first buyer of the ticker), and they don't know who Tony is (the next buyer), even though Tony brought his family to the game. Soon, the team will know exactly who owned that ticket throughout the entire value chain. The team will be able to market to all three of us directly for future sales, and on this particular transaction, the team will be able to participate in the gain along the way. So, if your ticket has a face value of $200, but Tony bought it for $600, right now the team just gets $200, but soon they'll be able to take a portion of that profit along the chain. That simple change unlocks 30 to 50 percent upside in just the ticketing revenue. There are so many near-term opportunities to help owners monetize and grow these incredible local brands, improve the fan experience, and participate in owning one of the most important kinds of content over the next twenty years. That's what we're laser focused on.

CHRISTOPHER:

As we went through our diligence on sports in general, what finally got me over the edge and made me a believer was the resiliency of the revenues. I don't think most investors fully appreciate how predictable and how consistent these revenue streams are. So, when you think about what's transpired, you've been spot-on with your projections of what was going to happen in professional sports. But there have been things over the last couple of years that have happened that you didn't expect. First, what are the things you expected to happen that have occurred? And then, what happened that you just didn't expect to occur in the last couple of years?

IAN:

Oh, man, that's a great question. When we started this thing and started talking to people, in March and April of 2020, there were no games. I had no idea when there would ever be games again.

TONY:

Did that provide discounts for you in terms of purchases at that time?

IAN:

What it did is provide me with anxiety. But we knew sports would come back and we were confident that sports as an industry, with its history of innovation, that sports would likely be an early recovery industry. We didn't know what the recovery would look like and we didn't know how strong the demand curve would be. It felt like it might be very regional. The snapback, the rebound, has been much stronger than our base case assumptions. As an example, the **NBA regular season gates closed two weeks ago—number** one season ever for total attendance. So, the speed and strength of that recovery is one thing that has surprised me.

So that leads to the next question. There's a lot of investors that get sports wrong, and they don't understand it. But what is it that you hear the most where people are really misunderstanding the business of sports?

I think they don't understand the valuation framework of these businesses. **On the revenue side you already noted the stability, predictability, and the durability of the revenue streams in North American sports are really unusual. They're more akin to infrastructure assets**—fifteen-year contracts on your stadium naming rights, five-to-ten-year contracts on your media rights at a national level, seven-to-twenty-year contracts at the local level for regional sports rights. That predictability is not well understood, but it is really valuable in a world of uncertainty.

The valuation environment in sports is also one that has been remarkably stable over the last fifteen years. Remember what I said earlier, institutional capital was never allowed to come into this space.

Another thing that the leagues are very, very protective of in North America is they don't let you use a lot of leverage on these businesses. For almost my entire career, the cost of capital has been getting lower and lower every year. When we started Arctos, there was about $18 trillion of sovereign debt that had a negative yield. If you're an institutional investor, that repricing of risk across asset classes made it really hard for you to achieve your actuarial returns or your personal return targets. As a result, you had to go out of the risk curve to achieve your return targets or just sit things out in cash earning no return and hope that things improved. Sitting on cash is really hard for most investors to do because of benchmarking and career risk. So, most investors felt compelled to put more into riskier and riskier strategies. As an unprecedented amount of global liquidity washed around the globe looking for things to buy, if it tried to invest in North American sports, the leagues prohibited that investment and the wave of liquidity bounced off and went in search of another opportunity. League debt limitations made it nearly impossible to use a lot of cheap leverage to buy a sports team, and institutions couldn't flood the market with capital. They weren't allowed to.

As a result, the valuation expansion that you had in so many sectors over more than a decade, it didn't happen in sports. In fact, sports and hydrocarbons are the only industries we've identified that had P/E (price to earnings) multiple compression from 2011 to 2021 because the combination of earnings growth and revenue growth in sports was higher than valuation growth. So, in this big unwind, this big repricing of risk over the last eighteen months, sectors that had their valuation metrics swollen from cheap debt and lower cost of capital have all seen valuation compression that has hurt returns.

TONY:

Haven't the returns been greater than the S&P and greater than the Russell 2000 on these four core sports organizations that you've invested in?

IAN:

What's interesting is the answer to that is yes, but more importantly in very different environments. So, the most accommodating decade of my career would've been 2011 to 2021. If you were invested in venture capital or leveraged buyout funds, you would've gotten like a 17 percent to a 20 percent return over a decade. Which is amazing. Public markets would've given you about a 10 to 11 percent return, which is also historically very, very attractive. Sports gave you 18 percent with no skill, just buying the broad market at no discount. But that was a pretty easy market environment, right? Just about everything worked. When the cost of money is falling every year, assets just become worth more if you just hold them. But in a totally different environment, the mid-1960s to the mid-1980s was a very different environment, with very high volatility and persistently high inflation. The 60/40 portfolio, that every investor kind of banks on, didn't work.

For twenty years (mid sixties to mid eighties), your compounded return from the S&P 500 was about 4 percent with inflation an average of 7 percent. So, you destroyed real wealth for twenty years if you were long equities. North American sports during that time frame, mid sixties to mid eighties, gave you a 16 percent [compounded return]. **It's been remarkably** resilient in its outperformance. **It has very low volatility for a lot of really nerdy mathematical reasons. It's got a lower negative correlation to other asset classes. And again, you don't have a lot of leverage.** So, you don't have the whipsaw of global liquidity impacting valuations like you do in other sectors. It's a really, really hard thing to find these characteristics.

TONY:

It ties into our next question. You know, Ray Dalio is a good friend of mine, and I asked him what the single most important investment principle was, and he called it the Holy Grail. And the title of this book is based on him. One of the reasons, obviously, that we're partners with you in this area is because it's such a non-correlated investment, on top of everything else you just talked about. But what would you say is the Holy Grail of Investing from your perspective?

IAN:

I talked to Ray about our strategy about a year ago. It was a fascinating discussion—he cut right to the lack of correlation. He actually flipped it into a slightly different mathematical construct and we started to talk about the cost to carry, because sports teams used to cost you money every year to own them via operating losses and capital calls. But that cash flow characteristic has changed over the last fifteen years. The cost of carry has flipped and that change has produced a big fundamental change on valuations in North America.

My entire career, I've been trained and sought advice and mentorship from successful and wise practitioners in illiquid markets. And **for me, the Holy Grail of a strong fundamental value investment philosophy is an intrinsic value arbitrage. Howard Marks and other value investors call it the margin of safety. Investing in things that are non-obvious, which means they are likely less competitive, at an attractive margin of safety in partnership with management teams and owners you believe in— if you do that while building a diversified portfolio of opportunities with these attributes, you will outperform the market because of that margin of safety and because of the performance of the people you've backed.**

TONY:

One of the questions I throw at people is this: If you had the world's attention for five minutes, what would you want to tell them?

IAN:

Oh man. If I had the world's attention for five minutes, what would I tell them? I'd probably tell them everything is going to be okay.

TONY:

That's great. I agree with you. But also tell me why?

IAN:

I think a lot of people are scared today, insecure. I think a lot of people are lonely. I don't think people have meaningful connections or as many meaningful interactions as we all need. **I would tell people, especially men, to reach out to other people that they respect and tell them they're doing a great job and that you love them. If you're friends with somebody and they're a good dad, tell them they're a good dad. Or if you think they are a great partner/spouse, tell them. Tell them that they are a great friend and how much you appreciate them.** I would tell people it's going to be okay.

CHRISTOPHER:

That's a beautiful thing.

TONY:

Beautiful. Let's talk about the investment business itself. You know, growing a large investment firm is a lot more than just having great investments. What do you think has been the primary reason for your success in your business?

IAN:

I think the edge that we have during the three years we've been building this thing is the people that we have here. We're very, very selective on who gets to come and be on this journey with us, and we've set some real parameters and filters around that process. We have six core values that are really important to us. One of the things that we talked a lot about as a founding group is, **if we're lucky enough to have success, there's going to be a lot of "shiny things" along the way. It's going to be really important to know when we want to reach down and pick one up, and when we need to keep on running and not get distracted.** So, we have these defined terms—our passion and our niche, from Gino Wickman's book *Traction*—they keep us focused. The core values . . . there's a lot of discussion around the value of diversity. **We are uncompromising in diversity; we want absolutely no diversity in values. If you are not aligned with our values, this is not the right place for you.**

TONY:

Do you mind sharing those six values with us? I'd love to hear that.

IAN:

Servant leadership, trust, teamwork, insights, character, and excellence. After our founding team spent a bunch of time with each other, starting to build the business, we actually hit the pause button and gave everybody a day off with a homework project. The homework project was, when we come back here tomorrow, you have to bring the two things you love about everybody here.

TONY:

That's great.

IAN:

Eight founders—that means you're getting feedback from seven people. There's a little bit of overlap and redundancy, so you're getting eight to ten things about each person. We went through this [list], trimming and consolidating, and at the end of that process there was this shared DNA. And so, our six core values are the shared core attributes of our founding team that we all loved in each other and that we are inspired to be more like in each other.

TONY:

That's beautiful. That's really beautiful. Thank you for sharing that. That's something any organization could grab and run with. What would you say would be the fulcrum point in your business that really allowed you to leap forward, you know, from good to great?

IAN:

So, about a year into it, it was easy to look around and be like, holy shit, this is incredible. But we actually had the opposite feeling. It was like, oh my gosh, we're going to blow it. How do we make sure we don't screw this up? Always having this imposter syndrome anxiety. **The one thing I know is that, in a year, our process won't look like it does today. The services we offer our owners will be different. The way we use data will be different. The kinds of data that we collect and analyze will be different. We have to make sure our people are comfortable challenging the way we think. We have to constantly reinvest and reevaluate and be totally fine ripping something up and saying, "That worked really well two years ago but stop talking about that because it doesn't matter tomorrow."** So, I think for us, about a year into it, we stepped back and said, okay, we have a chance to do something really special here. How do we define our right to win?

What are the best firms excelling at? And what does that look like? What did José and Behdad do at Clearlake? What did Robert (Smith) do at Vista? Robert dominated in his sector early, but then he doubled down and built the Vista playbook. He and his team keep reinvesting in this seemingly insurmountable intellectual property stack. We have to do that in sports. So, one of the things we did is we just stepped back and said, look at all these firms that we admire. And there are so many of them. What have they done that made them special? And what could we do in our industry to replicate some of those attributes?

CHRISTOPHER:

What are the few things that you wish you would've done differently when you started the firm?

IAN:

I wish I would've grabbed a couple of machine learning engineers, because when we started the firm three years ago, most people couldn't spell AI. Data science has been a big part of our business plan from the very beginning, but

I wish we would've over-indexed into that area. I know we're leading in that area. I know we're innovating and we're using data science in ways that most managers haven't even started to think about. But I wish we would've really doubled down on that early.

CHRISTOPHER:

Why are most investment firms and the vast majority of private asset management firms unable to scale?

IAN:

Well, first of all, some asset management firms shouldn't scale. Some, what they do really well just doesn't scale. And if they try, they will move away from their circle of competence, they will leave the market position where they have a right to win. I think the areas that firms can really excel at are pretty well documented: You can be an industry specialist or a country-specific expert. There are big macro/competency areas where you can dominate, like credit or infrastructure, but then there are organizational things you can dominate and excel at too. Culture, people . . . actually, a really easy thing to win in our industry is just treating people like they're human beings and that this might not be the only place they work their entire career. Just giving them grace and investing in them. You can win on organizational health and talent density. You can win in organizational management and people. If you have proprietary deal flow, real actual proprietary deal flow—where you have the luxury of being a hunter or a gatherer. Just harvesting whatever bountiful season presents itself, that is truly very rare. Originating differently, pricing risk differently, managing risk differently, managing the liquidity and monetization of your portfolio differently. Those are all areas where you can build core competencies and differentiation. Most great firms are really good at four or five of those things. But you have to know where, why, and how you have a right to win. And you have to have the confidence and humility to pressure test those conclusions regularly.

CHRISTOPHER:

It's fascinating to see exactly what you described, not only how hard it is to have those key attributes among the founding group, but also to make sure that persists through the generational transfers that occur inevitably over time. Some do it exceedingly well and some obviously don't.

IAN:

That is the biggest risk, in my opinion, in private markets—that generational transition. Investors don't understand how to underwrite it. A lot of times they're scared to ask about it. Those are hard questions to ask, but they are the most important questions. You have to be curious about how each firm is working, again "what is their right to win?" that's working, and you have to have the courage to double click and go deep into those topics because if the people you're backing aren't there in three or four years, the franchise has real risk.

TONY:

I love your language and thought process around the right to win. You do these things that earn the right to win. That's a very different way of looking at things than most people do, Ian. Speaking of investment talent, what do you believe are the key traits that separate the highest performers from their peers in your mind?

IAN:

Well, I do want to give credit where credit is due. The "right to win" is something that my friend Hugh MacArthur taught me, and he's been helping managing partners at private equity firms understand their right to win for a long time. What are the key traits to separate the highest performers from their peers? I actually think this is pretty simple. If you have a compelling strategy and thesis that has been vetted and supported by very sophisticated institutional investors and attracts capital, and **you do what you say you're going to do, and you do it with good human beings who are really talented, and you keep investing in those people and investing in your process, I think that's what the highest performing firms do.** They identify, defend, and grow their right to win.

CHAPTER 16

DAVID SACKS

COFOUNDER OF CRAFT VENTURES

Accolades: Cohost of the *All In* podcast and original member of the PayPal "mafia" with Elon Musk and Peter Thiel

Total Asset Under Management (as of August 2023): $3 billion

Area of focus: Enterprise and consumer technology

HIGHLIGHTS

- David Sacks has invested in over twenty unicorns, including Affirm, Airbnb, Eventbrite, Facebook, Houzz, Lyft, Palantir, Postmates, Slack, SpaceX, Twitter, and Uber.
- David began his career as founding COO and product leader at PayPal and then founder/CEO of Yammer, which he sold to Microsoft for $1.2 billion.
- He founded Craft Ventures in 2017 and now has $3 billion AUM across six funds. Portfolio companies include SpaceX, Reddit, Boring Company, ClickUp, SentiLink, OpenPhone, Vanta, Neuralink, Replit, and Sourcegraph.

TONY:

With all you've done in your life from PayPal to being an early investor in Facebook, Airbnb, and SpaceX—it's mind-boggling what you've accomplished and you're still a force of nature, not only in technology and as an investor, but also in politics to a great extent. And we're big fans of your podcast. Tell us a little bit about your origin story. How did this all come to be?

DAVID:

My family moved to America from South Africa when I was five years old. We became citizens when I was ten, and I grew up mainly in Memphis, Tennessee. I went to Stanford and graduated in 1994. That time period was around the birth of the internet in Silicon Valley. 1995 was an important year—the year that Netscape IPO'd. It was the first commercial browser for the internet. Unfortunately, I had graduated the year before and gone off to law school. It wasn't until 1999 that I came back to Silicon Valley. A friend of mine from Stanford, Peter Thiel, was starting a company. We talked a lot about what he was doing, and I eventually decided to join up with him. That company ended up becoming PayPal. So that was how I got into technology. Since then, I've mostly been involved in founding and investing in technology startups.

TONY:

And the type of startups you've been part of are some of the biggest in history. What's been your secret sauce in identifying these types of opportunities?

DAVID:

There are a few things I look for. One I call the product hook. **What is that simple, repeatable transaction or interaction at the heart of your product that users will want to do over and over again?** At PayPal, it was entering someone's email address and a dollar amount, and sending them money very easily. With Uber, you put a destination on a map and a car comes to pick you up. Google is the simplest of all. It's just that search box—a very simple interaction that users want to engage in over and over again. I think a lot of companies miss this because they think that if they keep layering on more and more features and adding more and more complexity, they can solve the problem of product-market fit. But if you can't get users to do something simple, it's very hard to get them to do something complicated. You want to start with something simple that users embrace and then layer complexity on top of it.

The other big thing that I look for is some sort of innovation on distribution. I call it the distribution trick—something unique that the company is doing to find users or buyers. At PayPal, we invented a lot of these tricks. Users could email money to someone who wasn't even a user yet. We embedded PayPal payment buttons inside of eBay auctions, bootstrapping off their platform. We gave people sign-up and referral bonuses. There are a lot of these tricks that PayPal pioneered that made the product go viral. If you look at other companies that have grown explosively fast, they're usually innovating on distribution, which is to say, reaching users in a new way. The reason that's important is that the world is so crowded that just building a good product is not a guarantee that you'll be successful. We wish it would be, but it's a big internet out there, and you need to find a way to reach your users in a cost-effective way, or they may never find you no matter how good your product is.

TONY:

You've had such an amazing group of friends, some of which are the most influential people in the world in tech. Who had the most influence on your life? And how did they help shape you in positive ways?

DAVID:

In terms of my business career, I was very lucky to work with two great founders in my first startup: Peter Thiel and Elon Musk. Those were the two CEOs I worked for as either head of product or COO. Getting to work with both of them was a great learning experience for me. They have very different styles as CEO. Elon is very hands-on, very involved in every part of the business, especially the product. And Peter is more of a delegator and focuses on big strategic issues. Both styles obviously have their merits and can work. When I founded Yammer after PayPal, I felt like I was able to take the best techniques that I had learned from both of them.

TONY:

Would you say you fall in the middle [of their styles]? Or do you strategically use one or the other depending on the situation?

DAVID:

I fall in the middle. Elon is incredibly hands-on with every part of the business. If you look at his org chart, he has a lot of reports because he keeps things very flat. I had a more conventional org chart. I liked to work through my executives, but there were two areas where I was more hands-on. One was the product. You can't fully delegate that if you're the one with the product vision. The other is that when a functional area was going well, I would give my executives more latitude, but if it wasn't going well, I would breathe down their neck until we fixed it. For example, if sales was hitting their numbers, I would mostly leave them alone, but if they were missing, they would really feel my presence and there would be a lot more inspections. You want to be hands-on where you think you have a special advantage or skill set or, certainly, if anything's going wrong. But you can trust your executives to operate more independently when they've demonstrated success in doing that.

CHRISTOPHER:

It's a fine balance to walk there. When you look at technology today, it's changing a lot. What are the greatest opportunities for investors?

DAVID:

The great thing about Silicon Valley is that there's been a platform shift roughly every decade. If you go back all the way to the eighties, the personal computer replaced the mainframe. Then in the nineties, we had the birth of the internet, and computing moved from on-premise to the cloud, or from the desktop to the cloud. Then we had the launch of social in the early 2000s. We had the birth of mobile in the late 2000s. **Now the big platform shift is to AI.** It always seems to happen about once a decade. It is a little bit of a I to say that AI is the big wave, but I think it is, and we're just at the beginning of this cycle. There's going to be a tremendous amount of opportunity for new as well as existing companies.

TONY:

If you look at AI right now, it's very much like the [early] days of the internet. There are a zillion companies forming and many of them are not going to be around long. When you look specifically at AI [companies], what are the ones that pull your attention?

DAVID:

There are a couple of things we're going to look for. One is a founder who has vision, tenacity, and creativity. Someone who really understands the space—AI is fairly technical, so founders who are able to combine a technical aptitude with a vision for where the space is going have a better chance at success. The people bet is even more important at this super early stage.

The other thing we'll look for are ideas that we think fit where the market's going or what the market wants. **We think there's a market opportunity in what have broadly been called "copilots" for professionals. We think there's going to be a copilot for doctors, a copilot for lawyers. Pretty much every profession you can think of, every job function you can think of, there's going to be an AI copilot to help that person do their job.** We think that will create a lot of opportunities for founders who can go deep in a particular area—they understand the job requirements and they understand AI, and they can match those two things together.

CHRISTOPHER:

What has happened in the last couple of years that you expected to happen, and what has happened that you didn't expect to happen?

DAVID:

Silicon Valley is going through a huge reset right now. We had the popping of the biggest asset bubble since the dotcom crash in 2000. In hindsight, the Fed's zero-interest rate policies, or "ZIRP," going back all the way to 2008, had a lot more impact than people wanted to admit. It had a big impact on the amount of capital that came into the industry. There was all this free money sloshing around looking for a return.

The conventional wisdom about VC, roughly a decade or two ago, was that it wasn't a business that scaled. It's not like public market investing where you can just invest billions and billions of dollars or even hundreds of billions of dollars very easily. It's very much a business where VCs are working hand-in-hand with founders. It's just never been an asset class that's capable of putting a ton of money to work. That was the conventional understanding. What happened was that during this zero-interest rate period, a lot of new money came into the industry.

A lot of public market investors came in thinking: We've seen how well these startups do when they go public, so we'll just invest in the last private round before they go public. They looked at the numbers and it appeared there was an arbitrage there. So they started investing in the last private round. Then they realized: Wait a second, the guys who are investing in the second-to-last private round are getting marked up by us, so there's an arbitrage there too. **They started using that logic, and they worked all the way down the stack, without necessarily having the expertise to evaluate early stage startups.** You can imagine the result of this. Money flooded into startups, and it drove valuations sky high. But as interest rates have gone up, liquidity has gone down, and there's been a popping of that bubble. So, the industry is going through a big reset right now.

The way that capital markets behavior translated into startup behavior is that a lot of founders thought money would always be available, that they could always raise a new round at a higher valuation. Money grew on trees, and founders got lax in their spending. I think founders lost focus on the idea of ever getting to profitability; it was all just about top-line revenue. The whole mentality was to grow regardless of how inefficient that growth was, regardless of how unprofitable it was. In their defense, founders felt like they had to play the game that was on the field. That game was that if you didn't show the most top-line growth and your competitor did, they would raise all the money and they'd be able to buy up the rest of the market. **You saw this dynamic in the whole Uber versus Lyft battle where they were both raising huge amounts of money and deploying it inefficiently but they felt trapped in a prisoner's dilemma—as long as there was an investor willing to fund the other guy, then you had to play the same game. This dynamic trained these companies to be very inefficient.**

Now that capital is not as available as it used to be, founders and startups have had to become much more efficient. We've gone from a situation where the only focus was on growth to one in which there's a more balanced focus. Founders have to think about the efficiency of growth, as reflected in metrics like burn, margins, and unit economics.

That's been a huge change in the industry because these bad behaviors built up over roughly fifteen years. There's an old saying that the market is an escalator on the way up and an elevator on the way down, and we just took the elevator down. It's been a rude awakening for a lot of VCs and founders.

CHRISTOPHER:

So, what are investors getting wrong today when they're thinking about technology and specifically growth and venture capital? What are they not seeing that they should be?

DAVID:

That's tough. We are in the midst of this big reset, and people are waking up to capital being much less available than it was in the past. The last decade or so was a very unusual period. I think we're going to be in a much more capital-constrained environment moving forward. Everyone's going to have to adjust their behavior accordingly.

CHRISTOPHER:

Do you think the valuations have fully begun to adjust for that or is it still further to go?

DAVID:

It's a good question. I would say that the valuation adjustments are happening in a somewhat uneven way. In a lot of areas, the adjustment has occurred and it's appropriate. But whenever an area gets hot in VC land, the valuations go crazy. For example, even though we're excited about AI, we are a bit concerned about how crazy some of the valuations are getting. We're starting to see companies with no revenue be valued at hundreds of millions of dollars. We've even seen some unicorn valuations without any revenue yet. We're back to multiples of a hundred times ARR (Annual Recurring Revenue) for hot AI companies. So, in that sense, VCs never seem to learn the lesson. Or they forget it when an area gets hot.

I'm a big believer in AI and believe it is going to create a lot of opportunity. The problem is that you still have a bit of a mania going on in some VC circles, so it's hard to find AI companies that are both promising and reasonably valued. We look for both.

TONY:

I met Ray Dalio about fourteen years ago and we became friends, and I asked him, "What's the single most important investment principle that guides you?" That's what this book is about—the Holy Grail of Investing. Ray told me at the time that it was finding eight to twelve uncorrelated investments because it reduces your risk by 80 percent and increases your upside. It is such a simple principle. What would be the Holy Grail of Investing for you?

DAVID:

Well, it's interesting. The type of investing I do is like the opposite of what he's doing. He's a macro investor, and I'm the most micro investor you can find. Not only am I investing in private companies, I'm investing in the earliest stage of private companies. I'm investing in the companies that just got started—many of which we know statistically aren't going to work out. The hope is that one or two do work out and can return the entire fund and then some. In my business, you're always looking for that power law company. The power law states that the most valuable investment in any given portfolio will generate the majority of the returns for that portfolio. So, it's almost the opposite of Ray's investing strategy.

I would not recommend this for the average investor. This is not a good way to construct a portfolio for the average investor. This is one asset class within what would be a balanced portfolio. Maybe you have a few percent of your portfolio in private companies, and then within that bucket you have this power law dynamic. We're always looking for that power law company. You can tell from what we've talked about today that I'm very much in the weeds when it comes to product. How is the product being distributed? How is it going to market? What is the founder's vision?

What are the intangible qualities the founder has that could make this an outlier company? It's very micro. The most important thing for startups is if you can find one that is catching fire. That's really the trick—to find something that's at the inflection point of the hockey stick.

We've developed our own understanding of what metrics are important for software startups. We look at not just their annually recurring revenue (ARR) and growth rates. We look at their customer acquisition costs. We have various metrics of capital efficiency. We talk to customers on our own. We try to make sure that the product actually is loved and is being referred by customers to others. We're always trying to look for signals that the company's taking off.

TONY:

And if you can find the right timing with those signals, you're then using the expertise of your decades of experience to help them grow. This is kind of a silly question for you because you have the world's attention in so many different ways but, if you have the world's attention for five minutes, what would you want people to know?

DAVID:

One of the themes I keep coming back to on my podcast is that the world that's emerging right now is a multipolar world. That's different from the world around 1990 when the Berlin Wall fell and the Soviet Union broke up. America was the only superpower left. Now we're in a world, roughly thirty years later, where a number of countries are becoming powerful and innovating with technology. Back in the late nineties when I got to Silicon Valley, there was really only one Silicon Valley, one epicenter for technology in the world, and that was true for a long time. Now you see that technology centers have sprouted up all over the world.

Innovation is hard. Often you need geniuses to achieve breakthroughs. But once a breakthrough occurs, anyone can copy it. Catching up is a lot easier than breaking new ground. And there are a lot of parts of the world that are catching up to the United States. I think that's going to require us to think about the world in a different way.

I'm a believer in American exceptionalism, but what that means to me is that we should try to set a good example rather than impose our values on everyone else. If we do a good job and create an attractive model, other people will want to copy us. But a heavy-handed approach is going to be fiercely resisted across the world. If we don't adapt our thinking to allow for the rise of others, the result will be a great deal of conflict.

TONY:

In order to build Craft Ventures into a great firm, it takes more than just great investments. What aside from strong performance has been a primary reason for the success of your business? And what was the fulcrum point of your business, if there is one, that allowed you jump from good to great?

DAVID:

The question for us is: Why would a founder want to have Craft on his or her cap table? When Ray Dalio or Warren Buffett decide they're going to buy Apple, they don't need the permission of the company. They can just go out in the public market and buy it. Apple doesn't really know or care if I own a share of their stock. They're agnostic on that question. But founders really know who's on their cap table and they care a lot. And so, we have to create a value proposition for them in the same way they have to create a value proposition for their customers.

We've spent a lot of time figuring out how to be helpful to startups. Obviously, it starts with the fact that I've been in their shoes before. I've created companies, and my partners at Craft all have operating experience and/or founding experience—they know what it's like to be on that journey. By specializing in SaaS, we can cultivate and share a lot of expertise and best practices relevant for SaaS founders. We created a tool called SaaSGrid that shows founders all the key metrics they should be looking at for their business; they just connect their data sources, and the charts and dashboards appear automatically. Finally, we have our platform team—operating partners who are specialists in areas where most startups need expertise they can't yet afford: recruiting, marketing, PR, InfoSec, legal, government relations, and the like. Whenever one of our portfolio companies needs help, there's an expert with decades of experience to help them. We focus a lot on the question: How are we going to add value to our founders?

TONY:

And, as you said, you're not somebody looking from the outside in. You're somebody who's been on the inside yourself. It's fantastic.

DAVID:

We're trying to build the VC firm that we wish we had when we were founders.

CHRISTOPHER:

With that in mind, what are some things that you wish you would've known or that somebody would've told you, before you started the firm?

DAVID:

I wish I had known how much Fed policy was going to impact our world! Maybe in a completely well-functioning economy, you wouldn't have to worry that much about it. But we're living in a time of great distortions. Fed policy swung very rapidly from a zero-interest rate policy to the fastest rate-tightening cycle ever—from zero to 5.5 percent in one year. You just can't underestimate the trickle-down effects of that; not only has it reduced capital availability and valuations, but it's also created a software recession. Tech companies are doing layoffs, and as they lay off employees, they buy less software because software is generally sold on a seat basis. The cycle feeds on itself. I think we've probably bottomed out and now we're seeing new opportunities with AI, but there has been a major recession in software for the last year or two.

CHRISTOPHER:

One of the greatest concerns right now in the marketplace is higher infla-tion for longer. Do you think that the reset has happened enough to where people will just go back to building businesses? Or do you think it continues to ripple?

DAVID:

Right now the market seems to believe that inflation is largely a solved problem, that you'll have inflation in the 2.5 to 3 percent range at the end of the year, and that there's a good chance we'll get rate cuts next year. The market is starting to price in this scenario, so if inflation rebounds and we don't get rate cuts, then there is downside risk to current price levels. That will trickle down to private markets because the public markets are our exit comps.

That's what we saw in 2022. When the Fed raised interest rates, the public markets crashed, especially growth stocks, and then it worked its way down to the private markets. The private markets take their cue from what's happening in the public markets. But right now, people think we've bottomed out and these problems are on their way to being solved, albeit things are not going back to the way they used to be during the heady days of ZIRP (zero interest rate policy).

CHRISTOPHER:

One of the things that I'd love to hear your feedback on is that as AI becomes more prevalent throughout the business community and disrupts and eliminates bodies and jobs, as it does that, it feels like it would also reduce the number of licenses [or the] number of seats, which would have an impact on software. Does that spiral because of the secular trend of AI? Or is this more cyclical [and] tied to the softness of the economy?

TONY:

Or is it just replaced by AI software sales of some sort?

DAVID:

I think we're still a ways away from AI that can completely replace human job functions. The category that is showing the most promise right now are these copilots. I think that is the right way to look at it. It's a human working with AI to be more productive than they otherwise could have been, or to do their job faster or in a higher quality way. It's about humans gaining leverage through productivity tools. Does that wipe out tons of jobs? I am skeptical of that. First of all, we're going to get a lot of new software companies creating new products. Those products have to be sold; they have to be marketed. So, first, we will have an explosion of company creation in order to create the AI tools we're talking about. That's one part of it.

The second part is that the customers of this AI software can now get more done. It lowers the startup cost for a founder to create a company. We have the famous story of Mark Zuckerberg creating the first version of Facebook in his dorm room at Harvard. He had the ability to code the first version himself. A lot of founders or would-be-founders don't have that ability. But now, thanks to AI tools, they're going to be able to do more of it themselves. So, there'll be more people who can get started creating more companies.

The history of innovation is that as we make humans more productive, it makes our species richer. It doesn't put people out of work. We always find new things for them to do. As long as people are adaptive and are willing to be in a constant process of learning, I think it will be beneficial.

The history of innovation is that as we make humans more productive, it makes our species richer. It doesn't put people out of work. We always find new things for them to do.

TONY:

A lot of people have a very daunting view of the future. There are always challenges, obviously, but it bothers me when I see young people talking about not having kids because they think the whole world's going to end in twelve years, which we all know is not true. There are plenty of challenges, but I'm curious: Where do you see the world going?

DAVID:

One of the reasons I'm excited to be in tech is that I think it has consistently delivered the most progress for people. Even as our politics become more dysfunctional or divisive, and so many parts of our society aren't working, technological progress is still working and does deliver a better future for people.

I've seen it over the course of my career. Over the last three decades, I've seen that technology keeps becoming a bigger and bigger part of our economy and of our way of doing things. It creates products that make our lives better and more convenient, helps cure diseases, helps us get the information we need, the learning we need. The real key is to have as many people benefit from it and be included in it as possible. That goes back to what we were talking about with learning; you need people to see learning as a continuous process throughout their lives as opposed to a degree that gets stamped.

CHRISTOPHER:

It is a great tie-in to a question we've asked everybody. When you're looking for people to join your team, what are the key characteristics? What makes them stand out?

DAVID:

In an investor, you want somebody who is scrappy and sniffs out opportunity. The funny term we have for this is a truffle pig—those pigs they train to find truffles. I don't know how they do it, but these pigs go rooting around in the dirt and somehow they dig up these valuable truffles. Good investors are like that.

CHAPTER 17

MICHAEL REES

COFOUNDER OF DYAL CAPITAL, COFOUNDER
AND COPRESIDENT OF BLUE OWL

Accolades: The market leader in GP stakes
Total Asset Under Management (as of August 2023): $150 billion
Area of focus: GP stakes

HIGHLIGHTS

- The largest investor in GP stakes, with a market share of approximately 60 percent in terms of fund capital raised for GP stakes over the last twelve years.
- The firm has a market share of nearly 90 percent for GP stake deals done with an investment size in excess of $600 million.
- Mr. Rees is cofounder and copresident of Blue Owl, which manages $150 billion and was formed in 2021 when his Dyal Capital merged with Owl Rock Capital.

CHRISTOPHER:

As a way to set the table, why don't you tell us your origin story—how you ended up in your current position.

MICHAEL:

I started my financial services career at Lehman Brothers, and somewhat serendipitously I was the fourth teammate to join the strategy group. And if you rank ordered the performance of the major groups at Lehman, fixed income was the bellwether, then equities, then investment banking, and then asset management. And so the first person hired into the group had the option to pick to be on the fixed income team. And the last one on the list was somewhat stuck with a nascent, sort of white-sheet-of-paper investment management division. And so I guess I was the one who got stuck with it. It kind of felt like I got the short end of the stick. It was a total build project; with the goal being that Lehman was going to try to grow rapidly into investment management to have a division on par with Goldman Sachs or Merrill Lynch.

At the time, hedge funds were the talk of the town. It was 2000, 2001, and hedge fund performance coming out of that time frame was pretty strong, and large hedge fund businesses were being built. The question was, should we buy one of these? We sat back and talked about it—part of the reason we decided not to is that no hedge fund that escaped Wall Street wanted to come back and be a part of a big firm. Also, we thought that these were highly entrepreneurial investors that were creating these businesses, and we wanted them to be highly aligned with them, not controlling them within the walls of a twenty-thousand-person organization. We asked, does buying a hundred percent of their business take away their motivation?

So, we came up with this crazy idea (at least it was crazy at the time): Let's just buy 20 percent of a few hedge funds instead of buying 100 percent of one. The rest is history for me. I've done close to ninety minority stake transactions over the twenty-two years since we sat back and came up with this strategy. You know, my life falls under the adage when you're a hammer, everything looks like a nail. **Everything I look at daily, every business I think about, I ask myself, "Could we buy 20 percent of this? Is it a great**

business run by smart people, and would aligning myself with them be a smart idea?" That was the beginning, and it has been a great run since the beginning.

And then as time moved forward, I had a real love for this space and I wanted to set up my own team—Neuberger Berman was a great place to do that. We spun the investment management business out of the aftermath of the Lehman bankruptcy, and starting building this minority stakes business at Neuberger. From its inception, the firm had this multi-product platform where each group had its own investment authority, and each team had the financial upside that came with building its own successful pod. We were able to convince investors that investing in minority stakes in alternative firms was a good thing to do. That signaled the start of the Dyal business within Neuberger. And we grew it quite rapidly. **Now we have about a 60 percent market share of all of the investment capital ever raised in the minority stake space. And when you look at just the larger deals, our market share is close to 90 percent for deals above $600 million.** So that origin story dates back to getting the short end of the stick at Lehman Brothers when I joined. And, luckily, I did.

CHRISTOPHER:

It's a great example of how life is happening for us and not to us, for those that take the opportunity and run with it. It's a fascinating fifteen-to-twenty-year run. Who was the most important person in your life, that shaped your success, and how did they shape that success?

MICHAEL:

It's a little cliché but my father and mother. I work with my brother and have for twenty years. It's been a familial approach to what we're doing. But, coming from Pittsburgh, largely a blue-collar town, my father was a salesman, my mother was a nurse. **They instilled in us as kids that this world is about hard work. It's about looking people in the eye. It's about a firm handshake.** The financial services and "Wall Street" industry has a lot of personalities, a lot of egos. And one of the things I hear a lot and that I'm really proud of is that myself, my brother, and the rest of the team have that humble, personable, Pittsburgh approach to the business. One based on trusted relationships where our word is our bond. We're the kind of people that you want to do business with as a partner for a long time.

CHRISTOPHER:

When we think about minority stakes, otherwise known as GP stakes, where's the greatest opportunity for investors right now?

MICHAEL:

We are still really strong believers in private assets and the markets at large. We still see a lot of incremental allocation to alternatives. We do see a rising tide and a long-term trend towards private alternative investments (buyout, growth, private credit, real estate). It will not be a straight line, but if you look at the global allocation of pensions, sovereign wealth funds, and individuals to these strategies, you see a lot of upside. But I guess your question is: Where is it most acute and where is the real interesting aspect of it?

We're believers in the consolidation trend of industries. It happens in nearly every industry we have studied. Here we are in the soft drink market with two main producers. Over time, the industry consolidates because there is power in scale. And I just think we're on a long-term trend that benefits the bigger businesses in the industry. That was a soft tailwind that was working to the benefit of the bigger firms from 2015 to 2021.

But 2022 and 2023 has really turned the soft tailwind into a really powerful tailwind. Hence why we're really focused now on truly scaled players that have the benefits of a global reach to investors in the Middle East, in Asia, possibly retail, and with networks like yours. And so, we think brand name is important, stability is important, and we think these types of investors put preference in a safe pair of hands. All of those things typically benefit established players that have been building a business over time with strong cornerstones and brand recognition. Our phrase, "the big get bigger and the strong get stronger," has been something we've believed in now for eight years. And the last eighteen months has really strengthened that belief.

CHRISTOPHER:

Do you think the outlook over the next three years is different from the next ten years, or do you think it's more of the same?

MICHAEL:

Private markets move at a slow, almost glacial pace. I think a lot of what is beneficial about private markets is that you have time on your side, and you can outlive the acute moves in the public equity and fixed income markets. So, three years is a blink of the eye in the private markets. So, I think more of the same and continued consolidation at the top, and growth. I do think the next ten years are going to be extremely strong for private markets. But I don't really see any acute trends that will change dramatically over the three-to-ten-year window.

CHRISTOPHER:

What has happened recently in the GP stake landscape that you expected to happen, and what has surprised you?

MICHAEL:

I don't know if a lot happened that surprised us in the last couple years. We haven't seen a dramatic shift in the performance of our managers from a fund perspective, owning what we believe are long-term, stable businesses. You know, you hear all of the investment chatter about software, and how amazing mission-critical software is because you get three-to-five-year contracts that have net retention rates near a hundred percent. That's all good and software will drive the economy. **That being said, I believe that private equity and the private markets are even better. Owning stakes in the GP of private market firms is a fantastic business where you see layering and layering of revenue streams just like in software.** That is the common model. Growth happens quite nicely as you layer fund after fund after fund.

I like software. I think a lot of our partners invest in software, but I'll take the private equity business and the private markets business all day long. I think high-quality, mission-critical private market firms are meant for times like this. **Whether it is COVID, whether it's the banking crisis of late, or just the overall rising inflation and interest rate environments that we've seen for the last two years. The private markets firms and the strategies they employ are built to weather that storm and be quite stable.**

CHRISTOPHER:

You've talked to many investors about GP stakes over the last eight years, particularly as Dyal has grown so dramatically. What is it that you see that investors typically get wrong about the space, or that they miss when they're evaluating GP stakes and the opportunity set there?

MICHAEL:

The phrase that bothers me the most, that I don't think I'll ever get over, is the term "cash out." People assume that the money we invest in a GP stake goes right into the pocket of the ownership group. And then, if they want to take it one step further, it goes into a fancy boat or a fancy car. **What really sparked the GP stakes industry and has created such strong growth is that when you look at a private markets firm, particularly a successful one, it consumes capital. There's a window of time during that growth trend of a firm when it needs incremental capital.** And so, most of the capital, the vast majority of the capital that we invest in GP stakes has nothing to do with the "cash out." It has everything to do with supporting the growth of these best-in-class firms. And one of the unique things that we hypothesized would be the case, and has turned out, is that the firms that want to do a deal are the ones that perform the best. Some investors say, "You're going to get adverse selection. You're only going to get called by the people that are nervous and not doing well, and they're going to try to sell you something." What we've seen empirically is the exact opposite. **It's that the firms that are doing the best and see the highest potential and opportunity in front of them—they are the ones that need the growth capital. If you're not growing, you don't need growth capital.**

CHRISTOPHER:

It's interesting because so many people do think that it's an exit strategy for these folks when in reality it's a growth engine for people as the primary motivation for these transactions.

MICHAEL:

Yes. Every investor knows that a tech company that's growing and developing its business needs to go through an A round, a B round, a C round, a

D round. That's sort of what the venture and growth market is all about. It surprises me that it's taken a lot of education over time to convince investors out there that a private markets business, a successful GP, would be the exact same thing. They need capital to fund their growth. And I'm happy to be the C, D, and E round for a lot of these really good firms.

CHRISTOPHER:

It's a very different way to frame the conversation because every business that wants to grow is going to consume capital at some point. And there are different places they can get it. But if the capital is not only available, but also is strategic and can add value to them, that is absolutely the best kind of growth capital one can access. So, if you had the attention of the world for five minutes to talk about anything that you think the world should be focused on, what would it be?

MICHAEL:

Well, as this banking situation plays out, I'm sort of in the minority that is thinking it's not over and maybe not even really getting started. I know this puts a line in the sand from a timing perspective, so we'll be able to judge if I was right or wrong, but I remember acutely being at Lehman Brothers. Bear Stearns happened six months before, and, you know, the situation we saw in 2007 and 2008 evolved over a twelve-to-eighteen-month window. I'm very hopeful that that isn't the case. But I think there are several more shoes to drop in the situation that was caused by a rapid increase in interest rates and unprecedented government liquidity being pumped into the system during COVID and, most likely, a liability and funding mismatch across a lot of midsized banking balance sheets. Hopefully I'm wrong, but if I could have the world's attention, at least the policymakers' attention for five minutes, I would say act quickly, powerfully, and convincingly, because there's nothing worse than a financial crisis that's caused by confidence.

CHRISTOPHER:

We had the initial big earthquake that got everybody's attention. The aftershocks can also be very problematic if they're not managed.

When you look at growing a large investment firm, what's been the primary reason for the success of Dyal?

MICHAEL:

The one thing that irks me from time to time when I meet with a private markets firm, or any investment firm for that matter, is the sentence: "I'm just going to focus on great returns, and everything else at my business will work itself out." I surprisingly have heard it hundreds of times over the last twenty years. The frequency is not going down. I think it couldn't be more wrong. This manner of thinking ignores all of the other aspects that go into making a great firm and a firm great. Investing (and doing it well) is certainly fundamental. But there's a lot more to a successful firm.

It's hard to have a batting average of a thousand. You're not going to get everything right all the time. What's been important at Dyal and Blue Owl is a focus on the whole business. Client service and client relationships are at the very top of the list of things that really take focus, making sure that you're not just coming around asking for money every few years, making sure you're trying to help investors to solve their problems. Maybe this comes in the form of a new product, maybe with advice in something you're seeing throughout the industry. To me, investment performance is very important. But how you run the rest of the business, how you interact with your clients are critical parts of building a money management business. We all saw what happened at the end of the nineties, when most hedge funds had no business but for the investing aspect. They were return generators; reporting was bad, client interactions were bad, operations not great. And it did cause problems over time. What we've seen is that a lot of the better firms over the last twenty years have decided to make their firm into a real business. They've decided to think about all aspects of their game and try to instill best practices across them.

CHRISTOPHER:

When you think about the growth of Dyal, what was the fulcrum point? What was that seminal event, if you will?

MICHAEL:

We intentionally had a focus on midsize hedge funds as our target for our early two funds. And those continue to perform well. But as we moved into fund three, we decided to launch a much bigger fund, not focusing on midsize private markets firms, but focusing on the larger best-in-class brand names. And when you're out there marketing a story, there are some investors that are willing to believe a story, but more investors want to see where the proof is in the pudding. The ability to raise capital for our private markets fund with investments with Vista, EnCap, Starwood, and Silver Lake, to come out of the gate with those great partners, really set the table and really put us in a great position. And that was certainly an inflection point for us. It showed the market and the Investor group that you can partner with really high-quality, best-in-class firms (which was doubted at the time) and that these investments should make for a better-than-average growth investment.

CHRISTOPHER:

What are a few things you wish somebody would've told you before you started your firm?

MICHAEL:

I guess it never hurts to reiterate that it's never easy. I think if it ever got to a point where it was easy, you'd know something was wrong. You really have to improve your game, month after month, fund after fund, whatever it is. And you have to earn your investors' trust on a continuous basis. That's probably something everybody should have written somewhere in their office. It's not going to get any easier. But it gets more enjoyable. And it's great to have a team that's worked together and collaborated for a long time.

CHRISTOPHER:

If you could do anything differently in your business with the benefit of hindsight, what would you have done differently? Or what would you advise someone else to do differently than you did?

MICHAEL:

I think even though we've grown very rapidly and have created a leadership position in this space, we really grew in a very methodical way. We didn't hire that second person until we had enough revenue to pay for that person. And the fund size we targeted was just enough to execute our strategy. From the beginning, we took a very cautious approach to growth. We were able to, knock on wood, stay slightly ahead of the competition. And we continue to feel really good about our competitive position.

But what you hear and what you see across the tech and venture world is that much of the growth in innovation comes from people in their twenties who have nothing to lose and who go at it a thousand percent, not a hundred percent. And so, maybe in our early stages we put 110 percent into this idea and grew it very methodically and consistently. Who knows where we would be if we would've gone a lot harder and a lot faster and really expanded the opportunity set.

I do think one of the hardest things in our industry is to find innovation out of the professional crowd that is in my age bracket because that group has a much larger focus on downside, and maybe there's more innovation coming out of the "young and ignorant" (that I certainly was) in one's twenties or early thirties and having nothing to lose. That's maybe an attribute that should be celebrated more.

CHRISTOPHER:

What is the primary reason that you believe most investment firms don't scale?

MICHAEL:

At the core, there are very low barriers to entry into the investment space overall, and that applies to alternative asset management as well. You can get someone to back you for your first deal or maybe even for your first fund. So we will always have a very wide base to the industry pyramid and a lot of new entrants. However, it's an industry where that first five-year window has a percentage of success that is very low. I do think if you can clear that hurdle . . . and get to a point where you have a high-quality group of core investors, and a process that has some consistency and experience to it, the moat starts getting deeper and wider.

We don't really focus on what happens when a firm scales that first $100 million fund to get to the $300 million. That's not my area of expertise, but that's where the weeding out happens. I think it's rare that a large-scale firm can't weather a tough market or soft period and get to the other side. For smaller firms, getting to the other side means ten, fifteen years. It's one of those industries that weeds you out quickly—chews you up and spits you out. But if you can break through that barrier, it's a pretty accommodating and stable industry if you build a solid foundation.

CHRISTOPHER:

It is unique in that regard. As you think about talent—obviously you've hired a lot of people over the years and Dyal and Blue Owl have grown quite dramatically—what are the key traits that you look for that separate the highest performers from their peers?

MICHAEL:

I think it differs dramatically depending on what type of firm it is and what the core objective of that firm or group happens to be. The question I try to ask is: What's the goal, and what's the best person that fits that organization? There are firms where you want to be full of graduates from Wharton and Harvard and Yale and Stanford. We happen to have a nice cross-section of Big 10 and Big East graduates. It's just a different type of hiring and team approach. We've found that the success of our teammates has really been driven by that ability to engender a partnership mentality and confidence with investors and with our GP stakes partners. It's not about being the smartest person in the room. It's about being a good partner to the person on the other side of the table. Granted you have to be smart and highly motivated, but school pedigree doesn't drive success for us.

It's not about being the smartest person in the room. It's about being a good partner to the person on the other side of the table.

CHRISTOPHER:

That's a really good way to look at it. It is very idiosyncratic based on the business and the personalities of that business and the people that will thrive and be fulfilled while working in that particular business.

TONY:

Michael, as you know, we're writing a book with an audacious title: *The Holy Grail of Investing*. It's a phrase Ray Dalio used to describe to me his most important principle in investing. What you've built over the years is amazing, and we're so proud and excited to be partners with you in GP stakes. When you look at investment, what would you say the most important principle, the Holy Grail, is?

MICHAEL:

As it relates to private investment with a human capital firm, it really is as simple as partnering with good people. I know that sounds trivial, and maybe shallow, but when you are looking to establish a relationship that you can't get out of and you really are thinking about your investment as permanent, you don't have the luxury of bickering, fighting, and getting divorced. So, we've found across fifty-eight different investments, fifty-five of them have been with good people. And we spend 90 percent of our time dealing with the three that have, you know, more challenging individuals.

This [Holy Grail] is not just about our relationships with them. It also means that when they are doing deals in their space, they're treating their other constituents with the same congeniality and partnership that we look for. So, we certainly benefit on the point-to-point relationship, but it also permeates all of their underlying investments. It surprises me that we've seen that phenomenon (that the success of our deal is a function of the "goodness" of the partner) really play out with almost a perfect correlation from the very beginning in this GP stakes business—but that's the truth.

TONY:

We all know the right people can take a terrible company and make it strong. How do you make those choices? What are some of the criteria you look for to know a company is going to be the right relationship?

MICHAEL:

The process of getting to know an organization can be long. It's been upwards of seven or eight years to get to know a firm and to help them through the process. Or it can be as short as four or five months. But you just really get the sense, when you get into the nitty-gritty of the negotiation, about whether the counterparty is viewing everything as a zero-sum game and just trying to win as many points as possible, or whether they're willing to take a view of the issues from both sides of the table. And that's the easiest lens to look through. If a partner is going to sit down and say, "I understand why these three things are important to you, and I'd like you to understand why these other three things are important to me," well, that is the kind of dialogue that really, really works and foreshadows behavior over the next decade or two.

In most cases, a firm that succeeded in getting to the size and scale that we're looking at is going to have that type of human capital within its walls. Every once in a while, though, you get too far down the path, and you realize this person is just arguing for every nickel and dime. It's a pretty good litmus test to really understand what the future's going to look like if you look at the term sheet negotiation as a predictor of the future.

TONY:

Even though it's simple, it's super helpful. If someone is trying to maximize every single dollar, they are not going be playing for the long term with anybody else, much less you. It makes total sense.

CHRISTOPHER:

One of the things that's really interesting about Dyal is how diversified they are. How do you look at the mixture between private equity, between buyout, between private credit, between real estate, technology, etc.?

MICHAEL:

We are fortunate enough to be investing in a great industry. And those that have gotten to the more premium end have built really nice businesses. And our goal is to really try to partner with those firms that are truly specialized in what they do. They are the best at X. Generalization, we think, is sort of a race for mediocrity. I don't think we have a view of whether an upstream energy manager is going to do better than a technology manager, but we want to be partnered with the best one of each. And having that type of diversification has certainly helped. There's a bit of a winner's curse in GP stake investing, and that means that the better a firm does, typically, the faster it grows and the more likely it is to need growth capital.

> There's a bit of a winner's curse in GP stake investing, and
> that means that the better a firm does, typically, the faster
> it grows and the more likely it is to need growth capital.

So, we're fortunate that we don't get a lot of phone calls from firms that are mediocre. We seem to only get phone calls from the good ones. And we can really try to understand and determine who's really special in the area in which they operate. There are a few really good generalists, but where you see your really high-quality firms that we believe have longevity is where they truly do something that's differentiated and specialized. And that's obvious in a lot of industries.

TONY:

Having interviewed several of the players for the book here, many of which are partners through you, you really see that in a Vista, for example. You see the level of specialization that [Robert has] in SaaS. It's mind boggling. When you look at the world we are in now, how do you think private equity is affected by rising interest rates, after forty-five years of slowly dropping interest rates? Does that affect it in a significant way, and does it affect your partners?

MICHAEL:

Tony, it's funny you mentioned the number forty-five. I was going to bring it up in my response. There are a handful of private equity firms that have been around between forty-five and fifty years, and they have generated tremendous returns for investors and generated tremendous wealth for their owners in so many different interest-rate environments. That spans the seventies, eighties, nineties. And we're still at historic lows of overall interest rates when you measure it over that period. Now, that being the case, there are a lot of investments that were made when rates were low, and rates have ramped quite quickly. And so that may put some strain on those recent investments. But measured over a longer arc, we still have accommodating rates and there is still a lot of growth out there.

In general, depending on what multiple you want to pay and how you want to think about your terminal value, you can make money with interest rates where they are today. It's just going to take a different type of value creation approach and it's certainly going to take a different valuation paradigm. **It doesn't have to be an era of free money to make a good return. It was certainly easy from 2009 to about 2020 to sort of just throw darts at the wall and a lot of things worked. I think over this next phase we'll certainly see a separation of high-quality firms from the rest.**

On the flip side, private credit is just slowly chipping away at the market share that banks had in lending. And there are a lot of reasons why it's better to work with a private lender that understands your business's needs and is willing to work with you through the good times and bad. Doesn't mean they're always going to give you a break, but they're going to want to see you do well. And that flexibility that a private direct lender brings to the buyout space is one that's going to continue to gain market share. **We've seen a lot of really talented people leave banks over the last decade or two, and a lot of them ended up in direct lending at private credit managers.** And I think they've just built a better mousetrap. We certainly are honored here at Blue Owl to have one of the best mousetraps out there. Overall, as an industry, we're only at a market share of about 9 percent or 10 percent. So, there's a lot of room to grow for private credit, and that makes up a meaningful part of our investment program.

TONY:

Last question, what gives you the most personal satisfaction in your life at this stage? I'm curious.

MICHAEL:

Oh, man. It's all about the team, and Christopher has been fortunate to get to know a number of the folks on the Blue Owl team. And I am honored each compensation season by the reactions that I get from the vast majority of the team here, which is appreciation for the financial wealth that we can all create together, but also a recognition that most of them would come in and do it for free. When you hear that, that people are willing to work their butts off for all this time, all because they love the camaraderie, they love the sport . . . well, that's the best feeling you can have as a business leader. So that's why I certainly come in each day to partner with great folks like my colleagues here at Blue Owl, like Christopher and the team at CAZ, and like a lot of our great stakeholders.

TONY:

I'm going to ask you one more since you've walked me right into it. So how do you build that culture? Is it coming back to the first principle used for investing—finding the right people?

MICHAEL:

There's not a great answer to it, but it's the good old-fashioned Pittsburgh airport test when you're interviewing. Getting to know an individual that you're going to spend a lot of time with, and it won't all be poring over spreadsheets. [Instead], there's a lot of time in airports and in cars where you have to feel a connection and a trust. That's what we look for. I think this group that we've assembled is truly special in the way they interact with each other and the type of friends that we've all come to be.

CHAPTER 18

BILL FORD

CEO OF GENERAL ATLANTIC

Accolades: Member of the Council on Foreign Relations, McKinsey Advisory Council, and chair of Rockefeller University
Total Asset Under Management (as of August 2023): $77 billion
Area of Focus: Consumer, financial services, life sciences, and healthcare

HIGHLIGHTS

- As of July 2023, GA has invested over $55B in more than 500 companies across multiple stages of growth. We have $77B of assets under management across more than 215+ current portfolio companies and deploy $8–9 billion in capital annually with ~60% invested outside the U.S.
- We are now active in six global sectors and five major geographies with a team of 272 investment professionals working across 16 global locations.
- General Atlantic is currently ranked ninth in Private Equity International's PEI 300 ranking of the largest private equity firms in the world, thanks in large part to Mr. Ford's leadership.

TONY:

So, we're working on a new book and I'm doing my third in the series. We've been interviewing the best investors in the world, and you guys obviously have to be near the top with your track record. What you've done at General Atlantic is just unbelievable. We wanted to start out, if we could, and just ask if you'd share with us a little bit about your origin story, how you ended up in this position, and the development and expansion of General Atlantic over these years since you began.

BILL:

Thank you, Tony. This is our forty-third year. We started in 1980 as a family office, and for our first decade, we were primarily managing capital for an individual named Chuck Feeney, who was a self-made entrepreneur from New Jersey.

TONY:

The same Chuck Feeney that was giving all his money away? I interviewed him. He is extraordinary.

BILL:

You probably interviewed him, Tony, because he is considered the father of the Giving Pledge. Warren Buffett and Bill Gates will tell you that because Chuck invented this idea of giving while living, he was very focused on giving back and ultimately made it his life's work. When we started General Atlantic in 1980, Chuck had already built significant wealth and was receiving strong cashflows from the Duty Free Shoppers business. At this point, Chuck then hired two people out of McKinsey—Steve Denning, our founder, and another professional named Ed Cohen. These two started the firm and, for ten years, we only had one investor: Chuck Feeney. He was building wealth for himself and also for what became the Atlantic Philanthropies.

Then, around 1990, Chuck had a life event and decided to leave the company entirely—exit operations, exit leadership—and commit himself fully to philanthropy for the balance of his life. He decided to put all of his money into the Atlantic Philanthropies and then give that money away during his lifetime. With this in mind, Chuck encouraged General Atlantic to go out and find other investors. That was 1990; I joined in 1991.

We then began a process of becoming a more institutionalized firm by adding other clients, starting with wealthy families, before moving into endowments and foundations, and then moving into institutions with large capital pools like insurance companies, sovereign wealth funds, and pension funds. But, as mentioned, our starting point was Chuck, who sold the Duty Free Shoppers business to Louis Vuitton in 1997 for $3.7 billion. Between that and what we compounded for him, he ultimately gave away about $10 billion during his lifetime. So, Chuck lived up to his idea of giving while living and that journey led to our style of investing and the firm's culture. [Chuck] cared about two things. One was philanthropy, and specifically, compounding his capital so he could give more back. The second was a conviction about entrepreneurs. **He had a deep belief that entrepreneurs were going to change the world for the better. So, the firm was built on the ethos of supporting entrepreneurs and helping add value to their efforts to build new companies and do more philanthropy.**

We still carry these ideas forward. Today, we continue to focus our efforts on giving back as a firm, while maintaining a passion for backing entrepreneurs. We invest across many sectors around the world, not just in technology in the U.S.—but what drives our investment program is a strategy called growth equity, which is essentially trying to identify companies that have made it past the venture capital stage and need help growing fast. By identifying the right entrepreneurs and companies, and participating in that growth, you can generate outstanding returns for your investors.

Over the period of thirty-plus years, General Atlantic has become truly global. We're in the U.S., Europe, India, China, Southeast Asia and Latin America, with about 60 percent of our portfolio outside the U.S. One of the greatest journeys for me personally has been working and building relationships around the world. We've always been ahead of the curve when it comes to seeing where innovation is going, and then built our human capital to capitalize on it. So, now we're nearly 560 people with sixteen global locations across five regions, investing about $8 to $9 billion a year in growth equity.

TONY:

Who's been the most important person in shaping your success in life? And what did you learn or pull from them that shaped you?

BILL:

That's a great question, Tony. Steve Denning and Chuck Feeney were hugely influential. As mentioned, Steve is the founder of General Atlantic, and the one who hired me. Many of our firm's core values come directly from him, as Steve was a values-driven person. After I took over the firm as CEO, Steve went on to become the chairman of the board of Stanford University and did that for a decade. He was a great mentor, and I learned a lot from him.

Chuck also shaped who I became, because he was this incredible man who did something that nobody does, right? At the time, Chuck was one of the wealthiest men in the world. He created an industry, travel retail, had the winning company, and was a brilliant entrepreneur. To pivot from that to a full stop and commit himself completely to philanthropy at fifty-five years old, and ultimately give all his money away, is remarkable. You don't meet many people like that. He was very impactful.

Finally, the last big influence has been all the entrepreneurs I've gotten to work with—people like yourself. Entrepreneurs are the most interesting people in the world. They see the world differently. They've been told about fifty times that their idea won't work, and they somehow persevere. They're people you could inherently learn from. I think about all the entrepreneurs I've worked with over the years and there are a lot that come to mind. For example, Larry Fink, Jamie Dimon, and James Gorman—those three I put in a category of mentors and people I deeply admire as leaders, who helped me grow and become successful.

Entrepreneurs are the most interesting people in the world. They see the world differently. They've been told about fifty times that their idea won't work, and they somehow persevere.

CHRISTOPHER:

That is a great group to be associated with in so many ways. Let's transition a little bit to the investment side. Your firm does more sectors now than many others, but it all fits in the bucket of growth equity. In the world of growth equity right now, in this economic cycle that we're dealing with, where do you see the greatest opportunity that people aren't paying enough attention to?

BILL:

I think three big themes are going to shape the investment environment in the next few decades and shape our opportunity set. One is the continued expansion of what I call the global digital economy. We've been seeing this happen for years, more and more industries, parts of the economy, and geographies are being fundamentally impacted by technology. We are in the midst of the fourth wave of computing that I've witnessed in my career. When I started, we were in the era of mainframe or centralized computing, in the eighties. We saw the advent of personal computing. Now, we are in the advent of artificial intelligence. This will reshape the computing landscape, the technology landscape, and will open up many possibilities for investment.

The second major investment theme is life sciences. **We are in a golden moment of biology and life sciences innovation, based on what we know about the genome and cell biology. AI supercharges all this innovation because of what it does for drug discovery. You're going to see a real acceleration in human therapeutics.** We know healthcare access is a huge issue, especially in emerging markets, but we need to rethink our healthcare systems to create more efficiency, more access, and better outcomes. So, while there's [investment opportunity in] life sciences, it's also a very large industry that needs disruption, change, and innovation. This is where AI can play an important role.

The third theme is energy transition. I look at a world that uses 110 million barrels of oil a day, and that number will eventually increase to 180 million barrels of oil a day. One, carbon can't even meet the energy needs of the world over the next two or three decades. And two, we need to work our way down from 110 [million barrels] to use cleaner sources of energy. The amount of innovation and investment that's going to be required to do that is going to be massive. It could be climate technology. It could be green energy generation. It could be carbon capture. Whatever it is, we need to think about the idea of shifting the energy base from carbon to non-carbon and dealing with climate problems.

TONY:

You say these are themes for decades, not themes for a couple of years.

BILL:

Yes, multi-decades. Themes that can have exceptional growth, can generate exceptional investment returns.

CHRISTOPHER:

We refer to it as wind at our back versus wind in our face.

BILL:

We want tailwinds, and these tailwinds will create opportunities for new entrants to come into the market and create value. If we have our human capital focused on that, we should be able to find good opportunities.

CHRISTOPHER:

What has happened that you expected to happen, and that you did not expect to happen, in the last eighteen to twenty-four months?

BILL:

The biggest major shift in the environment has to be U.S.-China relations. We've operated in a world where the integration of China into the global economy has been a tailwind and has been a net positive for global growth. Now, we're in a world where U.S. and China relations are going to be much more challenged, leading to a fundamental shift in the investment environment. It has implications for global trade. It has implications for innovation. It has implications for global investors.

CHRISTOPHER:

Related to that, what do you think investors are getting wrong today, where they're just not positioned correctly?

BILL:

I think many investors are underestimating the innovation that's going to come from technology, life sciences, and healthcare. It's very easy to underestimate the amount of prospective innovation that will keep coming and how long these trends will last—and I think life sciences and the tech space are the best examples of this. A year ago, no one would have had any expectations about how impactful AI was going to become, and how quickly it would become impactful. I think we're underestimating the impact of that on the investment environment and the investment opportunity set.

CHRISTOPHER:

Goes back to that old line: People overestimate what can be done in two years and underestimate what can be done in ten.

BILL:

That is perfectly said. Another thing is that it is easy to quantify what jobs may be lost from this technology shift, but it's very difficult to identify exactly what jobs will be created. I believe this is a moment where many people don't fully appreciate what positives will come from these developments.

Now, on the negative side as investors, we're moving from a world that was oversupplied relative to demand, which meant low inflation, and entering a world where demand exceeds supply. We might have fundamental inflation for a period of time, or, at least, we've run out of a deflationary capacity. I think that's a shift in the investment environment that's going to be with us for a while, and investors have to recalibrate. At some point the music ends on the two decades of easy money that we've had. Now, we're back in a world where we have a real rate of interest. We now have a reasonably high nominal rate of interest. We have a real discount rate for future cash flows that we didn't have before. Those are the big headwinds and big changes that make innovation more valuable because innovation is growth, and growth can outrun some of that.

TONY:

Ray Dalio is obviously a macro investor; it's not the same. But when he talks about his Holy Grail, meaning the ultimate principle he uses in the environment you're describing. When you're going to invest in companies, when you're looking for great entrepreneurs, what is your Holy Grail of investing?

BILL:

I want to go back to what you just said, Tony. We are micro investors operating in a macro context. We think about how big the market that this company is trying to serve is, and how fast it's going to grow. But we [also] think about how it is structured and whether there will be an attractive profit pool at the end. We're right into the micro of that. And, what's been the Holy Grail? It really comes down to three things. One, I just talked about, is market. Two, is it a big enough prize? Is it a business model that can yield high levels of profitability over time? Sometimes you can build a business in a great market, but the business model is fundamentally a 20 percent gross margin industry with 1 percent or 2 percent profit margins. You can build it, but you're not going to generate a very large profit. We actually do business model training with our teams about which ones are fundamentally attractive versus fundamentally unattractive. And the third is people and management. We call it management but it's really the quality of the entrepreneur. Is this the kind of individual or leader who can actually make something happen, overcome adversity and attract followership to build a team? Every time we're looking at our micro-opportunity, we're looking at those three variables in depth.

TONY:

You said you train your people to look at these business models. These are the attractive ones. Some are not so attractive. What are some of the criteria that you look at besides, obviously, margin in that area? And then, secondly, same thing on the people side. How do you know if it's the right leadership or the right entrepreneur?

BILL:

We look at pricing power, capital intensity, and high gross margins. Capital intensity creates a fundamental investment risk. You need more of it; it dilutes your equity base. It is usually a fixed cost that can't be managed, so we have a tendency to like low capital intensity businesses better. And pricing power. If you have pricing power, it usually goes hand in hand with higher gross margins and higher operating margins. The worst thing to be in is a commodity business where you have no pricing power and you're capital intensive. **So, we love those two things: pricing power combined with low capital intensity leads to high gross margins, high barriers to entry, and then ultimately high profit margins.**

And then, [for] people we do a lot of things. We do formal management assessments with other companies. We invest in understanding what got them to where they are, what's motivating them for what they want to accomplish, and what is in their background that they've actually accomplished that indicates they'll be able to accomplish the challenges ahead of them. And then there's always the intrinsic aspect. The one comment I've heard over the years that always resonates with me is that the best people are ambitious for the company and not as ambitious for themselves.

TONY:

I love that.

BILL:

That said, you should never take ego out of the equation—you need that. But some people are in it for themselves and what they can get out of it, whether that be wealth, power, or notoriety. Others are ambitious to really solve a hard problem. To me, that means ambition for the company, and what motivates them. They will let few things stand in their way to get to the outcome.

TONY:

That is so simple and so clear. These criteria are fantastic.

CHRISTOPHER:

Let's shift back to a little bit about your business side. Growing a large investment firm takes a lot more than just making great investments. So beyond strong performance, what's been the primary reason for the success of the business? And what was the real fulcrum in your business that allowed you to take the leap from good to great?

BILL:

The three things that have led to our success include our focus on talent, culture, and process. At the end of the day, we must have great people. If we aren't absolutely committed to being a talent driven organization, we will lose. So, we have a relentless focus on talent and human capital, and developing our people as best we can.

Second is culture. This is hard to develop and build, and it's easy to lose. So, having the people and a commitment to maintaining a culture—not just talking about it, but living it—is vital.

Finally, as I mentioned, you can't grow without process. Whether it's an investment committee process or portfolio committee process, you have to pay attention to implementing the right processes to allow the organization to remain effective and do what it does.

One other thing is that you can't get talent and culture without liberally sharing the economics. If the senior professionals keep too much of the economics, they will not be able to attract and retain the next generation of great people. It's remarkable how many organizations do not follow that, and they will lose their way on talent and culture as a result.

My predecessor, Steve Denning, would always be on the side of taking less, giving more, and that's allowed us to attract great people. People want to stay; they want to build a career here.

CHRISTOPHER:

You grew up through the organization and then took over the helm of the organization. What's something that you wish somebody would've told you before you took the role that you have now?

BILL:

I'm good with numbers and financials. I think I'm pretty good on strategy. I think I'm good on selling and communicating. And then, you very quickly realize [success] comes down to people. **All the joys of the job are about people, and all of its challenges have to do with people.** No one explicitly told me about that, and I had to learn from experience. If you're an empathetic, caring person, it's hard. It should never feel easy, and it isn't easy.

CHRISTOPHER:

You know, it's fascinating to me to watch why some firms scale and get large, like General Atlantic has become, and others have not. As somebody who's built a firm the way that you have, over a long period of time, why do you think some firms are able to scale and others are not able to scale?

BILL:

I think it has to do with sharing the economics, but there are other important considerations as well. It's also about sharing responsibility and decision-making. Some of the best investors are great individual investors, but they want to control the decision-making. If you build a firm around that—a small cadre of people who are excellent investors—you're obviously going to be limiting your scale to what they're able to do. I can think of many firms that had tremendous ten- or twenty-year runs around a set of individuals or an individual, and then ultimately started to peter out because they could not scale beyond that group. And that might be because of the [lack of shared] economics, but maybe more than that.

TONY:

You talked earlier about your relentless focus on talent that picks up on this as well. I'd love to go a little deeper on that. When you think about the universe of investment talent, what do you think are the key traits that separate those peak performers from their peers?

BILL:

That's hard to pinpoint, Tony. It's the hardest thing to do, and it's why you need time to let people grow and evolve. At the end of the day, it's a wonderful blend of IQ and EQ that make great talent. People must be smart and highly motivated to succeed. You have to have a little bit of that insecurity as well, but good talent will be able to manage their ego in a way where they can synthesize this information, be strong listeners, and make good decisions. Let me try to make that more tangible. Take somebody who says, "I really want to do this investment because I believe in my gut this is a 3x outcome. I'm convicted [sic] about it, and I'm convicted [sic] for the right reasons."

Someone's going to put their ego aside, use their intellect, and get to a point where they can say, "I have the ability to bring all this information and all this uncertainty together and still have conviction and push it through an investment committee." For me, it's been hard to figure out who gets to that place, but you start to see it as the years go on.

TONY:

It actually reflects what you look at with the entrepreneurs as well, right? You're looking for the value system: Is it me, me, me? Or is it something larger than me that I'm invested in? Which is consistent with the entire culture that starts all the way back with your founders, So that's really beautiful. Just one last question. I'm just curious, when you look around and see people that have entered the business and they have that sense of absolute mission versus those that don't, where do you think that comes from? I know it's different for everybody, but underneath it all, is there a pattern you notice?

BILL:

It's hard [because] you're always making decisions under uncertainty. You never have all the information. If you come here and say, "I want to do this because I want to be really rich and I want to be a great private equity executive," you're probably going to fail all the way. If [instead] you love competing and you say, "I really want to find great investments, I want to learn my craft and be really, really good at it." And if you're intellectually curious, so meeting people, learning new things, and seeing new markets motivates you. If you're that kind of person, then this is the most fun business in the world because it's always changing. It's never static, never the same. It involves people, and you are always learning something.

When we first started, private equity was a backwater. No one knew what it was. We didn't even have a name for it. People came into it because they loved investing and they loved, in our case, company-building and working with entrepreneurs. We're a $11 trillion industry and I worry about people coming in and saying, this is the winning job. That actually scares me as a recruiter. I want [people who] say, I want it because I love this. Then I know they can get passionate about it and acquire the right skills.

CHAPTER 19

TONY FLORENCE

CO-PRESIDENT OF NEA

Accolades: Founded over forty years ago, NEA was one of the original Silicon Valley venture firms with notable early stage investments in Slack, Airbnb, and Stripe.

Total Asset Under Management (as of August 2023): $25 billion

Area of Focus: Technology and healthcare

HIGHLIGHTS

- NEA's assets under management have more than doubled over the last decade, totaling more than $25 billion as of March 31, 2023.
- The firm's investments across the spectrum of technology and healthcare have resulted in more than 270 IPOs and 450-plus mergers and acquisitions.
- NEA has helped build more than one hundred companies valued at $1 billion or more.
- The firm's portfolio companies have generated over $550 billion in cumulative market value.

TONY ROBBINS:

You have a seventeen-year storied career at NEA, and you've basically taken this technology division to another level. You've taken some big companies public, and you've sold some. How did you come to be in this position—the grandfather of all these venture firms?

TONY FLORENCE:

Well, my origins date back to Pittsburgh, Pennsylvania. And a lot of what I feel is behind what I focus on today was built back then. I developed a passion for a couple of things but one of them is certainly just having a very long-term perspective on people and recognizing that people can change in so many ways. It really gets back to entrepreneurship and the core fundamentals of what we do here. **Most of us had a combination of other people helping create some luck for us and then [we] have created our own luck with that.**

I had the good fortune to work with NEA for a long time when I was running tech banking at Morgan Stanley—another place that was foundational for me. The origin was that I really wanted to go work with young companies and help them on their decade-, two-decade-, three-decade-long journey and try to play a small role in helping people fulfill their visions and dreams, and the network effect that would have. And so, I started in that journey a long time ago and, as you've done and Christopher has done, it's just one day after the other.

TONY ROBBINS:

Tell us a little about a company like, let's say, a Casper or a Jet.com, that I know you guys sold to Walmart. Tell us what you saw in the beginning, how you look at a company like that, how you decide to make the investments. I'd love to hear some of the criteria that you look through.

TONY FLORENCE:

I tell you, Jet is a great example. That starts with a founder named Marc Lore. Marc was my first investment at NEA back in 2009. And to me, this is the hidden gem, the most fun and rewarding part of what I get to do. I'm going to be working with Marc till I end up not working anymore. I'm on my third company with Marc; I invested in Diapers.com with Marc originally, which became Quidsi. We sold that company to Amazon, and I had a front-row seat to a founder that built a business [that] started in his garage literally reselling diapers. He was a dad that was frustrated going to CVS and [them] being out of stock.

When I met Marc, and he told me the original reasons why he built that business, I knew that he would not stop until it was successful. It didn't matter what was in front of him. **And so, one of the key things that we look for is that level of endurance and obsession that it's not for the money and it's not for any recognition.** For Marc, in that particular case, it started with his passion and obsession as a customer and his wife's frustration, but then it became: How can I help every mom in the country?

I remember, I left my first meeting with Marc, and I called my partner. I said, "I've got my first investment. You guys are going to hate it but I'm just telling you this guy's going to win. He's selling 10 percent gross margin products on the internet, and he is going to beat Amazon." Six years later, Jeff Bezos was calling him, threatening him one minute, and the next minute, sweet-talking him into coming (into) to the company. And then I had the board of Walmart calling me saying, "Hey, why don't you guys sell to us?" And so, **I realized that a guy from New Jersey who started an idea in his garage around selling diapers online built something that had relevance for the two largest retailers in the country: Amazon and Walmart.**

This little idea built to half a billion dollars (in sales) and hundreds of employees and hundreds of thousands of customers that loved that a mom didn't have to go to the store anymore and could get stuff delivered tomorrow. I learned a lot from Marc around the power of that high-frequency customer relationship. If you win that, the rest is easy. For every two moms that came in, one never came back and the other came back twenty-six times.

We sold that for $3.5 billion. Lots of details in that story, but Marc was the central figure and the reason. I'm on my third company with Marc now, called Wonder, which I think in a decade will be his biggest company.

So, if I can have one of those in a career, let alone a couple, that's the fun thing. I think one of the best things about being an investor and being a founder and an entrepreneur is you have to be a good steward of risk and opportunity. And so, in Marc and many of the other founders I've worked with, they lean into risk, but they'll listen to data and to the market and to people and feedback, and they're happy to evolve their thinking and what they do along the way.

TONY ROBBINS:

You've seen so much in the e-commerce space. I read an article where you described two different types of people: the person that's there to solve the problem like Marc, and the person who really just sees how to streamline or maximize. Where does Casper [mattresses] fall in that as just an example? I'm curious of that story as an example. And then, I'd love to know along the way who really influenced you the most?

TONY FLORENCE:

I think Casper was a little bit of a different story. There was an efficiency story that took shape there where they collapsed the distribution chain and then, ultimately, the middleman. That's the power of the internet ultimately. There's a streamlining of distribution and they happen to get lucky with a little bit of a marketing twist. They had a bed in a box that created a viral video and that caught fire and helped them break out of a pack, if you will.

And so, there was a little bit of luck involved, a little bit of ingenuity, a little bit of the we can do it better than they can, but I think that business model really spoke to me because everybody in the country has to buy a mattress. It's a problem and an experience that everybody's been through to certain degrees, and there's nobody that would rate that as a positive experience. And so, at a minimum, you had a market that everybody could understand and an experience that everybody either was neutral on or didn't like.

And so, a couple young kids, literally, somebody from University of Texas and a few others that he brought along the way, had an idea that you could collapse that whole supply chain and distribution chain and make it efficient. And you could actually get (a mattress) delivered in a box to your house instead of having it be delivered or [driven] on the roof of the car. And they developed a brand around it. You had an internet-based company that used marketing to effectively build a really big business.

We try to help pull out a vision. Hopefully, it's crystallized a little bit and we help along the way in small ways to amplify the things that they need to realize the vision. These guys wanted to build something unique, and they did.

TONY ROBBINS:

Who influenced *you* the most along the way? What did you learn from that person? Maybe there have been more than one, I'm sure, in your life, but who would stand out for you?

TONY FLORENCE:

Well, nothing starts and stops without your grandmother and mother. So, for me, it's the two of them. I was raised by both my mom and grandmother, and then by my wife. So, I think that I would probably say that I've hit my stride more than even I expected just because of their collective support and steadfastness. I've [also] been very lucky to have a lot of mentors along the way both at NEA and outside of NEA. And the founders that I work with are the ones that I draw inspiration from every day.

I was talking with one of them this morning and it just got me really energized, really excited. I was like, "Okay, let's go figure this out." And so, to some extent, it's a daily thing to get energized in this business. At this point in my life, I look for inspiration and little snippets along the way, not for something dramatic. I've got a great foundation from my family and that's what centers me. Everything else is just gravy at this point.

CHRISTOPHER:

NEA is called both a venture firm and a growth firm. Obviously, you now have capital to deploy. What do you see as the greatest opportunities?

TONY FLORENCE:

There's no doubt that when we realize our fullest potential on behalf of our limited partners, we do two things really well. One is that we get in early to a company and we can help them over a decade or two decades. Some of our best companies that are $50 billion market caps didn't start out that way. They started out with a $5 million (investment) check and a couple people. So, that's really where we can participate in the most value creation and we've architected ourselves to be able to do that at every stage along the way with the same level of passion around risk and opportunity that we had ten years ago when we first got involved in the company. That's what commitment means from NEA.

On a Sunday, when I get a phone call, even if I've been working with this company for a decade, it's as if nothing else matters and it's all in at the same level of effort that I had from the beginning. Today, we're very lucky that we can pick points in time in a company's development where we can take advantage of those things. So, at the earliest stages, we're seeing dramatic opportunities in AI and what we see in software development. So, we were leaning in heavily in early stage and mid-stage investments there. And then, at the growth stage, we're waiting for that opportunity to really accelerate but we're starting to see real value in growth-stage development companies.

These are businesses that are established, their risk has been removed from the business model, and they just need capital to grow. **And we've been in an environment where that's been very difficult for young companies to get capital and so we're just starting to see the pricing dynamics become much more favorable.**

CHRISTOPHER:

Well, we had the opportunity at breakfast when you came down and spoke at our Themes event in January to debrief on what happened in the world that was 2022. What happened recently in the world of venture and growth that you really did not expect to happen as you look back post COVID through today? What's happened that you really did expect?

TONY FLORENCE:

The thing that jumps to the top of my head is we had a credit crisis in tech with SVB that nobody would have predicted. Fortunately, we got ahead of it and pulled our capital out of SVB before there was an issue. But I think the speed at which a large public company like that collapsed was probably the biggest surprise of the year for us. It seems like it was a long time ago. The other thing that's interesting is the market snapped back pretty quickly, so that's been a big surprise.

I think the second is that the public markets have recovered so quickly, particularly with the large-cap tech companies. We thought we'd be in a more prolonged environment of malaise, and we'd have a more difficult interest rate environment. And the economy has been a little stronger, and more buoyant than we expected.

CHRISTOPHER:

That leads to the next question. What are investors getting wrong when they're looking at venture and growth right now? What is it that they're just not either fully appreciating the risk of or fully appreciating the opportunity of?

TONY FLORENCE:

Well, **I think crises create opportunity and so there's been a liquidity and a capital market, and an interest rate crisis created.** And so, this is the time where you want to be leaning in on secondaries and things that are nontraditional. We are trying to do that as we think about our business in the secondaries and in credit and other places. The second thing I'd say is that innovation does not stop. People who are founding companies today, they're not as worried about the Fed and about the recession as the three of us may think.

And so, **you have to be time-diversified in venture capital and early stage investments, especially, and you have to have the right duration outlook.** There are companies being created last year, this year, next year, that, ten years from now, we're going to look back and [say], "Wow, that was an amazing time to be investing in venture capital." So, I think what's happened in our business is that it's become a little more cyclical than it should be because these are long-duration assets. It takes a long time to build a company and you can't time when the next Marc Lore walks in with a great idea that's going to take eight years to build. But when he does, it's going to be an amazing outcome for your LPs.

So, you have to manage that with the environment. We closed a big fund in February. **We believe it's a good time, a healthy time, to be responsible but to be investing. And I think that's sometimes hard for limited partners to understand because, when it's scary and raining outside, sometimes that's the best time to have a long-term outlook.**

CHRISTOPHER:

If somebody gave you a bucket of money and said, "I don't want it back for twenty years, twenty-five years, thirty years, would you be excited about that? Would you be afraid about that? You talked about how long it takes for these businesses to build, but the typical LP structure of having to return capital is the nature of the industry that we operate in. Yet, it feels like permanent capital would be such a better solution in the world of venture and growth.

TONY FLORENCE:

There's no doubt about it, and I think that a bit of the Holy Grail for a lot of investment firms is to have more permanent capital. That's why a lot of firms have gone public. We are always in search of that long-duration partner. We've got a few. We have not taken advantage of it just because we've got traditional structures. But we are absolutely trying to think through what the right balance is.

Again, every dollar that we take, we take with extreme levels of accountability and responsibility and so you'd have to have the right expectation with that. I think the industry, over time, will continue to mature. I think we feel the same way about venture and growth.

Our fund life is twelve years, which is much longer than a traditional fund. Typically, these funds are eight years, maybe ten, so we are on the longer side because of that exact reason. But the good news is that it hasn't kept us from trying to maximize value for our limited partners.

TONY ROBBINS:

You bring up the Holy Grail. That's the title of this book, *The Holy Grail of Investing*. Ray Dalio is a good friend of mine, I was interviewing him, digging in with him, and I said, "What's the single most important investment principle that guides your decision-making?" And his answer that he called the Holy Grail was that you should have eight to twelve uncorrelated investments. I'm curious, what do you perceive to be the Holy Grail of Investing as you look at it through your lens?

TONY FLORENCE:

Well, it is, and it isn't, Tony, just to be direct. Anybody that's in our business that hasn't read everything that Ray Dalio has written or that you've written about him is probably shortchanging himself. We're lucky that we get to read that stuff. Our firm was founded forty-five years ago with a hundred-year vision, and it always had a couple key things. One is that it always had tech and healthcare. So, by definition, we have uncorrelated investing activities just by nature of that. We have diversification that's probably more similar to what Ray is saying. We also dynamically allocate capital, which is another one of his principles, within a fund structure, based on an environment. **We might over-allocate to certain areas or under-allocate to other areas, and we have that flexibility carved into what we do.** Then, we have time diversification.

What's nice about what we do is that I'll make an investment today, but I have seven to eight years of investment decisions to make on that company. So, I have lots of time diversification to see what technology cycles have played out. The original idea and the original product or technology that we invested in, is it still relevant today? We lean into that.

And then, lastly, I would say that, because of our scale, we take small bets that are very uncorrelated, that are more futuristic, that may not be in classic social media or e-commerce or AI today, but they may be in a robotics or automation company that has nothing to do with 95 percent of our portfolio but, if it works, could be super special. Or we take a small bet in an area of life sciences like CRISPR. Back when we invested in CRISPR technology, it was so crazy but yet that was against the grain on everything that had been done in life sciences. And so, we have the ability to have these small experiments, but in small investments that don't risk a lot of capital but provide that nice level of diversification that you're talking about.

TONY ROBBINS:

You've worked with so many entrepreneurs over the years. If you had to come up with one, two, or three principles that you think make entrepreneurs successful across the board, what would stand out to you?

TONY FLORENCE:

I hate to be repetitive, but I would say one is that they're obsessed with what they're doing. **They obsess over the opportunity, and they obsess over the risk. Both of those are important.** Number two, they have a very clear vision for themselves that they can go and build around, recruit around. That's very, very important and they're able to communicate it. And the third is that they have something inside of them that you know is working for you twenty-four hours a day. It's not just the obsessed part but it's a belief that this has to happen; there's a reason that they exist.

When I was talking to Marc yesterday about his new company, he's literally like, "Tony, there are millions of people that need this," and he actually believes in his heart that what he's doing is an important thing and it has nothing to do with a scoreboard.

TONY ROBBINS:

Growing a large investment firm requires a lot more than just making great investments or [having] great performance. What do you think has been the primary reason for the success of your firm over, what, forty-five years? And was there a fulcrum point in your business where it allowed the company to really take off?

TONY FLORENCE:

I think, like everything, it gets back to we're a human capital organization. So, everything is about the people and the team. If you look at NEA, most people that join here end up retiring from here. Most of our partners have been here for fifteen, twenty years. It is a very, very tight culture based on teamwork, trust, and excellence, and we try to live that every day. We obsess over this stuff. Everything that we do has to reinforce the teamwork, trust, and excellence of our culture. And when we see things that are not aligned with that, we [remove] it really quickly, whether it's a person or behavior. And we try to structure the way we do things, the way we work, the way we credit, the way we incentivize people, all to reinforce those key parts of the culture.

The second thing I'd say is that we have a concept of shared outcomes. **At the end of the day, we're just a small part of a company's journey and a founder's journey,** and we have a whole team. So, on average, eight to ten people at NEA will touch a company and that's really important. If you talk to a founder of ours, they might say some nice things about one partner, but what we really want them to do is talk about NEA. What we really want them to do is talk about how all the people at NEA love what they do and leaned in and had enthusiasm. That shared outcome concept is so vital.

The last thing is that we have a long-term focus on relationships. So, we have some of our limited partners that have been with us for thirty years.

TONY ROBBINS:

Wow.

TONY FLORENCE:

When you can sit there and work with somebody over one or two or three decades, that's something to really treasure and be proud of. So, we take that approach to founders [too]. That long-term approach to relationships matters.

CHRISTOPHER:

What are a few things that, before you took the reins, you wish somebody would've told you?

TONY FLORENCE:

I don't think somebody could have said this, but I feel very privileged, way more privileged to be doing what I get to do today than I thought I would. I get to work with great people. It's a hard business to get right in; there's a lot of decisions every day that add up to the long-term. And so, the long-term consequences of our decisions are what we debate the most. It's very easy to make a quick decision in what we do. What's hard is to make those decisions in the context of what this could mean for when we're not here.

And so, the basic tenets of what you would want somebody to be thinking for you is how we try to manage the firm. We're all aggressive. We're all type A people. We are all competitive, but sometimes you have to be measured and thoughtful in the way you make real decisions that can seem very small in the moment and very easy to make but have long-term implications. That's something that we spent a lot of time with, and [at the beginning] I probably didn't appreciate it as much.

CHRISTOPHER:

It goes back to what you said earlier which is that the firm was started forty-five years ago with a hundred-year horizon. That's such a beautiful way to look at it. If you could do anything over in your business with the benefit of hindsight, what would you do differently?

TONY FLORENCE:

I come from a bit of a nothing background in Pittsburgh and a conservative background from Morgan Stanley and so I obsess over not losing money. That's the thing, you don't want to lose money as an investor. But you got to take risk. In our business, I would say that we probably could [have taken] some more risk at certain points in time. So, if I look back to 2008 and '09, I wish we had probably taken a little more risk back in those days when we probably had a position of strength like we do now. I would say, right after COVID, things happened so quickly but there was a moment, a six-to-twelve-month moment, where there was an enormous amount of opportunity created.

In hindsight, we haven't made a lot of mistakes and we haven't stubbed our toe. But there were a bunch of things that I knew were great investments in those time periods [and] I just said now's not the right time to step on the gas because you just don't know. It's very easy in hindsight to say what I'm saying but, yeah, I wish we had done a few of those.

CHRISTOPHER:

We make the best decision we can with the information that's available to us at that point in time. You all have built what is a very unusual business which is a venture and growth business that has lasted for a very long time and gotten to enormous size and scale. What are the reasons why you believe most investment firms cannot scale or don't make that step to that long-term business?

TONY FLORENCE:

It's so funny, two weeks ago I had a dinner in New York with eleven or twelve PE and hedge fund heads or CEOs. We were all talking about this a little bit. I think it comes back to [that] there's a lot of psychology involved in being financial entrepreneurs. At the end of the day, an investment firm is typically run by financial entrepreneurs and it's hard to get aligned. You have personalities and people's lives change. We actually track the firms that were in a great position but didn't survive because we want to be humbly reminded of the fact that company X in 1996, '97, '98, and '99 were the best firms in our industry and they're nowhere today.

Why is that?

It's because, typically, the partners didn't get along, they had misalignment, they didn't have the long-term objectives right, and frankly, I think they didn't really want to sacrifice for scale. You got to really have a vision for what you want to be ten, fifteen, twenty years, and they're more in the moment. Just like building a company, you have to have a vision for scale, and you have to be able to put the pieces in place and be willing to continue to do that even when it's not obvious. A lot of venture firms have avoided scale. It's a very comfortable business to have four people around the table and they don't want to bring on partners and have the complications of making decisions and accountability. You have to really be willing to give back into the firm and the team more than you get—that's the bottom line.

TONY ROBBINS:

Tony, when you think about the universe of investment talent out there, what do you believe are some of the key traits that separate the highest performers from their peers? Because the building of the business really comes down to the people, right?

TONY FLORENCE:

You have to have a great investment team and you have to always be restocking the bench. In our business, we obsess over performance, so we take that very seriously on an annual basis and we try to make sure that we are hiring better people than we have today always and pushing ourselves. And I think you have to balance being willing to give people a lot of autonomy. You have to always balance that because you have to give people enough room to grow. Because we've been a growing firm, we've always had enough opportunity for people and creating that opportunity is really important to attract some of the best people.

TONY ROBBINS:

So, you're looking out for people that have their own sense of vision, the people that can build those same types of trusting relationships, the people that can balance the risk versus opportunity, those basic fundamentals that you talked about earlier then. Is that right, Tony?

TONY FLORENCE:

Yeah, absolutely. And I think, when you're recruiting people, you want people that are going to make you better, going to make the firm better, and going to bring something incremental. It could be a different type of background. It could be a different way of thinking; it could be a different level of ambition. Those things are good, and you have to be willing to take a little bit of that personal risk with people because that's important to continue to stay fresh.

CHAPTER 20

BOB ZORICH

COFOUNDER OF ENCAP INVESTMENTS

Accolades: EnCap is one of the top ten energy investors in the U.S. Zorich is a member of the Independent Petroleum Association of America and also serves on the board of several Houston charities, including the WorkFaith Connection and the Hope and Healing Center.

Total Asset Under Management (as of August 2023): $40 billion

Area of focus: Growth capital for independent energy companies

HIGHLIGHTS

- Zorich and his partners have successfully raised and managed $40 billion across twenty-four funds, attracting the trust and support of over 350 institutional investors from around the globe.
- Having an unwavering commitment to identifying and nurturing talent, EnCap has backed over 275 startup energy companies throughout their history.
- These teams used experience and focus to create billions of value for investors and were key instigators to the shale revolution.

To get started, please tell us your origin story, how you ended up where you are, and a little bit about the business.

I grew up in the Bay Area in what became the Silicon Valley. Born and raised there. Steve Jobs was five years behind me in high school, same high school, Wozniak one year behind. My dad was not an engineer, but a lot of other people's dads were. So, it was a competitive environment and was something I likely benefited from. Anyway, I went to college at UC Santa Barbara, got my undergraduate degree in economics, and met and married my current wife of fifty-one years. We moved to Phoenix, where I received my master's from Thunderbird and then we moved to Dallas, where I joined the Energy Department of Republic National Bank of Dallas in 1974. So, you know, about fifty years in the business. So, energy was not anything I knew anything about, but it was really the premier place within the bank to operate. Instead of participating in New York–originated loans, we were one of the leaders in energy financing. And one of the things I quickly learned about oil and gas is that it is difficult for those outside of oil and gas to understand. It is a very nuanced field. Engineers can ascribe a value to a property, but if you don't know what assumptions were used to generate the value number then you cannot understand the qualitative importance of the value ascribed.

Fast-forward, I went to London and I did some things with the bank—big North Sea financings—and I gained some confidence in myself and the ability to compete against very smart people. I also learned, when I went to London, that working for myself and getting up every day, and getting to go do things that would change the outcome of my life was fun. Harrowing at times, but fun. This experience caused me to embrace the concept of leaving the bank when that opportunity arose in the early 1980s. One of my best friends at Republic and I left the bank together to form a startup oil company in 1981.

We did that for five or six years in the early eighties, during a period of time when prices were going down. But we got to learn a lot more about oil and gas and about all of the technical and operational details that allow one to evaluate risk and values. If you recall, the oil market crashed in 1986 and we sold our company. We had five tiers of preferred stock, so we learned a lot about capitalization, capital structure, risk, bank debt, and so forth. At that point, I had almost fifteen years of experience in investing in and managing oil and gas risk. I moved to Houston to work for a money manager who managed pension fund money. They had a mezzanine debt product that was oil and gas related. In the middle of the crisis, I started my job with them. By 1988, it appeared to me that they were too narrowly focused on expensive debt. Mentioned that to my boss and my boss said that he wanted to continue focusing on the mezzanine product. While grateful for the opportunity, my desire to follow my instincts led me to think about doing something else. Discussed the opportunity to bring oil and gas financial product to the institutional community with my former oil company partner, and we decided to discuss the idea with two other top oil and gas Republic Bank friends, and the concept of EnCap was born. So that partnership has endured now for thirty-five years. **The real simple concept, Christopher, was to use our experience and contacts to deliver high-quality oil and gas investment product to the institutions.** So that's what we did.

CHRISTOPHER:

It's interesting because when you think about EnCap, you are oil and gas people who are really, really good at finance as opposed to finance people who think they're going to be good at oil and gas. I think that's been a real edge that EnCap has brought to the equation for a long time. Going back a little bit, who is the most important person that shaped your success, and how did they do that?

BOB:

You know, I've given a little bit of thought to that over time. **I really attribute my success to my partners and our collective character. You know, working hard, showing up, treating others as you want to be treated, and doing the right thing has driven all of us.** Maybe ultimately the attribution should go to our parents who raised us. Also, my wife is clearly responsible for helping support me in all the time and work it took to make EnCap a success. Without my partners, I wouldn't be as successful. So, I think when it comes to character, once you decide you're going to be in a certain lane, then you want to work with other people that also want to be in that lane. Looking back after thirty-five years I can only be grateful for the fate that brought us all together.

CHRISTOPHER:

What's the greatest opportunity for investors when they're looking at energy, you know, as we move forward from 2023 and beyond?

BOB:

Today, you've got this overlay—the world policymakers have decided that there's a weather model that indicates that too much CO_2 in the air will eventually superheat the earth. At least that's the summary thesis. There is some evidence that 600 million years ago, there was a lot of CO_2 in the atmosphere and the earth was very warm. Of course, a lot of things have happened over the 600 million years. I've read a lot about modeling, and because models have limited variables relative to the real world, they tend to overlook certain variables which can cause the outcomes to be quite different from the model. Econometrics and weather modeling are two good examples of being interesting but unreliable. So basing decisions and policies on an imperfect model creates an opportunity today. Simply put, we are not being efficient with the dollars we are investing relative to the impacting energy output. If you think about energy as though it were food and you are trying to feed the world, you need to invest in high-calorie food to be most efficient. You have to eat many pounds of kale for every pound of protein to get the same calorie intake. Similarly with energy, oil, gas, coal, and nuclear are your protein-equivalent dense fuels. Wood, solar, and wind are the kale low-density equivalents. Our policies are directing our capital toward low-density answers and away from high-density solutions. The result will be a train wreck as we will find ourselves short of the energy required to fuel the world's energy demand. **This makes this period unique and will result in unusual low-risk high-return investment opportunities when the policymakers wake up to the need for energy-dense solutions.**

> Our policies are directing our capital toward low-density
> answers and away from high-density solutions. The result
> will be a train wreck as we will find ourselves short of the
> energy required to fuel the world's energy demand.

CHRISTOPHER:

I would say that probably pretty close to 99 percent of people would never think about an energy investor today not being involved in the exploration side, but rather focusing on the engineering side. In this day and age, we just have to figure out how to get to it, as you put it. And so that's a very different risk-reward than what the vast majority of people realize is going on in the actual deployment of capital. And so, when you think about that train wreck, as you put it, of potentially underinvesting in fossil fuels, overinvesting in renewables, not getting enough yield from the renewables to offset the decline that's inevitable in fossil fuels, is that a three-year problem? Is it ten years?

BOB:

I think it is very apparent that it's happening. I don't think it's even close to being a mystery. But the combination of social media, the real media, wishful thinking, uninformed policymakers, and so on, they all kind of come together to create this misadventure that we're on. And it's obvious. It's going to happen. When does the Western world wake up to that? Hopefully three years but maybe ten?

Every country will be impacted differently by this train wreck. Those with energy resources—the U.S., Canada, Australia, Russia—will be in better shape; those without—China, Europe, Africa—will be at a disadvantage. Other non-energy issues will also create complications with energy maybe being the catalyst of a totally changed landscape.

TONY:

So, when you think about the last five, six, seven years, the energy world has changed a lot. But what has happened that you really expected to happen? And what has happened that you really didn't expect to happen?

BOB:

I think the failure of the European experiment, so quickly, it surprised me. You know, the failure of Europe's various decisions, whether they're stopping all nuclear, relying on Russian gas, building windmills, or building solar in Northern Europe. I lived in Northern Europe for three and a half years—I bet we saw the sun three weeks a year. Things like that have amazed me. And then the failure of the same policymakers anywhere in the world wanting to learn from that error is equally astounding. Most people in our industry kind of shake our heads at this and think it's obvious. There's a guy in Missouri who runs a co-op, an energy co-op, and he said exactly the truth: which is you cannot count on renewables as part of your baseload capacity. Because the wind may not blow, and the sun may not shine. So, if your people need energy 24/7 or some component of it, you can't rely on it. And if you're in charge of that process, and you're given a mandate that you use renewable first, it flips the logic. It's all turned upside down, unfortunately.

CHRISTOPHER:

You've been in the industry obviously for a long, long time. What has happened that you've expected to happen?

BOB:

Well, the success of the shales was very predictive. It's an interesting world we live in because there's always somebody saying something negative about everything. And yet, when you know your space, you can have confidence that what you're doing makes sense. And even though the oil industry was castigated for making a lot of bad investments, the truth of the matter is they made a lot of investments that were generally very good. What wasn't good was stability of pricing and cost structure. But when prices go up, cost structure will eventually go up, and that takes away a lot of the margin that was originally forecast by companies who bought the leases.

In our case, we tried to be very prudent about land prices paid and we only used leverage modestly against proven production-related cash flow. But we were not perfect. The bottom line is that the industry was by and large not irresponsible, but twenty-twenty hindsight measured by changing variables can make many industries look fragile from time to time, particularly those who used debt in any meaningful way.

CHRISTOPHER:

When you talk to investors now, people who are actually looking at the industry and considering making investments in the industry, what are they getting wrong when they think about investing in energy today?

BOB:

Honestly, there are so few of them, I don't think any of them are getting it wrong. I think a lot of people are staying away from fossil fuels because of their board and/or their committees. Some of them have come back and have continued to invest in things that make sense. EnCap is the top-performing fund in many of our investors' portfolios because we're returning a lot of cash and they can see it. But their boss can't go to committee with a fossil fuel investment for political reasons. Eventually, I believe this will change.

CHRISTOPHER:

So, switch gears just a little bit. If you had the attention of the world for five minutes, what would you tell them about the ramifications of not investing properly in traditional energy along with renewable or green energy?

BOB:

I think the message would involve focusing on fundamental truths and believing what your own brain tells you will happen relative to fundamentals. The importance of density relative to energy solutions is one of those fundamentals. The importance of energy relative to human flourishing. **We need policies that promote energy for human flourishing that also cause respect for the environment we live in.** This is a world problem and not a Western problem. **There are 7 billion folks who are not part of the West and they need energy and solutions to make it work for the world and they are capital constrained.**

CHRISTOPHER:

So, aside from the strong performance, which obviously you have had, what's been the primary reason for the success of EnCap?

BOB:

I'd say we're adaptable. I don't think any of the four of us could have accomplished what we accomplished just on our own. I think the strength of the rope with four strands to it is the reason for our success. And the ability to stay together and not cut each other's strand over that period of time has been highly beneficial for all of us and the success of EnCap.

TONY:

What was the fulcrum point that allowed your business to take the leap from a good business to a great business and really accelerate the growth?

BOB:

Well, without a track record, you can't establish yourself in this business. So, we built the track record of safe, consistent, solid returns in our early years. That was important. But then, staying within our focus area has also been important. **The exogenous events that include the shale revolution and our quick adaptability to that new set of economics and opportunity was one critical fulcrum point.** Others, who approached the business with a less technically driven decision process were slower to adapt. It allowed us to be very successful and grow substantially during that period.

CHRISTOPHER:

What are a few things you wish somebody would've told you before you started your firm?

BOB:

You know, it's honestly nothing because it would've robbed us of the joy of discovery. **I think you need to be tested by mistakes and learn from them and embrace them.** So, I'm happy our partnership got to search for the best practices as the opportunities unfolded. Maybe our common credit backgrounds made this process a lot easier to reach agreement on decisions along the way.

CHRISTOPHER:

None of us like going through what we go through in our path to growth, but when we look back with hindsight, usually we look back and go, you know, I'm glad I went through that because it made me stronger, made me wiser, made me realize different things. How would you have done things differently with the benefit of hindsight?

BOB:

I think with the objective being to finish strong, I'm perfectly happy the way it worked. Were there ways to make more money? Sure. Were there ways to do this or that, but those would've involved sacrifice on the family side, or a sacrifice within the partnership? It's hard to second-guess. You know, when the whole turns out in a complete baked cake that tastes good, it's hard to second-guess.

CHRISTOPHER:

Why do you think most firms are not able to scale?

BOB:

I go back to the adaptability thing. We saw many people struggle with shales because the technology was more complicated. Our partnership embraced involvement because the technical risk was actually lower. I think having a partnership, which I mentioned earlier, gave EnCap four different points of view on what was best and safe. And I think that's healthy. And the one thing you do learn is nobody's point of view is flawless. So, there are flaws, but I think you avert the biggest mistakes when you have more than one point of view to consider.

CHRISTOPHER:

You know, when you are talking about people, obviously people are a complicated animal, and so partnerships are complicated. What are those traits that separate the highest performers from their peer group?

BOB:

The character piece is number one. Everybody can perform differently yet still fit into the team, so to speak, if they have character. **We all showed up, worked hard, and were curious and able to defend our point of view within our boundaries of providing a safe, solid return on investment.** We had individual thoughts but a common goal of providing safe and sound investments to our institutional clients.

TONY:

Bob, one time I was speaking at one of the J.P. Morgan summits that they do for about 250 people and they're all billionaires. Ray Dalio was [speaking] right before me and he said that the Holy Grail of Investing is finding eight to twelve uncorrelated investments you believe in that will reduce your risk by 80 percent. There is no more important principle to him. That's part of the thesis of the book. We'd love to know what is the Holy Grail of Investing in your view, after decades of investing in the energy sector?

BOB:

You know, Tony, we view our investing much like we view our lives. You have to stick with values in order to be happy long-term. For us, what that means is reducing risk relative to what we're trying to accomplish. If you think about real estate, you think about your apartments full of people. They're paying you checks every month. That is pretty safe. If you think about oil and gas, the equivalent of that are wells that have been drilled and are producing and have a cash flow stream. And there are other methods even to protect against the rent payments, if you will, such as hedging that can reduce your risk. The other extreme would be exploration. You're going to a place where no well has been drilled before. And you can assume you're going to have a 10 percent chance of success if you're lucky and have used the best science available. We've always stayed away from those kinds of things. We don't like to fret about those kinds of risks. And so that's really been our Holy Grail, if you want to call it that. It is to establish some values around risk and around what we're trying to do. They can be operational, price, or production related. As you watch the facts unfold, you establish where you are and where you are not going to step with the business.

TONY:

So, one of the ways you've done that is by partnering with mature companies and then agreeing on that growth plan. Asymmetrical risk-reward is everybody's dream, obviously. But the way you do that is by reducing the risk as much as possible. I understand exploration. My hat's off to the people that can do that. I would be quite uncomfortable with a 10 percent chance of success in something.

BOB:

We actually partnered with lean but mature and seasoned management teams who were likely trained at mature companies. **We always tried to only partner with seasoned teams that viewed risk like we did.** Our capital was only released in quantity into situations where the growth had a high probability of success. That kept us primarily in the area of developing already proven concepts.

CHRISTOPHER:

The interesting thing about what Bob is describing, Tony, is how it fits with so many of the other concepts that we've talked about. While [EnCap] is not going out and doing real estate, credit, etc., inside of their space the same rules still apply—eight to twelve non-correlated asset streams, which in their particular case could be different basins in different parts of the country. It could be drilling in different areas of depth. It could be infrastructure versus upstream. All of these don't necessarily correlate to each other.

BOB:

The basic premise that supported the formation of EnCap is that oil and gas is complicated to invest in. An example would be understanding shale production. The big concept is that you had large geographic areas where there was a lot of oil in place, and simply by cracking the rock, you can get more oil or gas out. If you understood the dynamics of the reservoir and the history of the rock, you could then begin to understand which areas were going to give up economic quantities and which areas were not. There were ways to minimize risk and, at same time, apply reasonably proven technology to get economic returns. If you take that story to Wall Street, and you're going as somebody who needs their money not as somebody who is protecting their money, then there's a misalignment of interest. The guy with the gifted tongue possibly wins and the investor possibly loses. When that happens enough times, people start to stay away from the industry, and it gains a reputation for being high risk when, in fact, if you are deep in the weeds within the industry, you can understand the difference between the risk profile of different assets and different opportunities and assist the institutions you represent by keeping the risk profile low on the investment.

TONY:

You've certainly ridden decades of ups and downs that the industry goes through. And you've obviously had to manage your risk incredibly well to do as well as you've done on $40 billion of investment. I'm curious, what's your view of the most promising green energy? So much green energy has been promoted and yet doesn't seem to be ready for prime time. You guys have made investments in that area, if I understand correctly. What's your mindset?

BOB:

Our investment targets in that space are in areas where something is going to be safe, proven, but economically disruptive. We're not in the business to make a 3 to 4 percent rate of return on a piece of contracted infrastructure. So, we hired experts in that area that had been in the power business for a long time to be our investment staff. Their view was that batteries were the most disruptive space. Simply put, if you can place a battery in an area where existing infrastructure already exists, you have all the things you need to be able to disperse the energy from those batteries out into the grid in a very cost-effective way. **You can power the batteries up during low-cost times and dispatch power very similar to gas storage when prices go up.** That is one example of how we think about making a solid returning yet safe investment in the green space. And our first energy transition fund looks like it's going to be a very high rate of return over a four-year period. Good quality deals and management teams. Our second fund is going to be focused similarly but will include different opportunities.

You know, the Inflation Reduction Act doesn't mean a thing in terms of inflation reduction. But it is going to change the economic landscape. You can't deny the fact that subsidy is going to influence investment activity. When the volume of that subsidy is put into the marketplace, there's going to be a lot of money spent in a lot of directions and some of it will not turn out very well. **Our focus will be on areas with established proven management and technologies where the application can be implemented with a reliable economic benefit.**

CHAPTER 21

DAVID GOLUB

FOUNDER OF GOLUB CAPITAL

Accolades: Awarded "Lender of the Decade" by *Private Debt Investor* magazine
Total Asset Under Management (as of August 2023): $60 billion
Area of Focus: Private credit lending

HIGHLIGHTS

- David Golub has been named by *Private Debt Investor* as one of the thirty top change-makers driving the evolution and growth of the private credit asset class.
- Golub Capital has received numerous accolades, including the prestigious PDI Lender of the Decade, Americas, award in 2023 and has also been recognized as Lender of the Year in the Americas in 2015, 2016, 2018, 2021, and 2022.
- Mr. Golub has invested in over one thousand companies and has been a contributor to the *Wall Street Journal*, the *New York Times*, and *Bloomberg Businessweek*.

- Mr. Golub created the "Golub Capital Altman Index," which has become a key, widely anticipated measure of performance in middle-market private companies.

CHRISTOPHER:

How did you end up where you are today, leading one of the largest private credit firms in the world?

DAVID:

I love telling Golub Capital's origin story. Flash back a few decades and imagine the Golub family dinner table. My brother Lawrence is eleven, and I am nine. Mom and Dad are talking about psychotherapy. Again. By way of background, both my parents were psychotherapists. Just imagine how desperate my brother and I were to change the subject. So we did what kids normally do—we came up with a business plan to create a middle-market lending firm.

Okay, that's a tall tale. The only true part is that my parents were both psychotherapists. The truth of how Golub Capital came to be is really a story about serendipity and path-dependency.

I started my career as a private equity investor. My brother started as an investment banker and later as a private equity investor. **In the late 1990s, we both had the same insight, which was that the private equity industry was going to continue to grow and prosper. And with that growth, we saw a huge opportunity to create a lending business to serve private equity sponsors.** What happened after that included a lot of luck. The financial crisis distracted a bunch of lenders that were less careful about underwriting and financing than we were. And, as much as we had high hopes in the 1990s about how much the private equity industry was going to grow, it has grown much more than anybody expected. So, the Golub Capital origin story is like a lot of origin stories. It's one that started with a good idea—the idea of creating a partnership-oriented specialty lender to private equity–backed companies. **But how we got to be as big as we are today— that's as much a story about surprises, coincidences, and luck as it is a story about great design.**

TONY:

Along the way, who is the most important person in your life that shaped your success and how did they influence you?

DAVID:

I've had a lot of mentors who've been really important to me. My mentors have been critical in my development as a leader and in the success of my firm. One of my mentors was Jay Fishman. Jay was my first boss when I came out of business school and started my career at what was then Shearson Lehman American Express. Jay later went on to become chairman and CEO of Travelers. Jay taught me many things, but the most important was how to be a good leader and how to be kind at the same time. **Learn everybody's name, even the building staff. Go out of your way to be there for employees who get into difficulties. And be careful what you ask your people to do.** Jay had an aphorism about this. He said, "Be careful what you ask your people to do, because they'll do it."

One of the tricks in life is to learn from other people's mistakes in addition to your own. And one of the reasons I think mentors can be so valuable is, often, they can share with you wisdom that comes from decisions they wish they'd made differently.

CHRISTOPHER:

And many times they also have observed other people make mistakes, right? There's a lot of shared collective wisdom across their ecosystem and their network that they developed over time. Let's pivot to the investment world for a minute, and let's talk about private credit, and let's talk about the world that you operate in every day. Where is the greatest opportunity for investors who are looking at private credit today?

DAVID:

To answer your question, I need to start with a bit of a philosophy statement about how I approach investing and how we as a firm approach investing. Some people think investing is different from other businesses. They believe good investors are geniuses. Think Warren Buffett or Bill Ackman. I think those kinds of individuals are extremely rare. **I think good investing** businesses don't rely on a genius behind the curtain. Instead, good investing businesses are like other good businesses in the sense that they have some identifiable and really compelling sources of competitive advantage. So, in our business, the key to success is having a set of competitive advantages that give us an ability to produce consistent premium returns over time.

What kinds of advantages am I talking about? Let me tell you about several. First, we're big believers in relationships. We work with the same core group of about two hundred private equity firms over and over again. They represent a very small subset of the private equity universe, but they're 90 percent of our business every year. They like working with us—repeatedly—because they like our capabilities and our approach. We can help them with a wide array of their financing needs. We can do small transactions and large transactions. We have deep expertise across a variety of different industries. We can help their companies grow by providing more financing for acquisitions or capital spending programs. We can add value to their diligence processes. We're win-win oriented—so, if there's a hiccup, if there's a bump in the road, we're going to be very solution-oriented with them and not try to hold them up. Another example: We can give them solutions that they can't easily find elsewhere. We were a pioneer in the development of what's called one-stop, or unitranche, loans. It's a way of financing companies that makes it much easier to do acquisitions than the traditional multilayer capital structure that's very hard to manage.

Those are some examples of ways in which we come to the table with a distinctive approach. And that distinctive approach in turn makes us a compelling partner to our customers.

CHRISTOPHER:

So, you know the industry's changed here in the last year pretty dramatically simply because of the change in the interest rate regime. When people think about credit, they think about that as a negative. Just for the benefit of the audience, would you mind talking through why rising interest rates is less of an issue or even a positive for a private credit firm such as Golub.

DAVID:

Sure. **We've been big beneficiaries of rising rates.** We lend on a floating-rate basis; we earn a spread over a base rate called SOFR. So, a typical loan that we would make in today's environment would be SOFR (secured overnight financing rate) plus 6 percent. And SOFR today is about 5 percent. To your point, Christopher, a little over a year ago, SOFR was at roughly 1 percent. **So, where a typical loan that we were holding a year and a half ago would be paying us 7 percent, that same loan to that same borrower today would be paying us 11 percent.** That's good for our investors. The flip side is that borrowers have to pay a higher amount in interest expense, and that puts more pressure on them. It eats into their margin of safety. At some level of interest rates, the balance shifts from this being good for investors to being bad for investors because borrowers can't afford to pay the higher rates—but that's not where we are today.

CHRISTOPHER:

I think investors of all levels of sophistication failed to anticipate the rising rate regime and how it would change the perspective of different asset classes. It's one of the things that made us very, very optimistic about private credit as an asset class and particularly about acquiring stakes in firms that are in the private credit world because of the benefit that they are deriving from the higher rates. As you said, credit quality is still very important, and the ability to avoid defaults and those kinds of things. As we think out over the next three to ten years, what would you say is your outlook for private credit as an industry, and specifically, what impact could interest rates have over that period of time?

DAVID:

I think there's an important contrast between the short-term outlook and the medium- to long-term outlook. Start with the short-term outlook. We're in a bit of a strange time right now. We've been through this very rapid increase in interest rates. We are seeing this very rapid decline in inflation. The economy's a bit muddling. Equity values have dropped significantly. And as a consequence of that panoply of factors, and the uncertainty associated with them, we're seeing a slowdown in deal activity. Private equity firms are having trouble reaching agreement with sellers on price. Some private equity firms are putting off selling because they think things will be better in the future. So, right now we're seeing a favorable environment for the kind of lending that we do, but not as many new transactions as we'd like—the food is good, but the portions are small.

Now, let's take the longer-term view. While I can't tell you exactly when deal activity is going to speed up, I think it's very clearly a question of "when"—not "if." Looking out over the next three to seven years, our business has three fundamental tailwinds. The first tailwind is that the private equity ecosystem is going to grow significantly. We know that because there's about $2 trillion today of committed-but-uninvested capital in the private equity ecosystem. And that "dry powder" has a time fuse on it. Private equity firms have to use it over the course of the coming several years, or they lose access to it. I've been in this business for thirty years. I know that when you have that combination of factors, the capital's going to get used.

The first tailwind is that the private equity ecosystem is going to grow significantly. We know that because there's about $2 trillion today of committed-but-uninvested capital in the private equity ecosystem. And that "dry powder" has a time fuse on it. Private equity firms have to use it over the course of the coming several years, or they lose access to it.

The second factor is that historically the private equity ecosystem has looked for debt capital from both private credit players like Golub Capital and from the liquid credit market. **Over the last few years, the private credit market has been taking share from the liquid credit market, and I think that trend is likely to continue.** There are a variety of different reasons for this. One of the really important reasons is that the private credit industry's gotten big. And so, it's capable now of providing solutions for much larger companies than it used to be able to provide solutions for. In 2019, it was unusual to find a $500 million private credit deal. In 2023, we have had a $5 billion private credit deal. So, the second tailwind is that we're gaining (market) share.

The third tailwind is within the private credit industry. If you look at who's winning and who's not winning within the private credit industry, the winners are the larger players—those with scale, the capacity to provide a wide variety of different solutions, deep expertise across a range of industries, long track records of reliability. Again, this is predictable. If you imagine yourself as the CEO of a leading private equity firm, you too would choose to work with the largest, most scaled private credit players. So, the third big tailwind means that we and a couple of other large players are going to gain share within our industry.

CHRISTOPHER:

When you think about what's happened with the interest rate cycle, when you think about what's happened within the industry as a whole, what has happened recently that you did not expect to occur, and what has happened that you really expected to occur?

DAVID:

I'm going to start with what I didn't expect, although maybe I should have expected it. **One of the most consistent patterns in the history of finance is that banks make big mistakes.** Not every bank and not every year. In hindsight, I should not have been surprised that some banks were unprepared for the steep increase in interest rates we've seen since early 2022.

Something that does not surprise me is the continued outperformance of private equity. I've got a different take on this phenomenon than I've heard from many others. My take is that private equity competes very well against the two other principal forms of business ownership. The first of those is being publicly owned. Anyone who has served as an executive, board member, or advisor of a public company knows how challenged the public model has become. There is a heavy cost and regulatory burden, and unless you're a very large company, you don't get good research analyst coverage, you don't have good liquidity in your shares, and you don't get a strong valuation. **Being public for all but very large companies is a very flawed model.**

The second form of ownership is family ownership. This can be good for the entrepreneur-founder, but then things get difficult. Imagine an entrepreneur creates a company. The entrepreneur makes all the decisions—governance is simple! Maybe even one generation later this works because the entrepreneur only has a couple of kids and the kids all agree about how to operate the company. But as the group gets larger, maybe a third generation, it gets very difficult to maintain consensus among the owners. You need to navigate compensation for family members when some family members want to work in the business, and others don't. Some maybe want liquidity, and some don't want liquidity. It is just very, very challenging.

So, my take on the success of private equity is for many businesses it's just a better ownership model than either public ownership or family ownership. I think we're likely to see private equity continue to expand.

CHRISTOPHER:

There's so much press around some of the higher-profile transactions that either have worked or not worked over time in the private equity world. There's very little, and certainly not enough coverage in my opinion, of all the hundreds and hundreds of success stories where companies have been able to be improved dramatically. And so, it's a really interesting perspective to hear you say that related to private equity.

When investors are trying to decide where they should allocate assets, what are they getting wrong when they think about private credit?

DAVID:

I think what some investors get wrong about private credit is that they underestimate the incentives for mediocrity at big brand-name asset management firms. It's hard to be great at many different investment strategies. **Instead of focusing on giant firms with well-known brands, I suggest focusing on managers with clear, identifiable sources of edge.** Who has a proven track record in that niche? Who has competitive advantages that will enable them to sustain that track record over time? In many cases, figuring this out is not very complicated, but my experience is that often investors flock to a well-known name instead of doing the work.

CHRISTOPHER:

Let's pivot a little bit and give you the opportunity to talk to the world. If you had the attention of the world for a few minutes, what would you tell them?

DAVID:

I'm a giant believer in the impact of nonprofits. **We may be a polarized country politically, but I think almost all of us can agree that thriving, effective nonprofits have a hugely positive impact on American life.** So, my message, Christopher, is really simple: Get involved in a local nonprofit. Pick something that you're passionate about. It could promoting music and the arts, it could be serving the unhoused, it could be combating drug addiction—any of a variety of different things. I'd encourage everybody to find a nonprofit that they want to get involved with. I think you'll find it to be life-transforming.

TONY:

You talked a lot about having a clearly defined niche, and edge is the word you used. What else would you say has been important for the success of Golub Capital?

DAVID:

Success in business is complicated, but I tell you that every successful business I've gotten close to over time has had some core principles that are reflected in everything that they do. We've got two core principles. The first we already talked about—investing's hard, but it's not different from any other business. You can't rely on a genius sitting in the corner. You can't rely on a proprietary model. **You've got to figure out a set of competitive advantages, and you got to nurture those advantages over time so that you can outcompete your competition.** The second principle that underlies our business is that relationships matter. We're old-fashioned. We don't believe in the modern Wall Street mantra that everybody's a counterparty. We think good businesses work with the same parties over and over again. They work with the same suppliers, with the same customers, with the same investors. And they do that because they're able to develop a compelling value proposition for each of these groups so that each of these groups wants to work with that company, over and over again.

These two principles are very guiding. They have led us to sustain a very narrow mission: to be best at sponsored finance. We're not trying to be best at real estate. We're not trying to be best at oil extraction. We're trying to be best at making loans to companies that are controlled by private equity firms.

And we also have a very clear culture that, again, goes with the two core principles. Our culture is defined by two words: gold standard. And what we mean by gold standard is that we treat all our partners the way we would want to be treated if we were on the other side of the table.

CHRISTOPHER:

You've had a fantastic, long career at Golub Capital. But there are always things that we learn along the way that are sometimes less pleasant. What are some things that you wish you had been told before you started the business to spare you some of those less pleasant learning experiences?

DAVID:

That's a really long list. We've made a ton of mistakes over the years. **One of the things I have learned is the value of process and investment infrastructure. The non-glamorous parts of a business often don't get enough attention.** In lending, that's a mistake. We learned early that this was an area that we needed to really focus on, and it's become one of our core strengths. But I wish somebody had told me that at the beginning.

CHRISTOPHER:

It is inevitably the blocking and tackling that goes on behind the scenes that enables the business to prosper and to be successful. If you could do anything over in your business with the benefit of hindsight, what would you do differently?

DAVID:

You know, I don't mean to duck the question, but I feel very fortunate. There's not a lot I regret. There are things we could have done better; I'm sure I could name ten of them. They're not that important. I feel very lucky to have gotten right the important things—and a lot of those revolve around people. We have a phenomenal team.

CHRISTOPHER:

You and your brother and the rest of the team at Golub Capital have stayed very true to your niche and skill set. And it's interesting because there's a school of thought that the way that you scale a business in the investment world is by having lots of different offerings and lots of different verticals and lots of different segments. And there's been firms that have done that very, very successfully. You have chosen to do that in a very narrow focus. Very few firms with that narrow focus have been able to scale. What are the primary reasons that you think most investment firms are not able to get to that scale?

DAVID:

I think you make a really important point. If you think about most investing businesses, the challenge of scaling is that you need to go to your next best idea. Imagine for example, that you are a long-only equity manager, and somebody gives you $100 million. You do a great job with it, and then the next year, instead of having a hundred million to invest, you've got more investors, and you've got a billion dollars to invest. So, you've got to go from building a portfolio with your top twenty best ideas to one with your top one hundred best ideas. And your one hundredth best idea probably isn't as good as your twentieth best idea. What this illustrates is that most investment businesses aren't scalable because, fundamentally, the investment strategy isn't scalable.

Contrast that with our business. Our growth has actually put us in a position to be a more valuable partner to our private equity firm clients. It's the opposite of my long-only equity manager. **Growth doesn't diminish returns. Growth enhances our competitive advantages by enabling us to do more for our private equity firm clients.** I'd argue our growth has enhanced our capacity to sustain our track record of premium returns over time.

CHRISTOPHER:

It's really interesting the way that you describe it because what happens to most firms is that they, in the name of growth, end up having to sacrifice quality or sacrifice the level of work and diligence. When you think about the universe of talent in the investment business, what do you believe are the key traits that separate the highest performers from their peers?

DAVID:

I think there are a couple of different models to think about talent in the investing space. There's absolutely a set of investment firms where stars are critically important—where you need Michael Jordan. That's not how we operate. **For us, success is a team sport. No one's great at everything. Everybody's better in a collaborative setting.** So, what we're focused on all the time, micro level, macro level, in managing the firm is making sure we've got the right mix of people, and making sure that we are providing development opportunities to all of our folks so they can continue to grow over time. And we're able to measure our success in doing that in a couple of different ways. We can measure our success with our investors through our returns. We can measure our success with private equity sponsors through repeat business. We can measure our success with our financing partners through their desire to continue to work with us. And we can measure success with our team by looking at engagement survey data and retention stats. And in this era, when we've all read about the extraordinary growth of resignations during COVID or, more recently, all the articles about quiet quitting, I think you can tell an enormous amount about a company by looking at whether those phenomena are hitting the company. I'd argue that if you find a company that has high levels of engagement and low levels of attrition, you have probably found a winner. I think at the end of the day, while all of the strategy issues that we talked about over the course of our discussion are really important, if you don't have the right team, nothing else matters.

CHRISTOPHER:

We talk a lot about different businesses and the dynamics of the leadership. In your case, you've got your brother that you have worked with during the entirety of the business. And I don't know too many brothers that have built businesses as successfully as the Golub brothers have.

TONY:

And stayed together for that many decades as well. That's an art by itself.

DAVID:

Hey, we have passionate disagreements. It's not all a symphony of peace and happiness. But one of the great things about working with my brother has been that we can have passionate disagreements, and we both know we're going to wake up the next morning and we're still going to be brothers and we're still going to be best friends and we're still going to be business partners.

TONY:

David, the title of the book is *The Holy Grail of Investing*, which sounds over the top. But the reason is that when I did my first book, I interviewed fifty of the best financial investors in the world. When I talked to Ray Dalio, he said that the Holy Grail of investing is finding eight to twelve uncorrelated investments that I feel strongly about. So, the whole book is about all these alternative investment opportunities to help you fill that out. But we'd really like to ask you from your perspective, David, what is the Holy Grail of Investing for you?

DAVID:

My perspective, Tony, is that investing really isn't different from other businesses. If we turned around your question and we asked what makes a great business, I think there'd be enormous agreement around that answer. We'd talk about competitive advantages and ways in which the business has a moat around it, which makes it hard to compete with. For me, in our niche, which is lending to private equity–backed companies, it's all about our competitive advantages. **By nurturing those competitive advantages, we're able to continue to produce consistent premium returns.**

Now, Ray Dalio is a genius, and he can figure out, well, these are the ideas for the moment that are particularly attractive. I'm not a genius. My business does not rely on genius to produce really good, consistent returns year over year. What we need to do is continue to benefit from and to nurture these core competitive advantages. **This is what I would describe as the Holy Grail: You want to invest alongside managers who have a business and not just a fund—managers who benefit from some sustainable source of competitive advantages.**

TONY:

It's very similar to Vista with Robert [Smith]. The same mindset of knowing more about it than anybody else in the industry. Having all that specialization, having the ongoing clients that come back to him again and again. You both have done unbelievably well in different industries. One more quick question for you. I was with Sheikh Tahnoon recently, and he was being advised by all these people financially. One of them was a gentleman from SoftBank and he was saying to him that now is the time for private credit. He was promoting private credit over private equity even. And he gave all his reasons for it and so forth. I'm curious, why private credit now, why is it even more important than ever before from your perspective? Why should investors be considering it?

DAVID:

If you think about what changed in July 2022, we saw interest rates go up. We saw growth slow down. So, both of these are factors that are very significant headwinds for many different asset classes. For equities, for example, you're simultaneously taking down net income because you've got a higher expense and you are putting pressure on multiples. **Traditional fixed income performs terribly in a rising rate context. By contrast, our business has tailwinds.** We have a growing private equity ecosystem. **Rising rates result in higher profits (so long as we control credit losses). The banks are out of our market and not coming back.** Scale is a major source of competitive advantage. There a lot of reasons for optimism.

I think that lies at the core of your colleague's argument. And I think he's right; there are unusual opportunities right now in private credit with the right managers. But I'd still advise caution. You can make mistakes in any asset class. Maybe I'm going to sound like a credit guy, but I think if anybody ever tells you: "This asset class is fail safe"—hold your wallet!

CHAPTER 22

BARRY STERNLICHT

COFOUNDER, CHAIRMAN, AND CEO OF STARWOOD CAPITAL

Accolades: Starwood was one of the world's largest public hotel companies (they have since merged their hotel holdings with Marriot). They are also one of the largest multifamily owners, one of the largest public REITs, and one of the largest owners and operators of single family home rentals.

Total Asset Under Management (as of August 2023): $115 billion

Area of focus: Global real estate—all real estate asset classes across thirty countries

HIGHLIGHTS

- Barry Sternlicht is the cofounder, chairman, and CEO of Starwood Capital Group, which was founded in 1991.
- Starwood currently has $115 billion of assets under management and has invested over $240 billion over the last thirty years across all major real estate asset classes.
- Starwood's investments include market leaders in residential, hotels, office, industrial, and retail.
- The firm was founded during the depths of the savings and loan

crisis and now has five thousand employees across sixteen global offices.

- Mr. Sternlicht is on the board of directors of the Estée Lauder Companies, Baccarat Crystal, the Robin Hood Foundation, Dreamland Community Theater, the Juvenile Diabetes Research Foundation's National Leadership Advocacy Program, and the Business Committee for the Arts.

TONY:

Barry, tell us a little bit about your journey, how you go from [borrowing] $20 million to, if I understand correctly, $115 billion AUM today. That's quite a journey. Tell us a little bit about your origin story, if you would, just to give people an orientation.

BARRY:

Thanks, Tony. Sure. My mom was a schoolteacher, and my dad was an engineer, and he came to the country after World War II. During the war, he fought with the Czech partisans. So, I think probably the most defining thing about my career and my life is that my worst day was better than his best day, growing up in a war. I always like to keep that in perspective. We really are blessed. And he so loved this country, and the opportunities it presented which said, you can do anything if you work hard and commit.

We were middle class. We lived in a small home in Long Island, and moved when I was five to Connecticut. My mom taught while her three boys went to school. I went to public high school, a class of two thousand kids. And then I was told I could go to college, but it had to be within driving distance of the house. So, I went to Brown because I wasn't really a math guy. My selection process was the best college where I didn't have to take a math course. People know me as a finance wizard, and the secret is I'm not. I just know how to use a calculator really well, have a good memory, and as an artist in high school, I think with both my left and right brain. So, I majored in something called Law and Society. I called that "Lost in Society" because I was somebody who knew a lot of things, but not a lot of about anything. When I graduated, I had three jobs in two years coming out of school, and my last job was actually as an arbitrage trader on Wall Street. My father, being who he was, said, "Do you want to look at a little green screen for the rest of your life?" So, even though I was making good money, I decided if I could get in, I would further my education and go to business school. I applied to only two, and I got into Harvard and I still don't know how.

I thought I'd last five minutes when they found out I couldn't add and subtract. But I survived that, and did pretty well. I've always been good at talking, and half your grade is class participation! I took a job in Chicago working for a real estate firm called JMB because I got a call from a friend who was an alum of JMB. I was choosing between there or working on Wall Street at Goldman Sachs, which was the only job I could get. But I really liked design. I liked art, I liked architecture. I liked travel and people. So real estate, as a principal, seemed like a good place to start. JMB hired me and I rose rapidly at the firm. I was a pretty creative guy.

There was a finance professor at HBS (Harvard Business School) who taught Entrepreneurial Finance. I didn't take the course, but I was told to go to his last class, so, I did. And the professor said a couple things. He said, "Be careful what you ask for, because you may achieve it." That has been an interesting motto that I've thought about my whole career. And then he said, **"Find the freight trains in your life and get on them instead of in front of them."** I actually think about both of these all the time. You know, luck is when preparation meets opportunity. You create your own luck. You set the table to get lucky. And, I think you have to have chips on the table to be successful and play the game.

It's no skill to say no to everything. You have to take risks and you're going to fail. I think the most important milestones of my early career were the worst deals I did, because of how much I learned from those. My son just graduated from HBS last week and I was telling him that the most exciting part about investing and learning is that I actually approach every investment like I'm stupid. I think about what could go wrong—worry about the downside, and the upside will take care of itself. So, in investing, you try to take the right risks and never cross the line on ethics, ever. I think that among other things, that has been the reason Starwood Capital Group has been so successful. We've always put our investors first, and we've always done the right thing, even when they didn't know we were doing the right thing. We have the same fee structure in our funds today that we had in 1991. Investors get their money back, a return on their money, and then we participate. As my father said, "If you do the right thing, you can always feel good when you look in the mirror every morning."

So, in my career, I'd say the pivotal moment was that I got let go when I was thirty-one. I was working at JMB. I was the wunderkind. I was in Chicago. Then the savings and loans crisis hit, and I was let go. It was shocking. I took the bus to apply for unemployment benefits. But I was very close with the man who ran JMB, who was on the Forbes 400, and I was worth about $8,000. But we were good friends. I was at his house with his wife and his kids. I skied with him. He gave me a million dollars to start my firm. With two other families, we had our first fund of $21 million. That's where we started. We couldn't afford anything. We had no credit—we couldn't even get a fax machine. We borrowed offices from the AMA in Chicago. We even borrowed their employees and had them sit on our side of the building so that we could look more robust than we were. It's been quite a ride.

We first bought a bunch of apartments. I sold them to Sam Zell, and we tripled our investors' money in eighteen months. And then myself and my partner, who was a friend from business school, split and I went east. I took advantage of a really odd-looking public company that I tripped over and merged a bunch of assets that we owned with that company, and changed its name to Starwood Lodging. It had an $8 million market cap at the time [and] $200 million of debt. We bought a bunch of the debt, and then we merged and took control of the company. From there, Starwood started doing lots of deals. We bought Westin Hotels for $5 billion. And then we bought ITT Sheraton for $14 billion. We were a $7 billion company buying a $14 billion company, bidding against Hilton Worldwide. **All of a sudden, in three years, we were the world's largest hotel company measured by cash flow.**

TONY:

Wow, how did you outsmart them with that little bit of capital?

BARRY:

We always treated our public shareholders like they were our partners. So, Fidelity owned 10 percent of the company. I knew all those guys. We needed their support. We made a stock offer for ITT. Our stock was trading at a relatively huge multiple at the time. And Hilton made a cash offer. They weren't trading at the multiple we were because we were growing so much faster. Normally, the acquirer's stock falls after a takeover offer, but the portfolio manager of Fidelity's real estate group said, "Starwood stock is worth more than cash." When we announced the deal, our stock was $53 a share. And after we announced it, our stock went to $60. So, that offer was worth even more than our first offer, and then we threw in some cash. Hilton offered basically $81 a share in cash. We were $84, but it was stock and $30 in cash. The shareholders voted for us.

TONY:

And you were thirty-eight years old at the time?

BARRY:

I was thirty-eight. Sometimes youth and innocence can mean stupidity and, you know, you have to figure it out in full view of the public.

CHRISTOPHER:

It goes back to your point from your professor, which is to be careful what you wish for. You might get it. You had 120,000 employees all of a sudden.

BARRY:

And then I had three of everything. I had three CFOs. I had three chief counsels. I had three heads of IT, and [it was] like, eeny, meeny, miny, moe. So, I went out and got some help. I had people evaluate the team, and it was a bouncy ride. So, my day job became running Starwood Hotels, and I ran it for ten years. It was the best of times and the worst of times. In the media's eye, I was a genius and an idiot. I didn't really like the publicity that much. I'm a sensitive guy. And the press, you know, they loved me. And they hated me.

TONY:

You had some really interesting comments [in Miami] at the J.P. Morgan conference saying hospitality is going crazy. We've all seen it. The prices are going nuts. Everybody was cooped up for COVID. Tell us your view of the real estate market today and how your firm is looking at it.

BARRY:

Historically, it's the real estate industry that causes crashes. You know, '07, '08, the housing industry, the ninja loans, selling loans with derivatives, all this stuff was toxic waste. I was not a home builder, but we were instrumental as an industry in nearly taking down the entire world's banking system. You could borrow 110 percent of the purchase price of an asset, and it got silly aggressive. One of the other key factors when you invest in real estate is that it's not really a great idea to buy a property when debt is more expensive than the yield on the property. We call that negative leverage. [If] you're borrowing 9 percent and paying a 6 percent yield for a property, you're in the hole from the start. This was the market in 2007–2008. Of course, that wasn't the case in 2020, and 2021, no bank was really that aggressive lending after '07, '08. They kind of learned their lessons, and for a while, there was positive leverage in every asset class.

So, in late '21, the Fed said, you know, we can control inflation and rates will be "lower longer." As you know, the Treasury printed $6 trillion during COVID, and there were no goods on the shelves. The supply chain broke. Everybody ran to buy not only their groceries, but their golf carts, their vacation homes, their couches, their desks. With no supply, prices went bananas, used car prices went crazy, and inflation took off. When inflation hit the real estate world, the rents and apartments rose like 20 percent in our markets in 2021–2022. In forty years, I've never seen anything like that. It was insane. But then the government finally caught on and raised interest rates in a straight line, the fastest in history. So, basically, real estate got blindsided. However, the fundamentals remain okay. If you look at the real estate asset classes, the residential business is strong. Apartments across the nation are 95 percent occupied. Rents are rising, not 20 percent, but nationally like 4 percent, and that's a very healthy market. Normally, pre-pandemic, we'd be happy with the 4 percent increase in rents. With single family—they're not building as many single-family homes; people can't afford a new house right now because the mortgage is too expensive. There's a wave of new apartment supply finishing, but there will be nothing behind it. In the aggregate between single family and multi, Powell's policy will create an even bigger deficit of housing units. So, there'll be pressure on both home prices and apartment rents whenever we get out of whatever it is we're in right now.

And, as you know, the hotel market took off, especially the resort market, immediately when the pandemic began to clear. People went on vacation and worked from anywhere but the office. And that market has been really strong. Both occupancy and the rates. In the beginning, I was like, "Well, the airline ticket was very cheap." Now the airline ticket's really expensive and people are still traveling. It's actually one of the conundrums. I'm scratching my head. I don't understand it really, how these room rates are staying this high all over the world.

TONY:

Is it that there's this amount of money that's still in the economy from all the money that was shoved into people's pockets? And it was going to run out, if I understood it correctly, in October of this year. Is that still happening?

BARRY:

I think those Americans—the ones we have heard about that didn't have an extra $400 in their savings account, and then got several thousand dollars from the government—I think they're out of excess savings, or close to it right now. And they're on their credit cards. Credit card debt is through the moon and beyond. I'm watching delinquencies at Bank of America. They're saying they're normal, but I don't think they'll stay normal. Now, the reason all this is okay at the moment is that people are still employed. People are spending money they may not have, but they have a job, and they feel secure in their job. So, if the Fed actually gets what they want, which is to get the unemployment rate up and wage growth to slow, that could unwind a lot of things.

The one thing I'm talking to our clients about is the American "virtual" office.

TONY:

That's what I want to know. We're now complaining about working three days a week at the office. [People are] willing to go to work around the world, except here. It's crazy.

BARRY:

Oh, it's crazy. **You know, everyone's in their offices in the Middle East. I was in a building in Dubai yesterday that's as busy as can be. It's like you're in Manhattan pre-pandemic. And then Europe and Asia, Tokyo in particular, not only are people in the office, but the vacancy rates are really low. In most of the major cities of Germany, office vacancy rates are below 5 percent. That compares to 25 percent in San Francisco and above 20 percent in New York City.**

So, there's a couple issues in the U.S. One is this: We're delighted to work from Jackson Hole, and we'll work from the beach, and we'll work from wherever we are. And it was led by the tech companies, which are our biggest companies, the biggest component of the S&P 500. What they do, everybody notices. But now, Amazon, in their new headquarters in Virginia asked everyone to come back to work four days a week. Last week, Google said, we want to see you back in the office. Every CEO is going to fire the people who stay home, first. They're not even being subtle about it. All the CEOs are in the office, but nobody's in the office with them. When I started my career, when the boss was in the office on Saturday, guess who went to the office on Saturday? I might be playing a game on my computer, but I wanted him to see that I was there. It's a different generation, and I think their grit is defined differently.

TONY:

Where do you see it going? Do you think this is a ten-year period or this is a two-year period before people start to change lifestyle?

BARRY:

If you look at what's happened in office since the pandemic, there's been like a hundred million square feet leased in buildings built since 2015, and a hundred million square feet vacant in older buildings. So, there's been a shift in demand. People want really nice buildings that attract their employees to come back. I built a building in Miami, and we leased the whole thing in the pandemic. It's a hundred percent leased. There was no leasing broker. My team just did it. And we started out at $52 rents and the last rent was $95. So, there are parts of the country where office is doing fine—Nashville, Tennessee, Austin, Texas, even the Atlantas and the Raleighs are doing okay.

And then there's the derivatives of office. Life sciences are booming, data centers are booming. They're not really office, but people are converting office buildings to data centers. So, it's another use. Much like the retail business where the good malls are continuing to stay occupied and thriving, and the bad malls kind of went the way of the dodo bird. So, you're going to see the office markets kind of bifurcate. Really good buildings will be full, with good tenants. But there's a new assault coming to the office markets. And that's AI. AI is going after skilled workers like lawyers and accountants and also advertising agencies. And it's going to be really interesting to see because these are major users of office space, right? Who's going to backfill that space? Where's the demand going to come from? It's going to be a very stressful time for the office asset class for a couple of years. **The Fed can fix all this, by the way. Lowering interest rates would give people time to refinance and cover. Nobody knows what the proper price is for an office building today— you can't get financing.** And if you get financing, they're going to charge you like 10 percent for it. You might have bought that really nice building and a 6 percent yield. So technically you're, well you're not solvent.

CHRISTOPHER:

Barry, you talked about a couple of themes that a lot of investors know are coming. They don't know the magnitude. They don't know what's going fix it. They don't know how long it's going to last. From your perspective, what are most investors getting wrong right now when they look at real estate?

BARRY:

First, what I'm thinking about myself is the long term. Like, what industries won't be impacted by AI. And when I say won't be impacted, [I mean] the demand will stay in place. How you choose to get to your hotel or how you choose a house may change, but the demand for residential will be solid. I think investors tend to throw the baby out with the bathwater. That's what we look for. We look for the babies that are being thrown out with the bathwater. We look for the really good office building with a really good tenant roster, and we can buy it at a price that's way below replacement cost. We'll buy it with all equity or mostly equity, we'll put a tiny little loan on it, and then rates will come down and we'll refinance it. Investors know that in the history of the United States, the interest curve has never stayed inverted forever. It's never happened. It'll never happen. Short-term rates will come down.

TONY:

Investors have to marry the property and date the rate.

BARRY:

Exactly. And what you look for are great assets with the wrong balance sheet. Then you can fix the balance sheet. Or find a really distressed seller, and there are a lot of distressed people right now. There's a lot of distress, and you don't see it until the loan matures. So, the loans are maturing every month, and it's going to be a minefield for years and everything will be helped if rates come down. Right now, there's a lot of fear and anxiety in the market. But there's [also] a lot of dry powder. So, it'll work out.

And some of us will be bold and buy stuff, and people will think we're nuts, and we'll know that in the future they may be the best purchases of our lifetime. **I think if you pick the right markets, and you pay attention, real estate is the most practical application of common sense there is. It is not genius, but you have to be completely objective. Do not fall in love with anything.** People get it wrong. They get emotional. They don't pay attention to the details. And it is the physical real estate that matters.

There is one thing I'd say though: real estate's a little like the stock market. I don't know who said this, but the markets can be irrational longer than you and I can be solvent. That applies to real estate too. So, sometimes the flow of funds overwhelms fundamentals. Like if Europeans decide that they don't care what the yield is on that building in Greensboro, South Carolina, or Charleston or Murfreesboro or Orlando. They want New York or they want DC. They're never going to get fired for buying a beautiful office building on Park Avenue in New York. So regardless of what the fundamentals are, you can't find a buyer. I've had to learn to really watch capital flows, as well as fundamentals. And it's so true in anything you invest in, right?

TONY:

One of the reasons we wrote this book is that Ray Dalio became a friend of mine over the last few years, and when I first met him, one of the questions

I asked him was: What's the single most important principle in investing? He's a macro trader, obviously, but what's the most important principle that guides all your decision-making? He turned to me, and he said, "You mean, the Holy Grail of Investing?' Then he said, Holy Grail investing is finding eight to twelve uncorrelated return streams or investments that you really believe in because it reduces your risk by 80 percent. So, one of the reasons we wrote this book is to show people alternatives and their impact so that they can get those eight to twelve. So, I'm curious, in your business, what is the Holy Grail of Investing?

BARRY:

Good question, A couple things come to mind. One, I asked a friend who's very successful in the hedge fund world, I said, what was your worst investment? And he said, selling my winners early. When you have something that's really working for you, ride it. But, conscious that every day you hold it, you've bought it again. It's human nature to think if you haven't sold it, you haven't made any money. You sell your gains, and you hold on to your losses hoping they get better. That is a terrible strategy in the stock market, and a terrible strategy in real estate.

It's human nature to think if you haven't sold it, you haven't made any money. You sell your gains, and you hold on to your losses hoping they get better. That is a terrible strategy in the stock market, and a terrible strategy in real estate.

We owned a business called Intown Suites. It's a budget hotel company and charges $350 a week, not per day. We were making a couple of hundred million dollars a year in cash flow. And after debt service, it was a hundred million dollars of free cash flow. So, I'm like, why would I ever sell this? There's no new supply, no competition. Nobody can build anything profitably and charge $350 a week. So, we held it an extra couple years and made an extra half a billion dollars. We just sold it last year.

I'd say the other thing in real estate is that it's really important to think about what could be there, as opposed to what is there today. And then be really objective about your competitive set. Like, what are you competing against, and how can I you make this property better? So, I'll use Post Properties as an example. It was a really nice apartment company based in Atlanta. We owned an apartment building right next to a Post property, built the same year. They were physical clones. If you looked at their property, it was beautiful. Their landscaping was fantastic. They ran four (percentage) points higher occupancy, and $150 higher rent than us because it just looked better. That's what I call common sense. The only time I yelled at a GM in ten years at Starwood Hotels was when I walked into a W in Chicago, and the plants were dead at the front door. First impressions matter. You can't put dead flowers into a spreadsheet.

There's a company I worked for in my summer of business school called Arvida Davis. They built some of the greatest resort communities in Florida—Boca, West Boca, Longboat Key, Sawgrass, a whole bunch of really successful master-planned communities. They spent, I think it was, $15,000 a house on landscaping when everyone else was spending $5,000. Not very complicated. They sold their houses faster and at higher prices, and had an incredible return on investment. But that's just the application of common sense. The most overused term in real estate is below replacement cost. Well, if it's twenty years old or thirty, it's a product that's not relevant today, it doesn't matter what you pay for it! People get trapped in that catchall phrase. I say it's "relevant replacement cost." I was in Saudi Arabia a couple days ago and I was saying that our goal if we continue to play in the office markets will be to "act like the Saudis." We're going to buy that beautiful Park Avenue office building that somebody paid, you know, $1,200 a foot for, and we'll buy it for $200 a foot and rent it for $20 a foot, net. I'll be full because I'm now the lowest cost of supply. If you can buy it really cheaply, you can destabilize the market. You can rent to that competitive advantage and fill your building and everyone else can't match you because they didn't buy the building for $200 a foot.

TONY:

I started working with Paul Tudor Jones twenty-five years ago, and one of the first lessons he gave me, he said, let me show you this stock. And he shows me that it's growing and growing and growing. He asks, "What do you do?"

And I said, "Well, I'm not the professional investor, but I'd keep going." And he says, "That's exactly what I try to teach. Almost everybody sells." Then he said that one of the reasons Warren Buffett is as rich as he is, is that he hates paying taxes. So, he hangs on to things forever. How do you know when you have the wins though? When do you sell? I'm curious about your principle for that. You've got something that's a winner—when do you sell?

BARRY:

We try to sell, if you see a ton of new supply coming into a market or an asset category. If we think there's going to be a shift in capital flows, like people will lose interest in one thing and go into something else. I think, when you're running a fund, you have to look at the whole fund and then you look at: What are the best things I can ride and what is just a trade? Second, there's always a buyer for great assets.

I'm in Dubai and we opened a Baccarat Residence here. They sold all the penthouses first. All of them. Seven. Went instantly. My friend had an apartment in, what is it, 59th Street, the new building in New York City, the beautiful, incredible residential tower. He bought his apartment for $95 million. We were convinced he was going to lose $50 million on it. He never finished it. He put it on the market. A buyer from China came and paid him $200 million for it. He was just hoping to get his money out. **There's always a buyer for great assets.**

THE TRUE HOLY GRAIL

"For where your treasure is, there your heart will be also."
Matthew 6:21

Like a marathon runner finally crossing the finish line, I hope you have a sense of satisfaction and fulfillment after taking in the content of this book. We have covered a lot of ground, and my deepest personal desire is that the wisdom, strategies, and insights herein become foundational in your pursuit of financial freedom (as they have for me and my family). More important, I want to remind you of a core truth: **Knowledge is not power, it's potential power. Execution trumps knowledge every day of the week.** My original mentor, Jim Rohn, used to say, "Don't let your learning lead to knowledge. You will become a fool. Let your learning lead to action!"

So how will you build *your* Holy Grail portfolio? As Dalio taught us early on, which 8–12 twelve uncorrelated strategies might you consider implementing to maximize upside and reduce risk by up to 80 percent? What steps can you immediately take on your financial freedom journey? **Which begs the question: What is financial freedom for you?**

When I interviewed the late Sir John Templeton, one of the first great international investors to become a billionaire, I asked him, "What's the secret to wealth?" He said, "Tony, it's what you teach." I laughed and said, "I teach a lot of things. Which thing?"

With a big smile on his face, he replied, "Gratitude! You know, Tony, we've both met people who have a billion dollars, and they live in state of frustration and anger. They're miserable. So they're truly poor. And we both know people who seemingly have nothing, yet they're grateful for the breath of life, for everything. So they're rich beyond compare."

In our hearts we all know that it's not money that makes us rich. As I'm sure you've found, the greatest treasures are never financial. It's those moments of grace when we appreciate the perfection and beauty of it all. It's those moments when we feel something eternal and invincible inside us, the core of our spirit. It's the loving warmth of our relationships with family and friends. It's laughter. It's finding meaningful work. It's the capacity to learn and grow, to share and serve. **This is the true Holy Grail.**

For me (Tony), it's also the joy of helping people break through their limits and seeing them light up as they remember who they really are and what they're capable of achieving. It's the delight of seeing their lives become a celebration instead of a battle. It's the magical feeling that somehow I've played a role in the awakening of a marvelous and unique human being. It's appreciating that everything I've gone through has served not only me but others—that even the deepest pain I've experienced has led to something beautiful. In fact, there can be no greater gift than for your life to have meaning beyond yourself. This is the ultimate game changer. Find something to serve, a cause you can be passionate about that's greater than yourself, and this will make you wealthy. Nothing enriches us like helping others.

The second tip I got from Sir John Templeton was the importance of tithing, or taking a portion of what you have—regardless how small—and giving it to others in need. Templeton shared that he had never met anyone who had faithfully given ten percent of their income for more than a decade that didn't also become abundantly wealthy. And the tithe doesn't need to be a church. It could be charity, your community, or anything that makes a positive impact in the world.

This psychological shift from scarcity to abundance makes you truly wealthy and brings you a glorious sense of freedom. In making this shift, you're training your brain to recognize that there's so much more available for you to give, to appreciate, and to love. And remember: It's not just money that you can donate. You can also give your time, your talent, your love, your compassion, and your heart.

I often hear people say that they will give when they become wealthy. This is a farce. A childhood friend of mine was recently on a flight. The gentleman next to him was reading *Life Force*, my recent book on the future of regenerative medicine and precision health. They struck up a conversation, and the gentleman had nothing but positive things to say about the book and recognized that all the proceeds from the book were being donated. Despite loving the book, he brushed off the donation, saying, "but he is rich, so he can afford it." My friend smiled and decided to reveal our friendship of more than forty-five years. He told the man that I had been donating since I was a broke teenager and recalled many moments where I would dig in my pockets for five or ten dollars to give to a homeless man even though I had less than a hundred dollars to my name.

Here is what I know: Waiting until you're wealthy to donate is a massive mistake, because you will rob yourself of the fulfillment you deserve and will likely never become generous. And if a person won't give a dime out of a dollar they will never give a hundred thousand out of a million or ten million out of a hundred million.

As an aside, I want to thank you for purchasing this book, as 100 percent of the proceeds will be provided to Feeding America. I was fed when I was eleven years old, and my family often struggled to put food on the table. It changed the course of my life and started me on a journey to provide meals to those in need. We already reached our goal of 1 billion meals served, and I am now working on a global 100 Billion Meal challenge!

Having said all this, I want you to know that my daily prayer is to be a blessing in the lives of all those I meet. If you make the tools and principles in this book a part of your core, you'll be able to receive—and give—more than you could ever imagine. As this extraordinary abundance flows to and from you, you will feel truly blessed—and become a greater blessing in the lives of others. This is what it feels like to possess real wealth.

I'm thankful that you've allowed us the privilege of spending this time with you. I know that the titans we interviewed are also grateful to be a part of your story. I sincerely hope that the contents of this book have been helpful to you on your journey. Perhaps someday our paths will cross, and I'll have the privilege of hearing the story of how this book has helped you accelerate the building of the life you desire and deserve.

Please return to these pages whenever you need a reminder of who you really are and all that you can create. Remember that you are more than the moment. You are more than your economics. You are more than any challenging time you may face.

God bless you, and LIVE WITH PASSION!

Continue the journey with us! While a book is a snapshot in time, we will be providing ongoing education and resources with our podcast, newsletter and more . . .

www.TheHolyGrailofInvesting.com

ACKNOWLEDGMENTS

TONY ROBBINS

As I reflect on over four and half decades of my mission, so many incredible human beings have been with me along the way. I'd like briefly to express my deep gratitude to those who have touched this particular project.

First, my family, of course. This begins and ends with my wife, Bonnie Pearl—my Sage. I love you. I give thanks for the grace that breathes our love and our life. To my dearest daughter, Violet Pearl—the incredible gift that God brought into our lives in an unexpected and beautiful way. To Mary B., my right hand, best friend, and co-mother of our little Violet. To my son, Josh, without whom this book wouldn't have been possible. You have done some serious heavy lifting to bring this book to fruition, and I am forever grateful for how much fun it is to work with my son on such an impactful project.

To my dear friend and partner Christopher Zook and the entire team at CAZ Investments. I am forever grateful for our partnership and for the wisdom and insights you bring to the table day in and day out. This book will be a part of your legacy of impact. To Ajay Gupta, my brother from another mother, and partner in our joint family office, Robbins Gupta Holdings. Thank you for your never-ending friendship, loyalty, and late-night strategy sessions!

My deepest thanks, respect, and admiration for those who shared their precious time and life's work in our interview sessions. Specifically, to the thirteen brilliant minds that generously contributed their wisdom from decades of experience for the benefit of our readers. To Robert F. Smith, Vinod Khosla, Michael Rees, Barry Sternlicht, Michael B. Kim, Bill Ford, Bob Zorich, Ian Charles, David Golub, Wil VanLoh, David Sacks, Tony Florence, and Ramzi Musallam.

A special thanks to my dear friend Ray Dalio, whose core principle of the Holy Grail of Investing inspired both the title and mission of this book.

Thanks again to all my partners at Simon & Schuster, especially CEO Jonathan Karp. And my incredible agent and dear friend of forty years, Jan Miller.

To my core team at Robbins Research International—all of our fiercely loyal and mission-driven executive staff—I count my blessings for you every day.

To the folks at Tiny Wins for their brilliant visual design and execution.

My life has been powerfully shaped by deep friendships with four brilliant men. To my role models Peter Guber, Marc Benioff, Paul Tudor Jones, and Steve Wynn.

Of course, the mission of this book is to serve not only those who will be reading. And so my deepest thanks to everyone at the Anthony Robbins Foundation and our strategic partners, namely, Claire Babineaux-Fontenot.

And Dan Nesbit at Feeding America for helping us coordinate our next 1 Billion Meals Challenge!

To the grace that has guided this entire process, and to all those friends and teachers along the path of my life—too many to mention, some famous and some unknown, whose insights, strategies, example, love, and caring are the shoulders I have had the honor to stand on. On this day, I give thanks to you all, and I continue my never-ending quest to each day be a blessing in the lives of all those I have the privilege to meet, love, and serve.

CHRISTOPHER ZOOK

From beginning to end, the entire project of producing this book has been surreal. Three decades ago, I began listening to Tony Robbins's coaching when the only mode of communication was through a cassette tape. If someone had told me then that thirty-plus years later Tony and I would co-author a book together, I am not sure what I would have said. Yet I also know God has a wonderful way of uniting people at just the right time. Tony, words cannot express the impact you have had on my life, from a young man listening to your teachings to a seasoned investor now operating a company with a worldwide footprint. I will be forever grateful for the partnership and friendship that has developed over the past years, and I look forward to what the future holds.

Josh Robbins, this book would not have been possible without the heavy lifting you did from beginning to end. You are extremely talented and a joy to work with. I am honored to call you friend.

Ajay Gupta, I am thankful for our friendship and the extent to which you support our team, and specifically me. Your joyful spirit brings a smile to my day.

To the CAZ Investments team, I thank God for you daily, and this firm, our firm, would not be where it is today without each of you. Everyone on our team has had an impact and I would like to give a special thank-you to Matt, Clark, Mark, Steve, Lucia, Isaiah, and Heather for everything they have done to put us on the map. We would not be where we are today without your Herculean work. And to Bailey and Kirk, who went above and beyond to keep the whirlwind at bay so I could dedicate the time needed for this project.

I send my endless thanks to the shareholders of CAZ. You are the ones who took a chance on a young man with a dream. I will forever be grateful.

To my mom, Dee; mother-in-law, Winona; sister, Kimberly; and extended family, each of you has breathed life into me in different ways. I am the man I am today because of what you have meant to my life.

I send my love to my son and daughter-in-law, Christopher and Cecelia, who are always there to share in our excitement and provide encouragement. And to Christopher III (Tripp), my first grandchild, you bring light to each day. It is the three of you I often think of when I remember why I go through the daily grind and stress. You are my motivation.

Above all others, and with deep, abiding love, I want to thank my wife, Lisa. You are my best friend, my high school sweetheart, and my cheerleader. When needed, you set me straight, and when I am too hard on myself, you make me laugh. Outside of God, the only reason I can soar is because you have always believed in me. I cannot imagine what my life would have been like without you. You are my greatest gift.

NOTES

CHAPTER ONE: THE SEARCH FOR THE HOLY GRAIL

5 *Private Credit, an alternative to bonds*: Moriah Costa, "Private or Public: Investing in Private Credit vs Bonds," *MoneyMade*, October 18, 2022.

7 *The G.O.A.T. For those who aren't familiar, Ray is the founder of Bridgewater*: Bridgewater Associated, LP, Berkshire Hathaway Inc., June 30, 2023.

7 *Their "Pure Alpha" fund has averaged over 11 percent*: Carolina Mandl, "Bridgewater's flagship fund posts gains of 32% through June," Reuters, July 5, 2022.

8 *In August of 2023, a Bloomberg headline*: Ye Xie, "Bonds Are Useless Hedge for Stock Losses as Correlation Jumps," *Bloomberg*, August 2, 2023.

8 *Between 2010 and 2020, REITs had an 80 percent positive correlation with the S&P 500*: Roger Wohlner, "REITs: Still a Viable Investment?," *Investopedia*, September 22, 2021.

9 *A Georgetown University study found that "crypto assets followed the market's lead"*: Hannah Zhang, "Crypto Is Becoming More Correlated to Stocks—And It's Your Fault," *Institutional Investor*, February 9, 2023.

9 *"The same is true for almost a quarter (25%) of those ages 75 to 84"*: Anne Tergesen, "America's Retirees Are Investing More Like 30-Year-Olds," *Wall Street Journal*, July 4, 2023.

12 *Ultra-high-net-worth families (those with over $30 million)*: Henry H. McVey, *KKR Blog*, May 10, 2017.

13 *On a global level, private equity outperformed public markets*: Caryn Slotsky, "Global ex US PE/VC Benchmark Commentary: Calendar Year 2021," Cambridge Associates LLC, August 2022.

13 *As you can see in the figure below, as an entire asset class, private euity produced average annual returns of 14.2 percent*: Caryn Slotsky, "US PE/VC Benchmark Commentary: First Half 2021," Cambridge Associates, January 2022.

14 *In all three cases, the "peak to trough" declines of the S&P 500 were far steeper*: "Current benchmark statistics," Cambridge Associates, Q1, 2023.

14 *Case in point, in 2021, on the heels of the pandemic and a global supply chain crisis*:

"McKinsey Global Private Markets Review: Private markets turn down the volume," McKinsey & Company, March 21, 2023.

14 *This is just slightly below the stellar performance of 33 percent in year 2020*: "A year of disruption in the private markets: McKinsey Global Private Markets Review 2021," McKinsey & Company, April 5, 2021.

15 *Private equity heavyweight Bain Capital wrote*: Hugh MacArthur et al., "The Private Equity Market in 2021: The Allure of Growth," Global Private Equity Report, Bain & Company, March 7, 2022.

15 *In fact, according to the* Financial Times: Robin Wigglesworth, "US has fewer listed public companies than China," *Financial Times*, October 6, 2019.

15 *In fact, back in 2009, 81 percent of public companies were profitable*: "Share of companies that were profitable after their IPO in the United States from 2008 to 2021," Statista, June 30, 2022.

15 *When you look at the total value of all publicly traded companies globally*: "2021 Preqin Global Private Equity & Venture Capital Report," Preqin Ltd., February 4, 2021.

16 *Numerous studies have shown that adding private equity to a typical stock-and-bond portfolio*: Anthony Tutrone, "Private Equity and Your Portfolio," Neuberger Berman Global Insights, January 2019.

16 *In addition to the many trillions already flowing into private markets*: Austin Ramsey, "Private Equity Firms Are Winning the Fight for Your 401(k)," *Bloomberg Law*, January 31, 2022.

18 *A story in the* Wall Street Journal *summed it up*: Miriam Gottfried, "Buying Stakes in Private-Equity Firms, Not Just Their Funds, Pays Big," *Wall Street Journal*, November 18, 2018.

21 *The firm has grown to be one of the top 200 allocators*: "April 2022 Global Markets Snapshot," PitchBook News & Analysis, May 3, 2022.

CHAPTER TWO: GP STAKES: A PIECE OF THE ACTION

25 *"More than a quarter of the wealthiest people in America"*: Rachel Sandler, "Nearly Half of America's Richest Billionaires Have Fortunes in These Two Industries," *Forbes*, October 26, 2021.

27 *For the investment nerds like us*: Author's note: In typical private equity investing, the J-Curve means investors in a fund initially show "losses" while their capital is being put to work to buy assets in the fund. This is followed by a reversal once the gains start to materialize, creating a J-like curve on a graph.

33 *After all, the universe of high-quality private asset managers is very limited*: Erik Fogelstrom and Jonatan Gustafsson, "GP Stakes in Private Equity: An Empirical Analysis of Minority Stakes in Private Equity Firms," MSc Thesis in Finance, Stockholm School of Economics, Spring 2020.

33 *A* Forbes *article from 2022 explains it well*: Benjamin Summers, "GP Stakes:

What You Should Know About Designer Financial Structures," *Forbes*, November 18, 2022.

CHAPTER THREE: PRO SPORTS OWNERSHIP: SWINGING FOR THE FENCES

36 *The sports economists and various talking heads*: Dayn Perry, "Report: Dodgers, Time Warner agree to more than $7 billion TV deal," CBSSports.com, January 22, 2013.

38 *Fast-forward to 2002*: Michael Haupert, "The Economic History of Major League Baseball," EH.net (Economic History Association), 2007.

40 *North American Major League Soccer*: Joseph Zucker, "LAFC Tops Forbes List of MLS Team Values; 1st Billion Dollar Franchise," Bleacher Report, February 2, 2023.

41 *In 2019, ninety-two of the top one hundred highest-rated programs on TV*: Austin Karp and John Ourand, "Politics aside, sports still dominated the list of the 100 most-viewed programs of 2020," *Sports Business Journal*, January 11, 2021.

44 *By all accounts, this is a modern-day gold rush*: News release, "2021 Commercial Gaming Revenue Shatters Industry Record, Reaches $53B," American Gaming Association, February 15, 2022.

46 Bloomberg *reported that the Fenway Sports Group*: Alex Wittenberg et al., "Private Equity Funds Are Pushing Deeper Into Pro Sports," *Bloomberg*, March 24, 2022.

46 *And according to PitchBook, more than a third of Europe's Big 5 soccer leagues*: Marie Kemplay, "US private capital scores big in European soccer," PitchBook, August 3, 2023.

CHAPTER FOUR: PRIVATE CREDIT: LEADERS IN LENDING

47 *"As fewer companies have gone public in recent years"*: Stacy Francis, "Op-ed: Demystifying private credit amid a frozen IPO market," CNBC, June 21, 2023.

48 *In the pages ahead, we explore how private credit has grown*: Kelsey Butler, "How Private Credit Soared to Fuel Private Equity Boom," *Bloomberg*, September 22, 2019.

49 *Put it all together*: Akane Otani, "The 60/40 Portfolio Is Delivering Its Worst Returns in a Century," *Wall Street Journal*, October 14, 2022.

49 Bloomberg *reported that "bonds are a useless hedge"*: Ye Xie, "Bonds Are Useless Hedge for Stock Losses as Correlation Jumps," *Bloomberg*, August 2, 2023.

50 *Contrast this with private credit*: Jeffrey Bartel, "Private Credit Investing: Current Opportunities and Risks," *Forbes*, March 30, 2023.

50 *On November 9 of 2021*, Bloomberg *wrote*: Paula Seligson, "U.S. Junk Bonds Set $432 Billion Record in Rush to Beat Rates," *Bloomberg*, November 9, 2021.

50 *Not even a year later, on October 22 of 2022*: Giulia Morpurgo et al., "Global Junk-Bond Sales Drop Most Ever With No Signs of Recovery," *Bloomberg*, October 24, 2022.

52   *This is why many firms see a "golden moment"*: Jessica Hamlin, "Blackstone sees a 'golden moment' in private credit after bank failures," PitchBook, April 20, 2023.

CHAPTER FIVE: ENERGY: THE POWER OF OUR LIVES (PART ONE)

59   *That's down from 77 percent in 2000*: "China increased electricity generation annually from 2000 to 2020," U.S. Energy Information Administration (EIA), September 22, 2022.

60   *And while the entire world retired 187 gigawatts of coal plants*: Editorial, "John Kerry Tilts at Chinese Coal Plants," *Wall Street Journal*, July 17, 2023.

60   *The Paris Climate Accords*: "China permits two new coal power plants per week in 2022," Centre for Research on Energy and Clean Air (CREA)," February 2023.

61   *In 2023, we are on track to use more oil*: Alex Lawler, "OPEC sees 2.2% oil demand growth in 2024 despite headwinds," Reuters, July 13, 2023.

61   *It took natural gas fifty years to reach 25 percent of global energy market share*: "2021–2025: Rebound and beyond," International Energy Agency (AEA), 2020.

62   *The International Monetary Fund (IMF) predicts*: Neil Ruiz et al., "Coming of Age," International Monetary Fund, March 2020.

63   *They ranked #2 on the Fortune Global 500 largest companies*: Vivienne Walt, "Saudi Arabia has the most profitable company in the history of the world, and $3.2 trillion to invest by 2030. Who will say no to that tidal wave of cash?" *Fortune*, August 1, 2023.

66   *The state reported that since the closing*: Thomas Zambito, "NY's fossil fuel use soared after Indian Point plant closure; officials sound the alarm," *Journal News* and lohud.com, July 22, 2022.

66   *Then, in another desperate move*: Philip Oltermann, "Stop dismantling German windfarm to expand coalmine, say authorities," *Guardian*, October 26, 2022.

67   *In addition, they are investing half a trillion dollars*: Dan Murtaugh and Krystal Chia, "China's Climate Goals Hinge on a $440 Billion Nuclear Buildout," *Bloomberg*, November 2, 2021.

70   *Somewhat ironic, considering that*: "Democratic Republic of the Congo—Country Commercial Guide," International Trade Administration, December 14, 2022.

72   *In 2022, California mandated that by 2035*: "California moves to accelerate to 100% new zero-emission vehicle sales by 2035," California Air Resources Board, CA.gov, August 25, 2022.

73   *To put that into perspective*: "2021 Total System Electric Generation," California Energy Commission, accessed on August 27, 2023.

74   *We will need two times more copper*: "Critical minerals market sees unprecedented growth as clean energy demand drives strong increase in investment," International Energy Agency, July 11, 2023.

CHAPTER SIX: ENERGY: THE POWER OF OUR LIVES (PART TWO)

81 *We produce about 22 percent of the world's energy*: Shannon Osaka, "The U.S. is the world's largest oil producer. You'll still pay more for gas," *Washington Post*, October 8, 2022.

81 *Case in point, U.S. natural gas is about 30 percent cleaner*: Matthew Mailloux, "Where American Gas Goes, Other Clean Energy Can Follow," ClearPath, June 16, 2022.

81 *This is why the U.S. has been leading the charge*: "2022 Global Gas Flaring Tracker Report," The World Bank, 2022.

83 *Mike Wirth, the CEO of Chevron*: Carl Surran, "No new refineries ever built again in the U.S., Chevron CEO warns," Seeking Alpha, June 3, 2022.

85 *According to Reuters, the U.S. is poised to become the world's largest LNG producer*: Scott Disavino, "U.S. poised to regain crown as world's top LNG exporter," Reuters, January 4, 2023.

87 *The* Harvard Business Review *estimates that retired solar panels*: Atalay Atasu et al., "The Dark Side of Solar Power," *Harvard Business Review*, June 18, 2021.

88 *As a material scientist, Simon holds a staggering 140 issued patents*: "Patents by Inventor Simon K. Hodson," JUSTIA Patents, Filed from 1990–1995; Patent dates from 1992–1997, accessed August 27, 2023.

89 *He walked into the nondescript metal building*: "Operating with Ethics and Integrity; a proud history of responsibility," Consol Energy, accessed August 27, 2023.

90 *Case in point, Tesla and other EV manufacturers*: Mirza Shehnaz, "Tesla supplier warns of graphite supply risk in 'opaque' market," *Financial Times*, November 20, 2022.

90 *Scientists at MIT were recently experimenting*: Jennifer Chu, "Physicists discover a 'family' of robust, superconducting grapheme structures," press release, MIT News, July 8, 2022.

CHAPTER SEVEN: VENTURE CAPITAL: INNOVATION AND DISRUPTIVE TECHNOLOGY

102 Time *magazine explained that*: Alice Park, "Scientists Have Reached a Key Milestone in Learning How to Reverse Aging," *Time*, January 12, 2023.

CHAPTER EIGHT: REAL ESTATE: THE WORLD'S BIGGEST ASSET

106 *With 7.9 billion people on earth*: Paul Tostevin, "The total value of global real estate," Savills, September 2021.

110 *When added to another 740 million square feet of space*: "Obsolescence Equals Opportunity," Report, Cushman & Wakefield, accessed on August 27, 2023.

112 Fortune *magazine reported that the "housing market shortage is so acute"*: Alena Botros, "Housing market shortage is so acute and the office glut is so big that Boston will offer 75% tax breaks on office-to-residential conversions," *Fortune*, July 13, 2023.

112 *Midjourney, the most popular AI image creation tool*: "Profile, Midjourney Company Stats," *Forbes*, accessed August 27, 2023.

113 *New York City lost 468,200 residents*: Elizabeth Pritchett, "New York City has lost nearly half a million residents since start of COVID pandemic," FoxBusiness, May 19, 2023.

113 *California is so fearful of further exodus*: Arthur Laffer and Stephen Moore, "'The 'Hotel California' Wealth Tax," *Wall Street Journal Opinion*, March 5, 2023.

113 *Charles Schwab, CBRE, and Oracle are just a few of the many titans*: "19 Corporations & Businesses Fleeing California for Texas," blog entry, Concordia University Texas, June 16, 2021.

114 *In 2023, the* Wall Street Journal *named Nashville, Tennessee*: Sarah Chaney Cambon and Danny Dougherty, "Sunbelt Cities Nashville and Austin Are Nation's Hottest Job Markets," *Wall Street Journal*, April 1, 2023.

114 *The landlords of San Francisco's largest mall*: Natalie Wong et al., "The World's Empty Office Buildings Have Become a Debt Time Bomb," *Bloomberg*, June 23, 2023.

115 *As a result of the coming loan predicament for banks and tenants*: Neil Callanan, "A $1.5 Trillion Wall of Debt Is Looming for US Commercial Properties," *Bloomberg*, April 8, 2023.

119 *Today, 980,000 homes are for sale, a forty-year low*: "Housing Inventory: Active Listing Count in the United States," FRED Economic Resource, updated August 8, 2023.

119 *That's barely more than half a million homes for sale*: "United States Total Housing Inventory," Trading Economics, July, 2023.

119 *According to Realtor.com, in September 2022*: Hannah Jones, "Data, Economic Coverage, Housing Supply," Realtor.com, November 21, 2022.

121 *An Indian immigrant and former IT worker*: Will Parker et al., "A Housing Bust Comes for Thousands of Small-Time Investors," *Wall Street Journal*, May 23, 2023.

122 *The* Wall Street Journal *reported that*: Konrad Putzier and Will Parker, "A Real-Estate Haven Turns Perilous With Roughly $1 Trillion Coming Due," *Wall Street Journal*, August 7, 2023.

INDEX

ABOUT THE AUTHORS

TONY

TONY ROBBINS is an entrepreneur, #1 *NY Times* bestselling author, philanthropist, and the nation's #1 life & business strategist. He has empowered more than 50 million people from 100 countries around the world through his audio programs, educational videos, and live seminars. For more than four and a half decades, millions of people have enjoyed the warmth, humor, and transformational power of Tony's business and personal development events.

Mr. Robbins is the author of six international bestsellers, including the 2014 *New York Times* #1 financial bestseller *MONEY: Master the Game* and *UNSHAKEABLE: Your Financial Freedom Playbook* (2017). His most recent book, *LIFE FORCE: How New Breakthroughs in Precision Medicine Can Transform the Quality of Your Life and Those You Love*, was released in February 2022.

Mr. Robbins is involved in more than 100 privately held businesses with combined sales exceeding $6 billion a year. He has been honored by Accenture as one of the "Top 50 Business Intellectuals in the World," by Harvard Business Press as one of the "Top 200 Business Gurus," and by American Express as one of the "Top Six Business Leaders in the World." *Fortune* magazine's cover article named him the "CEO Whisperer," and he has been named in the Top 50 of *Worth* magazine's 100 most powerful people in global finance for three consecutive years.

Mr. Robbins is a leader called upon by leaders. He has worked with four U.S. presidents, top entertainers—from Aerosmith to Green Day, Usher, and Pitbull, and athletes and sports teams, including tennis great Serena Williams, UFC champion Conor McGregor, and the NBA's Golden State Warriors. Business leaders and financial moguls from Salesforce.com founder Marc Benioff to Ray Dalio of Bridgewater Associates have tapped him for personal coaching.

Mr. Robbins is a leading philanthropist. Through his partnership with Feeding America, Mr. Robbins has provided more than one billion meals through his "1Billion Meals" challenge, which was completed ahead of schedule. He is now working on a global "100 Billion Meal Challenge." Through the Tony Robbins Foundation, he has also awarded more than 2,000 grants and other resources to health and human services organizations, implemented a life-changing curriculum in 1,700-plus correctional facilities and gathered thousands of young leaders from around the world with its youth programs.

CHRISTOPHER

CHRISTOPHER ZOOK is the Founder, Chairman, and Chief Investment Officer of CAZ Investments (www.CAZInvestments.com). He has more than 30 years of experience investing in both traditional and alternative asset classes. Zook was recently honored with the Texas Alternative Investments Association's (TAIA) Lifetime Achievement Award in recognition of his contributions to, and sustained support of, the industry in Texas. He is a regular contributor to major media outlets, including CNBC, Fox Business, and Bloomberg.

In 2001, Zook founded CAZ Investments with one aim: to curate unique and exclusive investment opportunities for a network of investors—investments that most individuals would not otherwise have access to, as they are typically accessible only by major institutional investors. Fast-forward 23 years and CAZ Investments has more than 3,000 high-net-worth families (and numerous investment advisors) across the globe that have chosen to lock arms and invest as a unified front. Collectively, CAZ Investments is the equivalent of a large institutional investor, with superior access and buying power.

The mission of CAZ Investments is to lead with alignment. Zook and the shareholders invest their own personal capital first so that clients can rest assured that the correct incentives are in place.

Prior to starting CAZ Investments in 2001, Zook served in senior leadership positions with Oppenheimer, Prudential Securities, Lehman Brothers, and Paine Webber. Zook is actively involved in public policy and frequently serves as a resource to state and local officials. In 2019, Zook was appointed by the Texas governor to serve on the State of Texas Pension Review Board, where he serves as Chair of the Investment Committee. He also recently served two terms as a member of the Greater Houston Partner¬ship's Executive Committee and is past president of numerous charitable organizations. He is a graduate of Texas Tech University, where he was recently honored as a Distinguished Alumnus.

Zook is a lifelong Houstonian, and his greatest joy comes from being married to his high school sweetheart and from spending time with his son, daughter-in-law, and grandson.